# Nela's Cookbook

*Illustrations by Fela Krance*

# Nela's Cookbook

## BY NELA RUBINSTEIN

ALFRED A. KNOPF   NEW YORK

1   9   8   3

THIS IS A BORZOI BOOK
PUBLISHED BY ALFRED A. KNOPF, INC.

Copyright © 1983 by Nela Rubinstein
Illustrations copyright © 1983 by Felicia Krance

Library of Congress Cataloging in Publication Data
Rubinstein, Nela.
Nela's cookbook.
Includes index.
1. Cookery, Polish. 2. Cookery, International.
I. Title.
TX723.5.P6R83   1983     641.5     83–47959
ISBN 0–394–51761–X

Manufactured in the United States of America
First Edition

*To my family and friends*
*with love*

# Acknowledgments

I should like to take this opportunity to thank all the wonderful people who helped me with this book.

First, the late Blanche Knopf, who, thirty-seven years ago, believed in me enough actually to send me a contract, which, although I never dared sign it, remained a token of intent all these years.

My utmost gratitude goes to my editor, Judith Jones, for her priceless advice, warm encouragement, and extraordinary patience with the numerous drafts and revisions of the manuscript;

To Peggy Yntema, my collaborator, whose infectious enthusiasm kept my spirits up, and who with such good humor and energy seemed even to enjoy testing and retesting the recipes;

To Fela Krance, my lifelong friend, whose lovely drawings grace these pages and the jacket, and who has always been ready to lend a helpful hand or word;

To my daughter Eva, for her loving, invaluable, and most efficient work on the final draft of the book, and for the many memories she added to mine;

To Clara Clemans, my devoted friend and secretary for twenty years, who not only helped with the typing but performed so many unsecretarial tasks.

My warmest thanks go also to Basia Johnson, whose generosity in letting me use her apartment in New York made it possible in the last few months to bring this long-lasting project to a happy conclusion.

# Contents

# Introduction

For a very long time now, my family and many of my friends have insisted that I put down on paper the recipes for some of the dishes I have so enjoyed cooking, and, apparently, they have enjoyed eating, over the years. I finally gave in, little knowing what was in store.

Nearly three years ago, my very dear friend Fela Krance, whom I have known since we were both ten in Warsaw, offered to help me get started. Suddenly I realized what lay ahead of me. I began gathering the scraps of paper, backs of envelopes, telephone messages with scribbled recipes on the other side, my mother's little notebook, handwritten for me, of the old "family secret" tortes and many other delights of my Lithuanian-Polish childhood, including recipes from my grandmother, from our dear Lith-uanian cook, Barbarka Zinkevicus, and, finally, all my own memories, often incomplete, of dishes I had cooked over the past fifty years.

And that was only the beginning. In the first place, as most of my cooking has always been done mainly from memory—with a few dashes of instinct thrown in—I had made my little notes in a kind of shorthand, usually leaving out such minor details as measurements and oven temperatures. In the second place, what notations I did have were not only in Polish and Lithuanian, but in French, Russian, German, Spanish, and Italian, depending on their original provenance, and, finally, in English! I was faced with translating such measurements as *"garniec"* (a kind of bucket) or *"une bonne poignée d'ail"* (a good fistful of garlic). Fela, armed with a pencil and pad, spent months with me in Paris, quite literally intercepting seasonings as they fell from my hand into a pot in order to measure them—something I had never done in my life.

Then, when we had begun to conceive some semblance of form for the book, Peggy Yntema came on the scene. With the patience of a saint she helped me test, retest, and test again dish after dish, to say nothing of putting all those scribbles into "recipese"! I began to have hope—maybe at last my children would not be calling overseas in the middle of making something to ask "*Now* what do I do?" or "But how *long* does it cook?"—questions I desperately tried to answer from Paris or Marbella while one of them stood in Los Angeles or New York with dripping spoon or bubbling pot. First there was Eva, the eldest, who was married and with a houseful of children as well as her chaplain-husband's students and guests—she cooked all the time. (She may never forgive me for not doing this book twenty years ago when she needed it most!) Having been mixing, chopping, and watching pots for me since she was six, she seems to have acquired some of my kitchen ways—to say nothing of remembering countless anecdotes and stories—and she has been a great help with this book.

Some years later, my younger daughter Alina, having lived on yogurt and little else while in medical school, suddenly began cooking for her friends. Both my daughters have been after me for years, with very specific lists of what *had* to be in the book.

Now, a word about food in general. I have always thought it quite meaningful that almost every important occasion, religious or pagan, seems to involve a sharing of food. The very word "company" comes from com/pani/on—"with bread"—as though eating with another signifies and symbolizes a unity or trust. The examples are endless: bread and wine in the church coming from the Seder (which the Last Supper was), Thanksgiving, eggs at Easter standing for birth, new life, and so on.

I often wondered why I developed such a passion for cooking and came to the conclusion that from my early childhood to this day a meal for us has never been just the process of swallowing food, but a ritual of a kind. It brought the whole family together; it was a pause in our rushed life; it made whatever place we were in feel like home. When I was a child in Lithuania I learned from my parents to love and respect the good food from our fields and farms. Then the Great War exiled us to Moscow, where food during the Revolution was scant and poor. (I remember precisely the feel, like glue between the teeth, of that bread made of potatoes and hashed straw!) But our cook, Barbarka, managed somehow to keep us (and many cousins) fed, and my parents' kindness and warm hospitality made our meals together moments of relief from worry and fear. Those times taught me also never to waste food, or to take it for granted, lessons I know have been passed on to my children, and to theirs.

When World War I ended in 1918, my mother had to rehabilitate and oversee the estates that were her heritage, and so had to spend the winters in Lithuania. My sister and brothers and I went to school in Warsaw where our father was the director of the Warsaw Philharmonic, the Opera, and the Conservatory of Music. The director's private apartments were in a wing of the Opera House, and one could reach the main stage without going out. You can imagine how difficult it was for a little girl of ten, dreaming of being a dancer, to concentrate on her homework in the evenings! Needless to say, my lessons often went unfinished or undone, and I would run from our apartment through a maze of stairs and corridors, peering fascinated into room after room filled with costumes, wigs, props, boots, and ballet slippers, the very elements of that magical world of music and make-believe, until I reached the director's box. There, wide-eyed, I would listen and watch until I saw my father take his last bow. Afterward, we children would all sit up with him while he had supper, long past our school-night bedtime, drinking in eagerly all the stories and gossip of that wonderful world. In the mornings, of course, I was half-asleep and often late for school, but the many evenings we spent helping entertain our father's friends, musicians, singers, and artists became an invaluable experience for my future life.

After my marriage to Arthur Rubinstein this experience was greatly broadened when I accompanied him on tour. Being a famous "gourmet" he knew the best restaurants all over the world. Then I discovered that I had an odd but very useful talent: much as one might have a musical ear, I had the ability to decipher and identify the ingredients in even fairly elaborate dishes—and made a sort of game (and challenge!) of reproducing them at home without asking for recipes. Succeeding was great fun and gave me confidence to add or change or improvise, and finally to invent! My love affair with cooking had begun—and now after more than fifty years it has proved a very happy relationship.

Although eating well but reasonably is important to everybody, it may be especially so for performing artists whose hours and mealtimes are strictly dependent on concert schedules and must vary accordingly.

And so it happens that this book can offer you some fairly sophisticated dishes (like crayfish bisque), along with some old-fashioned and traditional ones (like walnut torte), and a few not only good but also quite simple (like scrambled eggs). My emphasis is not merely on dishes that can be produced at home, but on those that are better at home. After a few weeks of being "on the road" and eating in hotels and restaurants, no matter how good, I craved my pots and pans, my own knives, and the fresh flavors of real home food. Often I made "guest appearances" at our friends' houses, offering—and sometimes being asked!—to prepare one of my specialties like chicken cutlets, or, most often, *bigos.* I found myself cooking everywhere, in big and small kitchens, in modern food laboratories, on tiny gas burners in hotel kitchenettes. And once, in 1935, after five days of greasy borscht on the Trans-Siberian Express, I even made scrambled eggs in the diner—to the utter disbelief of the comrades on the kitchen staff, who had never seen a capitalist cook!

Arthur and I gave lots of parties, on tour and at home. There was a lovely one in 1938, when we opened the house of our dreams in Paris for the first time. And another, in California, which could have been disastrous, for the help inexplicably left suddenly the night before our tenth anniversary, our son, Paul, had mumps, and we had invited fifty guests to a sit-down dinner, then more guests for dancing, and a late supper for, as it turned out, everyone! Here are the menus for that evening:

### DINNER

Carp in Jelly, with Horseradish
Pink, Green, and White (Mustard) Mayonnaise
Pancakes with Meat Filling, Gratinéed
Green Bean and Artichoke Heart Salad
*Crème Brûlée* with Fresh Raspberries and Strawberries
Wafer Cookies (from a bakery)

### SUPPER

*Bigos,* with Potato Salad
Chicken Cutlets
Noodles with Mushrooms *(Lazanki)*
Cucumber Salad
Cut-up Fresh Fruit with Kirsch
Chocolate Mazurkas

As you see, these were generous menus. But all the dishes were practical ones I had cooked many times before, and I knew that I could cope. You will find recipes for all of them in this book, and also a group of menus I have found suitable for parties large and small.

My intention was always to cook quickly and not spend hours in the kitchen. I had so many other things to do! And I discovered that if I had planned carefully what I was to cook and in what order, half of the work was done. Good planning, organization, washing pots and pans while you cook are of utmost importance. And so is open-mindedness about new techniques and devices that will save precious time, and about manufactured products, which can be very good if you adjust your quantities to suit them. I use bouillon cubes, for instance. Having tasted all the brands, I now insist on Knorr's. But as any bouillon cubes are salty, I never salt anything into which the cubes will go. Once they are in the dish, I taste it carefully before seasoning, to avoid excessive saltiness, which kills all the aromas of food. Also, I use unsalted butter, which has a lovely fresh taste and does not add saltiness to dishes where it would be inappropriate. It is important always to taste and taste again. It is all very well to follow a written recipe, but one must also satisfy the individual palate. And ingredients vary with the place and the season—butter, cream, flour, oil, as well as vegetables.

One must be adaptable. Preparing meals is a joy if you do it with imagination, and with confidence. If something does go wrong, don't panic, but try to remedy it, or even change the recipe, to save your dish. Never admit your mistakes! And always be prepared to improvise.

I have learned to have a well-stocked larder, ready to produce a meal for two, three, fifteen people at the drop of a hat. (This book has many recipes one can prepare from things easy to keep on hand. Many of these are grouped in the chapter Little Entrées.) At home, which for me has meant New York or Paris or Marbella, in the south of Spain, old friends have always turned up from all over the world. Or new acquaintances are so nice that I want to show my liking by feeding them at home, at once! Or something splendid happens that requires a celebration: a success for one of our children, and now our grandchildren; a reunion with family or dear friends from Poland. My cooking is a token of my joy.

Cooking something good for my children, family, and friends has always been a way of expressing myself and showing them my affection. It is something I have always had time for and relished. And now I hope that using this book and making many of my dishes will convince you that cooking can be a joy, no matter how little time you may think you have or how limited your space may be.                                 *Nela Rubinstein*

# Nela's Cookbook

# Soups

# Broths

In my family everybody has always loved soup. At midnight, after a performance, the perfect thing to offer the artist was rich, hot broth. It seemed both to settle the stomach and to kindle appetite. Lunch, for us the principal meal of the day, often began with a cream of vegetable soup, which the children enjoyed (it was my way of making the children eat vegetables). Often soup was the main course. We Poles like it with a little complementary tidbit served on a separate plate; this can be as simple as a few croutons, to spoon into the soup or eat with the fingers, or it can be a small portion of a "made" dish—dumplings, filled pastries, etc.—one can also serve as a light entrée.

Almost all these soups can be made in the pressure cooker, which gives a nice full flavor and also saves time; directions are given with each recipe where using a pressure cooker is appropriate. And if you are really hurried, you can use canned broths or, better, bouillon cubes. (In certain recipes, these are essential for fortifying the water in which something has been poached. Not everything should be cooked in broth to begin with.) I like best the Knorr brand, as the cubes taste "real" and dissolve easily. With cans and cubes, be sure to taste the soup before adding any salt.

Except for fish stock, the broths described in this chapter are real soups, ready to serve. I don't use broths in the French manner, as *fonds de cuisine*. Long, slow reduction is a thrifty way to give something a rich taste, but for me all the freshness is lost. I'd rather use more meat and less time.

## BASIC BEEF BROTH

*Makes about 12 cups*

This is a good hearty broth, as a soup, or used in any recipe specifying "strong beef bouillon." (As a shortcut, you can use Knorr beef bouillon cubes dissolved in 1–1½ cups of water per cube.) For a fine aromatic broth, quite different from this, see the recipe for Boiled Beef with Horseradish Sauce, page 187.

I like to serve the broth with one of the garnishes in the chapter on Little Entrées, or I add to it one of these embellishments:

- 1 tablespoon per serving of cooked Rice (p. 122).
- Cooked vermicelli, about ¼ cup per cup of soup (for pasta doughs, see p. 100).
- Crêpes (thin pancakes rich with egg, p. 78) cut into very thin strips —about half a dozen strips per cup.
- A julienne of blanched vegetables, about 1 tablespoon per cup of soup.

I don't cook rice, vermicelli, or vegetables *in* the soup, because the separate, fresh tastes are more appealing. Dumplings, which are bigger and don't absorb so much soup taste, can be cooked right in the stock.

2 large, meaty soup bones
2 pounds (900 grams) beef shank, brisket, or short ribs
2 large onions, peeled
3 ribs celery
1 parsnip, peeled
2 carrots, peeled
3 white turnips, peeled
2 leeks, including some of the green
5 sprigs parsley
2 bay leaves
1 teaspoon thyme
10 peppercorns
1 Knorr beef bouillon cube (optional)
Salt to taste

Preheat the oven to 400°F (205°C). In a large pan, roast the soup bones in the oven, turning them once or twice, for about 15 minutes or until they are brown. Pour off and discard any fat from the pan. If any nice brown bits adhere to the pan, deglaze them with water and include them in the soup.

In a large kettle, put 4 quarts cold water and add the roasted bones, the meat, the onions, the celery, and the parsnip. Bring the pot to a boil and skim the liquid several times, until it remains clear. Then add the carrots, turnips, leeks, parsley, bay leaves, thyme, and peppercorns. Cook the soup slowly, covered, until the meat is tender, about 3 hours. Strain the broth, reserving the meat, and taste it. If it lacks strength, throw in the bouillon cube. Salt the stock carefully, tasting (if it is to be used in sauces, etc., it will cook down, and the saltiness will intensify). Let the broth cool, covered, then refrigerate it until the fat congeals and can be lifted off.

The broth will keep in the refrigerator for 5 days, or it can be frozen, but not indefinitely—say, for 2 months. The reserved meat can be useful minced in pancake or *pierogi* fillings.

*Note:* To color any brown stock like beef or duck, you may use dark caramelized sugar (details on p. 66), which has virtually no flavor, or you can roast an unpeeled onion for 1 hour at 350°F (180°C), then simmer with the broth (1 onion per 3 cups of broth).

*For the pressure cooker:* Brown the soup bones in the open pot, remove them, and brown the meat. Return the bones to the pot, and add the onions, celery, parsnip, and water to cover. Cook, covered, for 10 minutes after pressure is reached. Cool the pot under cold running water, uncover it, and skim the broth. Add the carrots, turnips, leeks, parsley, herbs, peppercorns, and more water, to cover. Cook for 30 minutes after pressure is reached. Cool and uncover the pot. Strain the broth, reserving the meat as above. Measure the broth, adding enough water to make 3 quarts (12 cups). Taste it, and add a bouillon cube if you want it stronger. Correct the seasoning. Cool, chill, and defat the broth as above.

## CHICKEN BROTH

*Makes about 7 cups*

This gives you a rich broth that jells slightly and may be served plain. It can also be used in any recipe specifying chicken broth, but, as a shortcut, you could use instead one Knorr chicken bouillon cube per 1–1½ cups of water.

I like to serve the broth with one of these embellishments:
- 1 tablespoon per serving of cooked Rice (p. 122).
- Dumplings cooked in the broth (p. 90).
- Separately cooked vermicelli, about ¼ cup per cup of soup (for pasta doughs, see p. 100).
- A julienne of blanched vegetables, about 1 tablespoon per cup of soup.

If I'm in a hurry, I use the pressure cooker and make Quick Chicken Stock (following recipe), which has slightly different proportions.

3 pounds (1350 grams) chicken backs, wings,
    necks, and giblets (not liver)
2 carrots, peeled
2 onions, peeled
3 ribs celery
5 sprigs parsley
6 peppercorns
Salt to taste

In 2 quarts (2 liters) cold water, place the chicken pieces, carrots, onions, celery, parsley, and peppercorns. Cook them slowly, covered, for 1½ hours. Strain the broth, discarding all the other ingredients, and let it cool, covered. Refrigerate it until the fat congeals and can be lifted off. Taste for seasoning. If you plan to use the broth in a sauce, salt it only cautiously, as further cooking will intensify the saltiness.

The broth will keep in the refrigerator for 5 days and can be frozen, but not indefinitely—say, for 2 months.

*For the pressure cooker:* See the following recipe.

## QUICK CHICKEN STOCK

*Makes about 3 cups*

This makes a nice fresh-tasting soup, which I might make for lunch for just two or three people or use as the base for a chicken dish. I don't bother to remove the fat before using the broth in a sauce, or for moistening a cutlet mixture or a pancake filling.

1 pound (450 grams) chicken backs and necks
2 carrots, peeled and quartered
1 onion, peeled and halved
2 ribs celery, quartered
Salt and white pepper to taste

Place in the pressure cooker 3 cups water and the chicken pieces, carrots, onion, and celery. Cook them for 15 minutes after pressure is reached. Cool the cooker under cold running water and uncover it. Strain the broth, squeezing as much broth as you can out of the chicken and vegetables. Discard these ingredients, and remove the fat from the broth if you are serving it as a soup. Season it to taste as you use it.

## Two Jellied Soups with Caviar

When we went to the Soviet Union in 1932, for the first time after the war, my husband was classified as a "special worker," which entitled us to food cards. The times were very hard then, Stalin in full power, and the stores empty of food; but those with dollars or *spec'es* with cards could find some items, in certain designated shops. When we ventured to one of them, we found the choices limited to smoked fish, a few sausages, and caviar both pressed and fresh. To our inquiry about what the card represented, the salesman said, "You can have a kilo of caviar or a kilo of smoked fish." It is obvious what our choice was.

For one whole month we ate caviar morning, noon, and night; my husband never seemed to tire of it. But I did, and would gladly have traded it for a decent piece of meat or white bread. Several months later, back in Paris and having supper at Maxim's, I sheepishly asked, "Arthur, could I have some caviar tonight?" He looked at me with reproach and said laughingly, "So now, here where a spoon of caviar is worth a fortune, you want it, and in Russia you did not deign to eat it. Shame on you!" But of course he ordered it immediately.

Now, caviar has reached quite impossible prices. But the small quantities of it, one black, one red, in my two soups make them taste and look so elegant—and yet are not ruinous.

### JELLIED CHICKEN SOUP
### WITH BLACK CAVIAR

*Serves 6*

6 cups (1½ liters) homemade Chicken Broth (p. 8)
1–2 tablespoons (1–2 standard envelopes) gelatin (optional)
6 teaspoons black caviar
1 tablespoon finely cut parsley

Test a little of the broth, by chilling a spoonful for 10 minutes, to be sure it will jell softly (not so stiffly as for unmolding). If it is too liquid, dissolve gelatin in ½ cup broth, heat the remaining broth, add the gelatin mixture, and chill. When the liquid begins to thicken, distribute it into 6 soup cups, sprinkle 1 teaspoon caviar over the surface of each, and refrigerate them. The caviar will sink a little, but will be trapped and suspended by the hardening jelly before it has a chance to collect in the bottom of the cup. Sprinkle each cup with a little parsley before serving.

## JELLIED CANNED CONSOMMÉ MADRILÈNE WITH RED CAVIAR

*Serves 6*

Be careful to get a very good brand of canned consommé; some of them taste too metallic, spoiling the tomato tang that makes a madrilène so good.

- 6 cups (1½ liters) canned jelling consommé madrilène
- 6 teaspoons red caviar (salmon roe)
- 6 teaspoons sour cream
- 1 tablespoon finely cut chives

If the canned consommé is already a little set, melt it before distributing it among the soup cups. Chill the cups of consommé until the liquid begins to thicken. Sprinkle 1 teaspoon red caviar over each cup, and chill again until the consommé has set. Before serving, garnish each cup with 1 teaspoon sour cream, lightly sprinkled with chives.

## ITALIAN SOUP

*Serves 6*

This is quite a substantial dish. Rather than the vermicelli one so often gets in restaurants, I use cooked elbow macaroni, because it keeps its firmness and doesn't get too soft during the mixing.

3 egg yolks
1 cup (¼ liter) sour cream
2 cups (½ liter) cooked elbow macaroni
6 cups (1½ liters) combined hot Basic Beef Broth
    (p. 5) and Chicken Broth (p. 8), or use 3 Knorr
    beef and 3 Knorr chicken bouillon cubes
    dissolved in 6 cups boiling water
½ cup (4 ounces or 115 grams) freshly grated
    Parmesan cheese
Pepper to taste
Salt, if necessary

In a saucepan, beat together the egg yolks and sour cream. Add the cooked macaroni and mix well. Slowly pour the hot broth over, stirring continually. Heat the mixture, slowly, without boiling. Add the cheese and mix it in with a fork. Taste the soup and grind in pepper to taste. If you used homemade broths, you may need salt (but of course Parmesan cheese gives you some). Serve immediately.

## DUCK SOUP WITH BARLEY

*Serves 4*

Without the barley, this is a basic recipe for duck broth or stock. It is important to cook the barley separately in water before adding it to the soup; if you cook it in the stock, it takes on the duck flavor and the soup becomes rather dull and without contrast.

Carcass of a roast duck, with giblets (but not the liver)
1 onion, peeled
1 carrot, peeled
2 ribs celery
3 sprigs parsley
⅔ cup (1½ deciliters) fine (small) barley
1 teaspoon oil
Salt and pepper to taste

Chop the duck carcass roughly and simmer, covered, for 1½ hours with the giblets, onion, carrot, celery, and parsley, and enough water to cover (at least 4 cups). Meanwhile, soak the barley for 40 minutes in 2 cups of cold unsalted water with 1 teaspoon oil added. Then set the pan over heat, cover it, and simmer for about 40 minutes, or until the barley has expanded but still has a little "bite." Check the barley package directions and add water during the cooking if necessary: some packaged barley will absorb more than three times its volume of water.

Strain the duck broth and add the cooked barley. Check the seasoning, salt and pepper to your taste, and serve.

*For the pressure cooker:* Most manufacturers advise you not to pressure cook barley because the vent may become clogged, but barley is safe for some new models; check the booklet that accompanied yours. As for the duck, combine the chopped carcass with the giblets, onion, carrot, celery, and parsley in the cooker. Add water to cover and cook for 30 minutes after pressure is reached. Cool and uncover the pot, strain the broth, and add more water, if necessary, to make 4 cups.

# Beet Soups

There are a few simple reasons that beets are so popular in my part of Europe. One is that they are plentiful and easy to grow, therefore inexpensive; another is that they keep well during the long winters. Also they have a rich, interesting, and slightly sweet flavor, while their ruby color alone must always have added a cheering note to even the humblest soup in the poorest pot.

You will find here the six beet soups I make most often, but I leave you to imagine how many others there are, from the most basic meal-in-one to the most refined and delicate—with recipes for different kinds of *barszcz* (barsh-ch), the Polish spelling, and borscht, a phonetic interpretation of the Russian.

I begin here with a Ukrainian borscht, very rich and full of other ingredients—really a meal in itself. *Barszcz* with Cream is Polish, enriched with egg yolks and cream—which was a great favorite with my husband.

Clear *Barszcz* is really a strong beet consommé. I have always served it, very hot and in deep coffee cups, at postconcert suppers, to my husband and many other artists who arrive thirsty, hungry, a bit tired, and in need of something immediately. Somehow the *barszcz,* with its slight sweetness, is instantly reviving. Many gracious hosts at such parties sometimes forget that most performers dine lightly, or not at all, before "going to work," but afterward would choose a cup of hot soup or a scrambled egg, *right away,* over any delicacy after an hour of waiting, *and* cocktails!

Quick *Barszcz* is *really* quick and is based on pickled beets. It approximates the taste of *kwass buraczany* (kvahss boorah-*chah*-nih), a mixture of beets allowed to ferment and used much like the starter for sourdough breads. Kept in a crock, it is replenished and always available to add the slight sourness that goes so well with the natural sweetness of beets.

Beet Tops Soup, called *Botwina* (Bot-*vee*-nah: remember, in Polish all *w*'s are pronounced like *v*'s, which don't exist in the Polish alphabet), has a quite special flavor, different from soups based on just the beet itself. It is also hearty and filling, excellent for cold winter meals.

The last recipe is one for a summer *barszcz, Chlodnik*—a kind of Slavic gazpacho—soup-and-salad in one, cool, smooth, rich, nourishing, and full of little surprises. One could hardly ask more of any dish!

## RUSSIAN BORSCHT
(*Barszcz Ukrainski,* pronounced barsh oo-cra-*hins*-ki)

*Serves 6 as a main course*

This is a meal in itself, served with a starchy dish like steamed potatoes, Kasha (p. 120), or navy beans. I like to cut up the cooked meat and serve a little of it in each soup bowl.

1 pound (450 grams) fresh pork shoulder
1 pound (450 grams) beef shank or short ribs
2 tablespoons lard or oil
4 large cooked fresh beets, peeled and cut
  in julienne; or about 1 pound (450 grams)
  canned julienned beets with their juice
2 onions, peeled
2 carrots, peeled
1 parsnip, peeled
2 bay leaves
10 peppercorns
½ head cabbage
Large piece lemon zest or 1 whole unshelled walnut
4 fresh tomatoes, peeled, quartered, and seeded; or
  1 pound (450 grams) canned whole tomatoes
Salt to taste
1 tablespoon lemon juice (optional)
½ cup (1 deciliter) sour cream (optional)

Brown the pork and beef in the lard or oil. See the note, page 262, on cooking beets. In a large pot, place the meat with 6 cups (1½ liters) water and the cooked or canned beets; if you are using canned beets, include their liquid; for fresh cooked beets, add an additional cup water. Tie the onions, carrots, parsnip, bay leaves, and peppercorns in a large piece of rinsed cheesecloth (for easy removal later). Add them to the pot, and simmer the soup, covered, for 1½ hours.

Shred the cabbage and blanch it for 5 minutes in a large quantity of boiling water with a large piece of lemon zest or a walnut, which helps to remove the unpleasant odor of boiling cabbage. Drain and add the cabbage to the soup. Add the tomatoes and simmer the soup for 30 minutes longer.

Before serving the soup, discard the onions, carrots, parsnip, bay leaves, and peppercorns. Remove and chop the meats. Taste the soup, and add salt and lemon juice if necessary; this *barszcz* is mild flavored and should not be acid. Serve it with pieces of meat and a little sour cream, if you like, floating on top.

*For the pressure cooker:* Brown the meats in the open pot. Quarter the onions, carrots, and parsnip, and add them to the pot with the bay leaves and 1 cup water and 1 Knorr beef bouillon cube. Cook for 10 minutes after pressure is reached; cool the pot and uncover it. Remove and discard the onions, carrots, parsnip, and bay leaves. Strain and defat the broth (the pressure cooker extracts more fat than an ordinary pot). Return the broth to the pot with the cabbage, tomatoes, peppercorns, and the meat. Add the julienned beets and cook for 15 minutes after pressure is reached. Taste and add salt and the optional lemon juice, to taste.

# BARSZCZ WITH CREAM

*Serves 6–8*

This *barszcz* is quite rich in taste. Do be very careful about adding salt, sugar, and vinegar in tiny amounts, for the balance must be just right, and vinegars vary. I like plain cider vinegar, the kind every store in the United States can supply, but can only be had *"à prix d'or"* in Paris at such elegant shops as Hédiard and Fauchon. So in France my everyday substitute is red wine vinegar.

With this *barszcz*, I particularly like to serve (on a little side plate for each person) crêpes with a filling of calf's brain, sautéed (p. 81), or Boiled Potatoes with Bacon and Onion (p. 279).

6 large cooked fresh beets, cut in julienne, or
   1½ pounds (675 grams) canned julienned
   beets with their juice
6 cups (1½ liters) Basic Beef Broth (p. 5), or
   use 3 Knorr beef bouillon cubes dissolved
   in 6 cups water
2 teaspoons or more vinegar
2 teaspoons or more sugar
Salt to taste
Pinch of pepper
6 egg yolks
6 tablespoons heavy cream
Finely cut fresh dill

See the note, page 262, on cooking beets. Add the cooked or canned beets to the broth, add the vinegar and sugar, and simmer for about 10 minutes, then taste. (Do not overcook, or it will get brown.) Strain the broth, discarding the beets unless you have another use for them, and taste. Add a little more sugar and vinegar, if necessary, and salt and pepper. Beat the egg yolks and cream together in a bowl, stir in some of the hot broth, and return the mixture to the pot, keeping the soup just below the simmer and stirring constantly until it thickens enough to coat a spoon. Taste it: Sugar? Vinegar? Salt? Add any of these cautiously, tasting again. Serve the soup in cups with a sprinkling of fresh dill, if available.

*Not for the pressure cooker:* This soup takes so little time in an ordinary pot that the saving of time would be negligible. Moreover, you would not be able to judge the color of the soup.

## CLEAR BARSZCZ

*Serves 6*

Always serve clear *barszcz* in deep coffee cups or the consommé cups, with little handles, that one can drink from easily. When eaten with a spoon this vivid broth has a particularly irrepressible urge to leave bright little pink dots, especially on starched white concert shirts.

When Eva was eighteen, dining before a ball and faced with clear *barszcz* in a shallow soup dish, she tucked her napkin unceremoniously all around her strapless gown—and was the only guest not dipping napkin corners into champagne for repairs.

Serve clear *barszcz* with *Pierożkis* (p. 116), or Boiled Potatoes with Bacon and Onion (p. 279), or Crêpes with Calf's Brain Filling (p. 81). Another perfect accompaniment is *Coulibiac* (p. 113).

8 cups (2 liters) Basic Beef Broth (p. 5), or
  use 4 Knorr beef bouillon cubes dissolved
  in 8 cups water (if using canned, follow
  directions for dilution)
6 medium cooked fresh beets, peeled and cut in
  julienne; or 1½ pounds (675 grams) canned
  julienned beets with their juice
1 bay leaf
2 teaspoons vinegar
2 teaspoons sugar
Salt and pepper to taste

In a saucepan, simmer the beef broth, beets, and bay leaf over a low fire for 10 minutes. (Do not overcook, or it will get brown.) Add the vinegar and sugar, and taste. Add salt, if necessary, and pepper to taste. Serve very hot.

## QUICK BARSZCZ

*Serves 6*

For this version of *barszcz* you use canned *pickled* beets, with their juice. (Don't get the kind that have been thickened with cornstarch, like Harvard beets.) You rely on the canner for a well-seasoned broth, and once you have found a brand you really like, then, in emergencies, you can be sure of a nice soup in no time.

1½ pounds (675 grams) canned pickled
  julienned beets with their juice
6 cups (1½ liters) Basic Beef Broth (p. 5),
  or consommé, or use 3 Knorr beef bouillon
  cubes dissolved in 6 cups water
2 tablespoons (or so) vinegar or lemon juice
  (optional)
Pepper to taste
1 tablespoon (or so) sugar (optional)
Finely cut dill or parsley

Stir the beets and their juice into the broth and heat together for 10 minutes. Strain the soup, discard the beets, and season to taste with vinegar and pepper. (If you used bouillon cubes, you will want to correct their saltiness with sugar.) Sprinkle the broth with the dill or parsley.

*Variation:* For a quick creamed *barszcz,* mix 2 tablespoons flour with ¾ cup heavy cream, stir in a little hot broth, return to the pot, and cook slowly, stirring, for 2 minutes or until thickened.

*Not for the pressure cooker.*

## BEET TOPS SOUP
### (*Botwina*, pronounced bot-*vee*-nah)

*Serves 6*

I love small young beet greens as a vegetable. Mature beet greens are better in soup, which is good by itself or as a component of *Chlodnik* (following recipe). Alas, in Paris one can seldom get beet greens at all.

- 2–2½ cups (½ liter–6 deciliters) mature beet stems and leaves (all the stems and about half the leaves from a bunch of 4–5 large beets)
- 5 cups (1¼ liters) Basic Beef Broth (p. 5), or 3 Knorr beef bouillon cubes dissolved in 5 cups water or equivalent amount of canned consommé
- A few drops of vinegar or lemon juice (optional)
- 6 tablespoons heavy cream (optional)
- 4 tablespoons chopped, cooked, or canned beets (optional)

Chop the washed beet stems and leaves. Cook them, covered, in 1 cup water for about 10 minutes, or until they are soft. Add the beef broth or consommé. Taste and add a little vinegar or lemon juice; it should be just slightly sour. I like to serve this soup with a little cream stirred in and a sprinkling of chopped beets.

*For the pressure cooker:* Place the chopped stems and leaves in the pot and add about an inch of water. Cover and weight the pot, and cook only until pressure is reached. Cool the pot, mix the soup with the broth or consommé, and season and serve as above.

## CHLODNIK
(pronounced hh*lod*-nik)

*Serves 8*

This exquisite ice-cold soup is smooth, piquant, and as pink as a petunia. On really hot days in Marbella, when a searing wind comes up from Africa and we have to keep watering the terrace tiles or else put on shoes, *chlodnik* is a most refreshing thought. This is partly true because it isn't cooked, just assembled like a salad, so the cook and the kitchen stay cool.

It is quickly made, but you should allow several hours to chill it well. If you have space, refrigerate the tureen, the soup bowls, and the garnish bowls well beforehand. If you are serving at a buffet lunch outside, ease the tureen into a big bowl of crushed ice.

The version below is my favorite, but, as with most traditional dishes (*chlodnik* is Polish), many variations are possible. To smooth the soup, you can substitute yogurt or even buttermilk for the rather calorie-laden sour cream. For a shortcut, you can omit the beef broth and the pickled beets by reserving some of a Clear *Barszcz* (p. 18) made in advance (though, in that case, you might add a few pickled beets to the *chlodnik* anyway). And you can vary the garnish, provided the flavors and textures are nicely balanced.

6 cups (1½ liters) Basic Beef Broth (p. 5), or
　use 3 Knorr beef bouillon cubes dissolved
　in 6 cups water
6 ounces (180 grams) canned diced beets
6 ounces (180 grams) canned diced pickled beets
1½ cups (3½ deciliters) Beet Tops Soup (p. 20)
2 cups (½ liter) sour cream
2 medium kosher dill pickles, peeled and diced fine

Combine all the ingredients. Chill them well.

Prepare and chill in separate bowls the following garnishes:

2 medium cucumbers, peeled, seeded, and diced
6 large cooked shrimp, peeled and diced; or 12 cooked crayfish, diced
2 hard-boiled eggs, peeled and quartered
Finely cut herbs: 1 tablespoon fresh dill and 3 tablespoons scallions
　(mostly the white part)

Before serving, taste the chilled soup. You may wish to add sugar or a few drops of vinegar or even salt. It is always important to taste a soup after chilling it well, as the cold mutes some flavors a little.

## SAUERKRAUT SOUP
### (*Kapuśniak,* pronounced kap-*oos*-hnyak)

*Serves 6–8*

This is one of those pickley, sweet-sour soups so popular in Central Europe. I wonder if our long, hard winters weren't responsible for dishes like this, since in my childhood one had to rely so much on brining and preserving for fresh, sharp flavors.

Like the hearty Russian version of Clear *Barszcz* (p. 18), *kapuśniak* can be a very substantial main course. (I serve it that way often, with steamed potatoes.) *Kapuśniak* is traditionally a hearty peasant dish, but I have tried to make it more subtle and well balanced.

    1 pound (450 grams) fresh or canned sauerkraut
    4 cups (1 liter) Basic Beef Broth (p. 5), or use 2 Knorr
        beef bouillon cubes dissolved in 4 cups water
    2 pounds (900 grams) pork spareribs
    2 bay leaves
    8 peppercorns
    2 medium carrots, peeled and sliced
    2 ounces (60 grams) dried mushrooms (optional)
    2 tablespoons sugar

Rinse the sauerkraut lightly in cold water and drain it well. In a large pot, place the beef broth (or the bouillon cubes and water), spareribs, bay leaves, peppercorns, carrots, and dried mushrooms, if used. Cook, covered, for 1½ hours until the meat is done.

Remove the dried mushrooms and cut them into strips. Return them to the pot and add 4 more cups of water.

Melt sugar over medium heat until it colors and caramelizes. (For details on caramelizing, see page 66.) Add the sauerkraut and the caramelized sugar to the pot, cover and cook for 30 minutes.

Cut meat off bones and slice in strips about an inch long; return to soup. Taste, add salt if needed, and serve.

*For the pressure cooker:* Place in the pot the spareribs, the bay leaves, the peppercorns, carrots, and the mushrooms (optional). Add enough broth to fill the pot two-thirds full. Cook for 30 minutes after pressure is reached.

Cool and uncover the pot. Add the sauerkraut and 2 tablespoons caramelized sugar. Cook 5 more minutes after pressure is reached. Add more broth, or water and bouillon cubes, to make about 8 cups liquid altogether. Taste for seasoning and serve.

## KIDNEY AND DILL PICKLE SOUP
### (*Ogórkowa,* pronounced oh-goor-*kov*-a)

*Serves 6–8*

Like *Kapuśniak* (p. 23), this is a rich, slightly sour Polish soup, but it is not sweet-sour. The pickle and kidney together produce a curiously dense flavor, which is offset and a little modified by the addition of potatoes, which also thicken the soup lightly. I find it very satisfying in cool weather.

    1 veal kidney, about ½ pound (225 grams),
       or a *young* beef kidney
    6 cups (1½ liters) cold Basic Beef Broth (p. 5), or use
       3 Knorr beef bouillon cubes dissolved in 6 cups water
    5 medium kosher dill pickles, diced
    1 cup (¼ liter) juice from the pickle jar
    3 medium boiling potatoes, peeled and diced
    Pinch of pepper
    3 tablespoons sour cream (optional)
    1–2 tablespoons finely cut dill or parsley

Soak the kidney for 1 hour in cold salted water. Discard the water and trim the kidney of fat and membrane. Slice it ⅓ inch thick and cut the slices in quarters. In the soup pot, cover the kidney with cold broth, or use cold water and add the bouillon cubes later. Bring to a boil and simmer 10 minutes, skimming the broth until it is clear; add the cubes if you are using them. Add the diced pickles, the pickle juice, and the diced potatoes, and cook for 10 minutes more. Pepper the soup to taste and serve with the optional sour cream, sprinkled with herbs.

## *Three Sorrel Soups*

I'll begin with a quick version, because that may be the only kind of sorrel soup available to you. Fresh sorrel, used in the following recipe, is sometimes hard to get, but you can buy canned or bottled *schav* in any Jewish grocery or in most supermarkets.

This soup is a joy to serve at parties, because it is a surprise to most guests and yet they always seem to enjoy it. I like to serve it with a garnish of hot, buttery Polish stuffed eggs (*Oeufs Farcis à la Polonaise,* p. 123) on individual side plates, or just with a quartered hard-boiled egg per person.

# QUICK SORREL SOUP, WITH SCHAV

*Serves 6*

3 tablespoons flour
3 tablespoons butter
6 cups (1½ liters) Basic Beef Broth (p. 5), or
   use 3 Knorr beef bouillon cubes dissolved
   in 6 cups water
¾ cup (1¾ deciliters) sour cream
10 ounces (285 grams) canned or bottled *schav*
   with juice
GARNISH: 6 hard-boiled eggs, plain or Polish style
   (p. 123)

Cook the flour in the butter, stirring, until it is thick and smooth. Add the beef broth and cook until it is thickened and the flour no longer tastes raw. Add the sour cream off the boil (so it won't curdle). Just before serving, stir in the *schav* with its juice. Serve with the egg garnish.

# FRESH SORREL SOUP
*(Soupe à l'Oseille)*

*Serves 6*

I would love to see sorrel in every garden. There are two kinds, a broad-leaved, cultivated variety and a smaller-leaved, wild type; both grow abundantly. Both are bright green until they are cooked, then the leaves turn a drab, dark olive color.

1½ pounds (675 grams) fresh sorrel
3 tablespoons butter
6 cups (1½ liters) Basic Beef Broth (p. 5), or
    use 3 Knorr beef bouillon cubes dissolved
    in 6 cups water
3 tablespoons flour
¾ cup (1¾ deciliters) sour cream
GARNISH: 6 hard-boiled eggs, plain or Polish style
    (p. 123)

Pull the stems off the sorrel, rinse the leaves, and cut them in strips. Over medium heat, toss the leaves in the butter, cover the pot, and stew them over low heat for 5 minutes. They exude a good deal of moisture and need no water. When you uncover the pot, you will find a limp dark mass and some brownish broth; let the nice smell reassure you! Take a little of the beef broth and dissolve the flour in it, mixing until smooth. Stir this mixture into the sorrel and gradually add the rest of the beef broth, stirring until it is evenly thickened. Simmer the soup, covered, on low heat for 5–10 minutes. Stir in the sour cream and serve with the egg garnish.

## POTAGE GERMINY

*Serves 6*

This is a rich pale yellow soup, being thickened with egg yolks and heavy cream, and is not quite so lively in flavor as the lighter sorrel soup in the preceding recipe. I usually serve it with croutons or cheese sticks.

1½ pounds (675 grams) fresh sorrel
6 cups (1½ liters) Basic Beef Broth (p. 5), or
    use 4 Knorr beef bouillon cubes dissolved
    in 6 cups water
6 egg yolks
1½ cups (3½ deciliters) heavy cream

Stem the sorrel, rinse the leaves, pat them dry, and shred them extremely fine. Have the broth at the full boil. Throw in the sorrel and cook for 3 minutes. Beat together the egg yolks and cream, add a little soup to them, stirring, and lift the pot off the heat. Stirring, return the broth-yolk–cream mixture to the pot, and stir the soup over very low heat until it is thickened and satiny; don't let it boil. Serve it at once.

With bottled *schav,* instead of fresh sorrel, you can make a quick *Potage Germiny.* Thicken the hot beef broth as above, then swirl in 10 ounces *schav* and its juice.

# Hearty Vegetable Soups

### ADAM'S VEGETABLE SOUP

*Serves 6*

In this mild, mellow soup the balance of flavors is important, and so I am quite precise about measuring equal amounts of each vegetable. The pieces must be cut quite small before they are sautéed, so that the cooking is even and so that there are more surfaces to get that good butter taste. If you plan to serve them floating in their broth, cut the vegetables in julienne; if you are planning to purée the soup, chopping will do. The puréeing produces a lovely golden color, and a smooth texture that is enhanced by serving plenty of croutons.

1 cup (¼ liter) julienned or chopped celery,
    including a few leaves
1 cup (¼ liter) julienned or chopped carrots
1 cup (¼ liter) leeks, with some green as well
    as white, cut in fine crosswise slices, then
    rinsed and drained
1 cup (¼ liter) potato, julienned and soaked in
    cold water
2 tablespoons butter
4–6 cups (1–1½ liters) Quick Chicken Stock
    (p. 9), or use 2–3 Knorr chicken bouillon cubes
    dissolved in 4–6 cups water
Salt and pepper to taste
2 tablespoons finely cut dill, parsley, or chives
½ cup (1 deciliter) sweet cream or sour cream
    (optional)

In a soup pot, turn the celery, carrots, leeks, and drained potatoes in the butter. Add 2 cups cold water, cover the pot, and simmer for 30 minutes.

Add 4 cups of the chicken broth. (Adding it at this stage, rather than cooking the vegetables in it, preserves their fresh flavor.) Taste the soup. Add more broth gradually, tasting, if you like. Add a little salt and pepper, to taste.

If you purée the soup and it seems too thick, add a little more broth.

Sprinkle the soup with the dill, parsley, or chives, and serve. The sweet or sour cream, if you are using either, may be stirred in or passed separately.

*For the pressure cooker:* In the open pot, sauté the vegetables as above. Add, first, 2 cups water, cover the pot, and cook for 3–4 minutes after pressure is reached. Cool and uncover the pot. At this point, if you are planning to purée or blend (my personal preference), do so before adding more liquid. When the soup is blended, add broth until desired consistency is reached. Taste and season.

## POTATO AND LEEK SOUP

*Serves 6*

This is a simple variation of a soup everyone likes and almost everyone makes. I do it without sautéing the vegetables, so that it is not rich, and I add a little sour cream, rather than the usual sweet cream. It need not be puréed, but if you want to, then it should be thoroughly blended or processed to make a satiny soup. To serve it cold, I prefer to purée it; and, since the soup thickens as it cools, I dilute it with rich milk or with half-and-half.

> 1½ cups (3½ deciliters) baking potatoes,
>   in ¼-inch dice
> 1½ cups (3½ deciliters) leeks, white part only, cut
>   very thin crosswise, with the rings separated
> 6 cups (1½ liters) Quick Chicken Stock (p. 9), or
>   use 3 Knorr chicken bouillon cubes dissolved
>   in 6 cups water
> ½ cup (1 deciliter) sour cream
> 5 grinds white pepper
> Salt to taste
> 4 tablespoons finely cut chives or scallions

Simmer the cut potatoes and leeks in the stock until done, a matter of 5–6 minutes. Stir in the sour cream. Purée the soup if you wish. Taste. Add the pepper, and salt if necessary. Taste again. Serve sprinkled with chives or scallions.

*For the pressure cooker:* Cut the vegetables larger, the potatoes in ½-inch dice and the leeks in ½-inch rings. Cook for 5 minutes after pressure is reached, then cool the pot, uncover it, and taste and season as above.

## WATERCRESS SOUP

*Serves 6*

The peppery taste of watercress is softened here by the blandness of potatoes. This soup is a bright, speckled green and has an appetizing fragrance. It is good served cold, but chilling thickens it, so you will probably want to dilute it with chilled light cream.

One large bunch watercress, about 3 cups
   (¾ liter), loosely packed
2 medium baking potatoes
5 cups (1¼ liters) Quick Chicken Stock
   (p. 9), or use 3½ Knorr chicken bouillon
   cubes dissolved in 5 cups hot water
½ cup (1 deciliter) sour cream

Rinse, dry, and roughly chop the watercress. Peel the potatoes and cut into 1-inch dice. In a heavy casserole, cook the watercress and potatoes slowly, covered, for 20 minutes in 2 cups of the broth. Purée the soup and strain it. Tasting at intervals, add the reserved broth, or not quite all of it if you want a stronger watercress flavor. Either add the sour cream to the soup (below the simmer), or, if you have dieters around, pass it in a bowl.

*For the pressure cooker:* Rinse and chop the watercress and dice the potatoes. Put the cress, potatoes, and 2 cups broth in the pot, and cook for 5 minutes after pressure is reached. Cool and uncover the pot. Complete the soup as above.

# PEA SOUP

*Serves 6*

For Split Pea Soup, see following recipe. This soup calls for fresh or frozen green peas, a version of the French *potage St. Germain,* but not so oniony. It should taste very fresh, even a little sweet, and it has a strong, pure color.

If you plan to use frozen peas, see the note at the end of the recipe; they are timed a little differently.

1 tablespoon butter
1 pound (450 grams) shelled fresh peas (buy 3 pounds,
    or 1350 grams, in shells); or two 10-ounce packages
    (285 grams each) frozen green peas
4 scallions, white part only, chopped
5 cups (1¼ liters) Quick Chicken Stock (p. 9),
    or use 2½ Knorr chicken bouillon cubes
    dissolved in 5 cups water
2 tablespoons heavy cream
Sugar, if necessary
1 tablespoon finely cut fresh tarragon, dill, or chervil
GARNISH: croutons

In a saucepan melt the butter and add the peas, chopped scallions, and 1 cup of the broth. Simmer gently, covered, for 20 minutes. Check during the simmer to be sure that the peas are moist, and add a little broth if necessary. Add the cream and purée the mixture. Reheat it, stirring in the remaining broth. Taste the soup, adding a little sugar if necessary and sprinkle with chopped herbs. Serve it with croutons in a separate bowl.

*Note:* If you use frozen peas, thaw and drain them. Place in the saucepan with the butter, chopped scallions, and 1 cup of broth. Cover and simmer for 10 minutes only. Complete the soup and serve it as above.

*For the pressure cooker:* Substitute 1 quartered onion for the scallions. Cook for 4 minutes after pressure is reached. Cool and uncover the pot. Complete the soup and serve it as above. (If you are using frozen peas, mince the onion first, and cook for 2 minutes after pressure is reached.)

## SPLIT PEA SOUP OR LENTIL SOUP

*Serves 6–8*

This makes a hearty main course for a winter meal. I think the bay leaf and the beef broth are a bit unusual, but for me they round out the good but still slightly "green" taste of dried legumes and give the soup a lot more fragrance.

½ pound (225 grams) split peas or lentils
2 medium carrots, chopped coarse
2 medium onions, chopped coarse
2 ribs celery (no leaves), chopped coarse
1 large fragrant bay leaf
6 peppercorns
A ham bone (optional)
6 cups (1½ liters) Basic Beef Broth (p. 5), or
    use 2–3 Knorr beef bouillon cubes dissolved
    in 6 cups water (use only 2 cubes if you
    have a ham bone)
GARNISH: 3 frankfurters, sliced thin to make
    ⅔ cup (1½ deciliters) hot croutons

First look at the package directions for the split peas or lentils. Hardly any ever seem to need presoaking nowadays, but make sure. Wash these legumes in cold water, pick out any unsatisfactory ones (again, very unlikely nowadays), and skim any little flakes or specks from the surface of the water.

Drain the split peas or lentils and put them in a large pot with the carrots, onions, celery, bay leaf, and peppercorns, and the ham bone, if you have one. Add the broth, cover the pot, and cook over low heat for 1½ hours, stirring occasionally and adding water if too much has evaporated. Taste the soup for seasoning. You might want to dissolve a bouillon cube in it if it is not strong enough.

Discard the ham bone and purée the soup. Serve with the sliced frankfurters floating in the tureen and pass the croutons separately.

*For the pressure cooker:* There is some risk, with most pressure cookers, in cooking dried legumes. Their thick splutters may clog the safety vent. I am told that some new-model pressure cookers make provision for this: check your accompanying handbook. You would cook the soup exactly as above, shortening the simmering time to 30 minutes (after pressure is reached). Cool the pot and uncover it. Taste a pea or lentil, and cook a few minutes longer if necessary.

## Two Mushroom Soups

Ordinary fresh supermarket mushrooms are perfect for both of these soups. The second soup is very different in taste and color because of the addition of dried *cèpes*.

## MUSHROOM BISQUE

*Serves 6*

This is a velvety, semipuréed soup enriched with cream.

1 pound (450 grams) mushrooms
½ small onion, peeled
2 tablespoons butter
6 cups (1½ liters) hot Basic Beef Broth (p. 5),
    or use 3 Knorr beef bouillon cubes dissolved
    in 6 cups water
2 tablespoons flour
½ cup (1 deciliter) heavy cream
Salt and pepper to taste

Grind, blend, or process together the mushrooms (including the stems) and the onion. Turn them in the butter, cover, and cook for 5 minutes. Add 2 cups of the hot broth. Mix the flour and cream to a smooth paste, dilute it with a little hot soup, and return the mixture to the pot. Simmer the soup, stirring, until it has thickened and you don't taste raw flour. Add the remaining broth and taste the soup for seasoning. It shouldn't be very thick, and you may even like to dilute it with water or additional cream.

*Not for the pressure cooker:* It makes the mushrooms too soft.

## MUSHROOM SOUP WITH BARLEY

*Serves 8*

I think the tastiest dried mushrooms of all are the French *cèpes,* very expensive but so flavorful you use them in tiny quantities. They have to be soaked before use, and their delicious soaking liquid is used too.

Note that in this flavorful soup the barley is cooked separately, not in the broth. I do this so that it will keep its rich, nutty taste, and also so that I can control its consistency, which should be just slightly chewable.

⅔ cup (1½ deciliters) medium-fine barley
2 dried *cèpes* (about 1 ounce)
2 tablespoons butter
1 pound (450 grams) mushrooms, caps only
½ medium onion
7½ cups (1¾ liters) Basic Beef Broth (p. 5),
  or use 4–5 Knorr beef bouillon cubes
  dissolved in 7½ cups water

Soak the barley in 2 cups cold water for 1 hour. Meanwhile pour over the *cèpes* just enough hot water to cover and let them soak.

Cook the barley in its soaking water for about 30 minutes or until it is *al dente*, but just barely. Reserve it, leaving it in the soaking water, which will soften it a bit more, while you proceed with the recipe.

Melt the butter in a pot. Slice the mushroom caps and add them to the butter. Grate over them the onion with its juices and sauté for 8 minutes, or until the mushrooms and onion taste quite done. Drain the barley and add it. Add the beef broth. Slice the dried mushrooms very finely and add them with their soaking liquid. Reheat the soup, taste it, and correct the seasoning.

*Not for the pressure cooker.*

# Clear Vegetable Soups

## CELERY SOUP

*Serves 6–8*

This is a clear soup (though you may thicken and purée it, as suggested in the variation below), with the finely cut celery floating in it. The flavor should be stimulating and aromatic. It is a nice substitute for consommé before a copious dinner, since it makes you feel hungry and keen.

The quantity of celery you use depends on the quality: in Spain, where our celery is dark green, limp, but full of pungent flavor, I might use just a few ribs. Here the crisp pale celery hearts are mild tasting, and two or three of them are not too much.

About 1½ pounds (675 grams) celery hearts,
   with leaves
2 tablespoons butter
6 cups (1½ liters) Chicken Broth (p. 8),
   or use 3 Knorr chicken bouillon cubes
   dissolved in 6 cups water
Pinch of pepper
1 tablespoon finely cut dill or parsley
½ cup (1 deciliter) vermicelli, measured before
   cooking and cooked separately (optional)

Cut the celery in very thin slices, crosswise, and simmer it, covered, in the butter until it is wilted. Add the broth and cook for 15–20 minutes. Add the pepper and dill or parsley and taste. Correct the seasoning, add the cooked vermicelli, if desired, and serve.

*For the pressure cooker:* In the open pot, turn the celery in the butter. Add the broth, cover the pot, and cook for 4 minutes after pressure is reached. Add the dill or parsley, taste for seasoning, add the cooked vermicelli, if desired, and serve.

### Variation: Bisque of Celery

Mix ⅓ cup (¾ deciliter) heavy cream with 2 tablespoons flour, blending them well. Add a little hot soup, blending well, and return to the pot. Cook until the soup has thickened slightly and you no longer taste the raw flour. Purée the soup, reheat it, and serve. (Omit the vermicelli, but pass croutons separately if you like.)

## TOMATO SOUP

*Serves 4–6*

Although it has almost no calories, this soup is somehow mouth-filling, which makes it a nice choice for dieters. It has more body than a really clear soup, and a full, satisfying taste. For nondieters, serve it with noodles or luscious French Dumplings (p. 90).

3 large, ripe tomatoes, quartered and seeded
1 medium onion, chopped coarse
2 ribs celery, chopped
2 bay leaves
6 cups (1½ liters) consommé
    (better than beef broth for this),
    fresh or canned

In a heavy pot, stew together on low heat the tomatoes, onion, celery, and bay leaves, covered, for 20 minutes. Purée them, strain, and combine them with the consommé. Reheat the soup, taste it, adding salt and pepper if necessary, and serve it very hot.

*For the pressure cooker:* Cook the tomatoes, onion, celery, and bay leaves for 5 minutes after pressure is reached. Complete the soup as above.

*Variation:* For a thicker soup, add 2 slices of crustless white bread and 1 cup of tomato juice to the vegetables before stewing them, and proceed as above.

## QUICK TOMATO SOUP

*Serves 6*

This takes about 5 minutes to put together from canned ingredients, and nobody will ever suppose that you took a shortcut if you just season it carefully. For instance, if the soup tastes a little salty, add sugar a few grains at a time, tasting, and put some heavy cream on the table, so that each person can swirl in one or two spoonfuls according to his palate and his figure.

If there is time, I like to make this into a hearty first course by simmering French Dumplings (p. 90) in the strained soup.

>Three 16-ounce (½-liter) cans stewed tomatoes
>    (choose the kind flavored with onion, celery,
>    and green pepper)
>4½ cups (1¼ liters) Basic Beef Broth (p. 5), or
>    use 3½ Knorr beef bouillon cubes dissolved in
>    4½ cups water, or canned condensed beef broth
>    (with half the water recommended on the label)

Swirl the tomatoes and broth in a blender or processor. Straining is optional. Heat the soup, taste it and correct the seasoning, and serve.

## GAZPACHO

*Serves 6–8*

I like gazpacho puréed not quite smooth, with just a little texture, and served in a thick earthenware pot to keep it cool, with its garnish in several small bowls. The garnish always has croutons fried in olive oil, and crisply diced vegetables you vary according to your fancy.

There are as many ways of making this refreshing cold soup as there are Spaniards, and the only thing they all seem to have in common is a thickening of soaked white bread. In Marbella my gazpacho begins with a stroll around the garden, which is not arranged in rows. My gardener likes to improvise, in that climate of no rains but heavy dews, where the midday sky is blue as enamel. I find the cucumber plants hidden among shrubs for shade; peppers grow in pots under the bougainvillea vines of the terrace pergola; and the tomato plants climb eight feet high on poles arranged in pyramids. They develop very thick skins to protect themselves from the burning sun, and when we pick them they are hot right to the center, and sweet as honey. For me gazpacho is a reminder of the amazing climate of its origin.

5 slices stale white bread
1½ pounds (675 grams) ripe tomatoes
2 medium cucumbers
1 red bell pepper
1 green bell pepper
2 cloves garlic, peeled
3 tablespoons olive oil
3 tablespoons wine vinegar
1 teaspoon salt
¼ teaspoon freshly ground black pepper

Soak the 5 slices of bread in 2 cups cold water. Quarter the tomatoes and shake out the seeds. Peel, seed, and coarsely chop the cucumbers. Seed and coarsely chop the peppers. Mince the peeled garlic cloves. Put all with the oil, vinegar, and salt and pepper in a blender or processor. Blend or process them until they are fairly smooth, then pass the soup through a sieve. Chill it, and taste it for seasoning when it is cold.

Prepare and chill in separate bowls the following garnishes:

White bread, for croutons (dice it and fry it in olive oil)
Sweet onion (Spanish or Bermuda), diced fine
Green pepper, seeded and diced fine
Cucumber, peeled, seeded, and cut in ½-inch dice

Before serving gazpacho, add a few ice cubes to the tureen. Surround the tureen with the garnish bowls.

# $\mathcal{F}ish\ \mathcal{S}oups$

## FISH BROTH
### (a stock, not a soup)

*Makes about 2 quarts*

Other good fish stocks are given as part of recipes such as *Soles aux Petites Légumes* and Sole with Mushrooms (pp. 166 and 165). They are quite similar to this one; but this is an all-purpose, full-flavored stock you would use in a fish recipe that had no sauce or vegetables.

Fish stocks are made on the opposite principle from meat stocks, which in the old-fashioned cuisine are simmered almost all day to extract every bit of flavor from the bones. (Not in my cooking; I'm a bit extravagant with bones, and don't cook them so long, as I like very fresh flavors.) You can't simmer fish for a long time. The only way to keep that bracing ocean taste is to use a lot of fish scraps and cook them quickly.

Most good fish stores will charge you very little for fish heads and "frames" (skeletons) with plenty of flesh on them (since filleting is fairly wasteful). Chop them up, to get at the good, gelatinous spinal marrow, which gives a stock so much taste. Fish skins and fins are flavorful too, and so are lobster shells.

For an emergency fish stock, try to get Knorr's fish bouillon cubes, which taste genuine and fresh, or use bottled clam juice. In either case, be careful about salting your dish.

4 pounds (1800 grams) fish heads and frames with skins
6 medium carrots, peeled and quartered
6 ribs celery
2 large onions, chopped coarse
2 teaspoons salt
8 cracked white peppercorns
8 cups (2 liters) water

Put all the ingredients in a large pot, cover, and simmer for 20 minutes, then strain the broth through rinsed cheesecloth. The stock keeps, refrigerated, for 3 days. I think it is not quite so good after freezing.

*For the pressure cooker:* Put all the ingredients, but with only 4 cups (1 liter) water, in the pot, and cook for 5 minutes after pressure is reached. Cool the pot under cold running water, uncover it, strain the broth, and add 4 cups of water to make 2 quarts in all.

## CREAMY FISH CHOWDER

*Serves 6*

This is a light, delicate soup that our cook, Barbarka, used to make with the freshwater fish commonly available in Poland: pike *(szczupak)* and river perch *(sandacz),* for instance. In America, you could use either of these, or brown trout, muskies, small-mouthed bass, etc. Generally I make it nowadays with any lean white saltwater fish, since I live in or near seaports in America, France, and Spain. This soup has little in common, except for fish, potatoes, and a little cream, with what New Englanders call chowder. (For a very rich and luxurious fish soup, see the recipe for *Soles aux Petites Légumes,* p. 166.) If you have good fish stock, this soup takes only minutes to make.

3 medium baking potatoes, peeled and cut in
   ½-inch dice
6 cups (1½ liters) fresh Fish Broth (p. 41)
1 firm-textured lean white fish steak, ½ inch thick;
   or about ⅔ pound (310 grams) fish fillets
6 tablespoons cream
2 tablespoons finely cut parsley (optional)

Simmer the diced potatoes in the fish broth (which they will lightly thicken) for about 10 minutes, or until they are soft but not mushy, and reserve. In a little of the broth, simmer the fish, skimming carefully, until it is just done, that is, until the flesh has become opaque. (This will take about 10 minutes for the fish steak, less for fillets.) If necessary, skin and bone the fish. Flake it into the reserved fish/potato broth and strain in the fish-simmering broth. Stir in the cream and serve, if you like, sprinkled with parsley. Since the stock is well seasoned, it is unlikely that you will want salt.

# Sauces and Notions

# Sauces

Home cooks are at a great advantage in this department, because we have only to make one or two sauces at any meal, and we have elbow room and a chance to plan. So we can use a little broth from the dish we are preparing and make a sauce that truly complements it and extends its natural flavor, or we can make a deglazing sauce in the sauté or roasting pan, collecting and dissolving all the delicious caramelized brown bits. Most of my recipes that call for sauces at all have their own built right in.

This is of course very different from the restaurant method, where the chef doesn't know in advance what will be ordered and must be able to produce a great number of sauces at a moment's notice. So when he makes a mushroom sauce, he is likely to combine sautéed mushrooms with the *espagnole* he has been simmering all day, along with several other "mother" sauces and a group of standard syrups and demiglaces. In our travels, after enjoying a few hotel or restaurant meals, I got very tired of those few, standardized flavor combinations—excellent though they were—because they showed right through whatever additions and garnishes each variation required: new veils on the same old hat.

My cooking is not really complex. The main ingredient is always the one you taste most. So when I make a mushroom sauce, you taste mushrooms (and beef scarcely at all), and my onion sauce is oniony. This chapter has only one wine sauce. I use very little wine anyway, normally not as a base but as an accent, cooked just long enough not to taste raw. And, although fat is a wonderful carrier of flavor, I don't like to use much. In the old school of restaurant cooking, many sauces were rich to the point of saturation so that, after sitting a bit on your hot dinner plate, they would separate slightly and you would see droplets of fat.

This is a short chapter, containing only the sauces that are mentioned in the entrée recipes without being integrally part of them. A few dessert sauces are given in the dessert chapter. Vinaigrette, with variations, is described along with salads on page 294, and so is Mayonnaise. *Refrito* is much used as a sauce or a sauce base in Spain, but in this book it is called for specifically in only one recipe, as a base for fish stew, page 52.

Caramel making is described here in detail, since caramel is part of so many of my recipes, both savory and sweet. So is clarified butter. Both of these are included, following the sauce recipes, as "notions," by which I mean minor culinary adjuncts of no special type, about which I have hints or opinions to offer.

## BÉCHAMEL SAUCE
### (Basic White Sauce)

*Makes 2 cups*

For a quick reminder, here is the basic formula:

| THIN BÉCHAMEL | MEDIUM BÉCHAMEL | THICK BÉCHAMEL |
|---|---|---|
| 1 tablespoon butter | 2 tablespoons butter | 3 tablespoons butter |
| 1 tablespoon flour | 2 tablespoons flour | 3 tablespoons flour |
| 1 cup (¼ liter) liquid | 1 cup (¼ liter) liquid | 1 cup (¼ liter) liquid |

I like the very mild flavor and the velvet texture of a nice béchamel made with milk or a good stock (in the latter case, it is properly called a velouté) and quite often use it plain, or as a vehicle to carry the juices of a particular dish. Most of the following sauces illustrate béchamel variations, and you will find many more instances incorporated in recipes throughout the book.

One always begins with a roux: equal quantities of flour and butter, cooked and stirred together slowly for 2 or 3 minutes without browning. The mixture becomes a rich pale gold color and sizzles gently. Then you can add the liquid, blending it carefully with a whisk to keep it smooth, and boil it for a minute or two, still whisking, as the sauce thickens.

A thin béchamel is one that will just cling lightly to the spoon. A medium-thick béchamel has the proper consistency for gratinéed dishes. A thick béchamel is really a paste, not a sauce with which to nap your dish. It is a "binder" to hold chopped ingredients together, or to thicken the juices that some ingredients exude in cooking, or to make a base for soufflés.

You will notice that the basic formula does not mention seasonings. This is because one must take into consideration all the components of a dish before adding salt, pepper, etc.

In many of my dishes, the béchamel is enriched with cheese or sour cream. Don't let it boil or even simmer after such an addition, as there is a risk of curdling. This is also true if there is an enrichment of egg yolks (something I use rarely, on top of a flour thickening).

A plain flour thickening is light and neutral; that is, it doesn't distort or much enrich the flavor of the liquid. It is not fattening, since you get so little flour per serving. (Even with butter, it is not very fattening, and the dish tastes so satisfying!) Sometimes I use flour without mixing it first with butter into a roux: for example, sprinkling it on mushrooms as they cook for a sauce—they cook in butter, why add more?—or reserving a little sauce liquid, thickening that with flour, and returning it to the pot. It will not taste pasty. "Pastiness" is the taste of *raw, soaked* flour. Just cook flour long enough to let it expand properly and become truly incorporated in the sauce.

Sometimes it enhances the flavor of a roast to retain a little of the fat in which the meat has been browned or of the meat's own fat. In this case I would skim off all but a tablespoon or two of such fat, add flour, and cook this roux before adding liquid.

## DILL SAUCE

*Makes 2 cups*

This is good with boiled beef or chicken.

3 tablespoons flour
3 tablespoons butter
2 cups (½ liter) Chicken Broth (p. 8),
  or use 1 Knorr chicken bouillon cube
  dissolved in 2 cups water
2 tablespoons finely cut dill

Cook the flour in the butter, stirring, until it is thickened and smooth. Add the broth, stirring, and cook until it is thickened and the flour no longer tastes raw. Add the dill, and simmer slowly for 10 minutes. Taste the sauce for seasoning.

## GARLIC BUTTER

*Makes about six 2-tablespoon servings*

This very simple sauce is nice for steaks of meat or fish, and for ground-meat cutlets. If we have a guest who has the misfortune not to enjoy garlic, I omit it from the cutlets but pass this sauce separately.

3 cloves garlic
1½ sticks (6 ounces or 180 grams) butter, melted
1 tablespoon lemon juice
Salt and white pepper to taste

Peel the garlic. This is quickly done by laying on it the flat blade of a knife, then smacking the blade with your fist, which loosens the skin so that it slides right off. Slice the garlic cloves, put them in a pan of melted butter, add the lemon juice, and let the pan sit for 30 minutes or so, to let the garlic flavor permeate the butter. Then cook it over low heat for a few minutes, taste it for seasoning, add salt and pepper if desired, strain out the sliced garlic, and serve.

*About garlic in general:* It doesn't keep very well, so I prefer to buy one loose head at a time rather than those little heads that come in boxes. For very finely minced garlic, don't use the press, but mince it on a board with your big knife. Then sprinkle it with salt and mash it with the flat of the blade. Mince it again, mash it again, and in a moment you will have almost a garlic purée. Be careful thereafter about salting the dish. To get the smell of garlic off your fingers, rub your hands with baking soda, wait a minute, and rinse them off. (Baking soda is not abrasive, but rather soothing to the skin.) Incidentally, the lemon you have just cut for the juice is also good for getting rid of the garlic smell; simply rub it on your hands.

## MUSTARD SAUCE

*Makes 2 cups*

As everybody knows, this is nice with broiled fish and with beef. I urge you to try it with boiled "new" potatoes.

3 tablespoons flour
3 tablespoons butter
2 cups (½ liter) Basic Beef Broth (p. 5), or use 1 Knorr
    beef bouillon cube dissolved in 2 cups water
1 tablespoon dry English mustard Colman's, for example)

Cook the flour in the butter, stirring, until they are well blended. Add the broth, stirring constantly, and the mustard. Cook the sauce until it has thickened and the flavors are well blended.

## MUSTARD AS A CONDIMENT

*Makes ⅓ cup*

This is very nice with a salty cold meat like ham or cured tongue. It has to be used quickly, because it does not keep.

1½ tablespoons dry English mustard (Colman's, for example)
1 teaspoon honey
2 tablespoons boiling water
Potato starch or cornstarch, if necessary

Pour over the dry mustard the honey and boiling water and mix well. If you like a thicker prepared mustard, carefully dissolve the potato starch (preferred for smoother dissolving) or cornstarch in a little water and add it to the mustard mixture while it is still warm.

## REFRITO
### (A Tomato Base for Soups and Sauces)

*Makes about 2 cups*

In Spain, where it is used for all kinds of dishes, this simple, fresh-tasting preparation is available everywhere, in cans; here it can be found wherever there is a Hispanic population. (In New York it is available as *"Sofrito"* under the Goya label.) It has a sweeter, milder flavor than the usual canned or bottled sauces for pasta, and some people prefer it for that purpose. It is good with eggs, surrounding an omelette, for instance, and can be spooned over browned stew meat before simmering.

Since it may be frozen I like to make a good quantity of *refrito* whenever we have really ripe tomatoes. In the refrigerator it thickens to the consistency of mayonnaise and will keep up to 10 days.

On page 140 you will find a recipe for a wonderful Spanish Fish Stew with *Refrito,* which represents an ideal way of using this.

3 tablespoons oil
5 ripe tomatoes (about 2½ pounds or 1125 grams),
    seeded and cut in eighths
1 green bell pepper, seeded and sliced
1 red bell pepper, seeded and sliced
5 cloves garlic
1½ cups (3½ deciliters) chopped onions
    (about 5 medium onions)
About ¾ teaspoon salt

Heat the oil in a skillet. Add the tomatoes, peppers, garlic, and onions, mixing well, and cook until the mixture is very soft. It should reduce to half its original volume, and have the consistency of a paste. Purée or process it and pass it through a sieve to get rid of the tomato skins, or put through a food mill, which will do both. Processing lightens the color somewhat. Add salt to taste.

*Note:* If making this specifically for the Spanish Fish Stew with *Refrito,* I add ½ small hot green pepper, seeded, to the mixture before cooking it. To make the sauce base less sweet, decrease the quantity of onions.

## CURRY SAUCE

*Makes about 3½ cups*

I like to reheat cold cubed meat or leftover chicken in this sauce, whose flavors strike a harmonious balance between the curry and the celery. For another curry sauce, which has the curry cooked in, see the egg dish on page 126.

I am assuming, of course, that you have found a brand of curry you like, or one that you doctor a bit with powdered spices to suit your taste.

1 cup (¼ liter) finely chopped celery,
    including branches and leaves
½ cup (1 deciliter) finely chopped onion
2 tablespoons butter
3 cups (¾ liter) Chicken Broth (p. 8) or
    Basic Beef Broth (p. 5), cooled, or use
    1½ Knorr chicken or beef bouillon
    cubes dissolved in 3 cups water
3 tablespoons curry powder
2 tablespoons flour
4 tablespoons cream (optional)

Sauté the celery and onion slowly in the butter, stirring, for 5 minutes.

Add to the cool broth the celery and onion, the curry powder, and the flour and blend or process it until it is smooth. Stirring constantly, heat the sauce to the boil and cook until it thickens. Taste it for seasoning and enrich it, if you like, with a little cream.

## TOMATO SAUCE

*Makes about 2½ cups*

This savory sauce is especially delicious with Fish Cutlets (p. 154), Eggs
Mollet, and, of course, any kind of pasta. If you do not have summer-fresh
tomatoes, use good canned plum tomatoes, and if you are in a hurry, try
the variation that follows using stewed tomatoes, to which the onion, green
pepper, and celery have already been added.

    2 tablespoons olive oil
    1 pound (450 grams) ripe tomatoes, or two 14-ounce
        cans plum tomatoes (½ cup liquid drained off)
    1 cup coarsely chopped onions
    ½ cup (70 grams) seeded and chopped green pepper
    1 stalk celery, chopped coarse
    3 large cloves garlic, peeled
    2 teaspoons Herbes de Provence
    3 bay leaves, crushed
    2 teaspoons sugar
    Salt and pepper to taste
    1 tablespoon finely cut fresh dill (optional)

In a saucepan heat the oil; then add all the vegetables, the herbs, and the
bay leaves. Cook over medium flame, stirring occasionally, until the mixture
has reduced to about half its volume—about 30 minutes or a little more.
Now add the sugar, and salt and pepper to taste. Put the sauce in a blender
and purée; then strain (to remove the bits of tomato and pepper skin and
bay leaf). Add the optional fresh dill.

*Variation:* Use two 14-ounce cans of stewed tomatoes and eliminate the
onions, green pepper, celery, and sugar. If you wish for a stronger tomato
sauce, stir in 1–2 tablespoons tomato paste after the sauce has cooked down;
then strain.

# HOLLANDAISE SAUCE

*Makes 1½ cups*

This is for fish and for many vegetables, especially asparagus and artichokes. The proportions below would serve six to eight people, but you can easily halve the recipe for a smaller number.

4 large egg yolks
1 tablespoon cider vinegar (or lemon juice)
Pinch of salt
Pinch of white pepper
2 sticks (8 ounces or 225 grams) butter,
    softened, or at room temperature

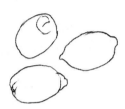

In the top of a double boiler, off heat, beat the egg yolks with a whisk until they are well blended. In the double boiler bottom, heat a little water just to the simmering point and set the top over it—the top must *not* touch the water. Beat the egg yolks vigorously until they thicken slightly, then add the vinegar or lemon juice and the salt and pepper. Beating continuously, begin adding the butter, by hazelnut-size lumps, waiting until each lump is absorbed by the egg mixture before adding the next. Beat a bit more after all the butter is added, then taste for seasoning.

*Note:* Be sure to keep the water in the bottom at or below simmer, or occasionally take the whole double boiler off the heat.

### Variation: Mousseline Sauce

Whip ½ cup (1 deciliter) heavy (or whipping) cream and add to the Hollandaise just before serving. I prefer the lighter, blander Mousseline to Hollandaise for some dishes using poached white fish.

# SAUCE AU VIN BLANC

*Makes 2½ cups*

This is good with any fish.

2 tablespoons butter
2 tablespoons flour
2 cups (½ liter) fish stock for Sole with Mushrooms
    (p. 167), or boil 1½ cups (3½ deciliters) Fish Broth
    (p. 41) with ½ cup (1 deciliter) dry white wine
    until the wine no longer tastes raw
2 egg yolks
⅓ cup (¾ deciliter) heavy cream
Pinch of salt
Pinch of white pepper
Pinch of nutmeg

Cook the butter with the flour until smooth and thickened. Add the fish stock, stirring, until the sauce is thickened and the flour no longer tastes raw. Beat the egg yolks with the cream, add to this a little of the hot sauce, return to the sauce, stirring, and cook without boiling until the sauce thickens a little more. Season the sauce with the salt, pepper, and nutmeg, taste it, and serve.

## MUSHROOM SAUCE

*Makes 3 cups*

This is not a brown sauce with mushrooms, but a sauce *of* mushrooms, lent a pleasant piquancy by the use of sour cream. It is nice with boiled beef, with cutlets of ground meat or chicken, with kasha, or with other vegetables.

2 cups (½ liter) sliced mushrooms, caps only
2 tablespoons grated onion
2 tablespoons butter
2 tablespoons flour
2 cups (½ liter) Basic Beef Broth (p. 5)
    or Chicken Broth (p. 8),
    or use 2 Knorr beef or chicken bouillon
    cubes dissolved in 2 cups water
6 tablespoons sour cream
Salt and pepper to taste

Sauté the mushrooms with the onion in butter, until the mushroom juices have exuded and about half evaporated. Sprinkle them with flour and mix well. Add the hot broth and cook slowly, stirring, until you no longer taste the flour and the mixture has thickened. Add the sour cream, taste the sauce, and season it with salt and pepper. If you made the broth with bouillon cubes, be careful with the salt.

## ONION SAUCE

*Makes 3 cups*

The addition of a little caramel and vinegar brings out the natural sweetness of onions in a way I like. This is an old-fashioned, warm, rich sauce. It is good with boiled beef, or fresh beef tongue, or meat loaf, or cutlets.

3 large onions, chopped
4 tablespoons butter
4 tablespoons flour
2 cups (½ liter) strong beef broth, from
   cooked tongue if possible (p. 211),
   or use 2 Knorr beef bouillon cubes
   dissolved in 2 cups water
1½ tablespoons cider vinegar
7 tablespoons sugar

Sauté the chopped onion in butter until it is golden-brown. Sprinkle it with flour and mix well. Add the hot broth and cook slowly, stirring, until you no longer taste the flour and the mixture has thickened. Add the vinegar. Caramelize the sugar (melt it in a small, heavy pan, stirring carefully, and cook it until it is brown; for full details on caramel, see p. 66). Add it to the sauce, and taste for seasoning.

## FRESH HORSERADISH

Horseradish is a root with a mottled tan exterior that comes in many sizes and even shapes, with gnarls and knots. In some countries—France and Spain, for instance—it is difficult to find nice big horseradish roots; here it is much easier. I am very fond of it as a condiment with vinegar, or fresh in a sauce. The flavor of the freshly grated root is so far superior to the bottled variety that it is really worth the slight effort of preparing it oneself.

The following instructions are based on a horseradish root approximately 8 inches long and from about 2 inches thick at the top to about 1 inch thick at the bottom. The unpeeled root, or part of it, can be kept as long as a very large carrot, and if it is, or becomes, a bit limp, should be soaked in cold water for an hour, or overnight, in the refrigerator.

1 horseradish root, approximately 8 inches long
1 teaspoon sugar
Dash of salt
2 tablespoons cider vinegar

Peel the root and grate it (on a fine grater, such as you would use for hard fresh Parmesan cheese). This is a bit trying—if you have a food processor, do use it. Either way, be very careful of the fumes: they are quite strong, and good ventilation is necessary. If you have a processor, cut the peeled radish into uneven little pieces, nowhere thicker than ½ inch—you should have about 1½–1¾ cups, loosely packed. Put these in the beaker of the processor, with the steel blade in place.* Add 2–3 tablespoons water and process, stopping several times to push the radish off the sides, until you have an evenly "grated" mass. You should have about ¾ cup gratings if you did the work by hand, and about 1 cup if with a processor. Put the radish into a bowl twice the size needed to hold it. Add the sugar and salt, then (keeping eyes and nose averted!) pour about ½ cup boiling water over the mixture, stirring; it will swell considerably.

The horseradish is now ready to use as it is, or in a sauce, or to be stored for a few days in a tightly covered jar in the refrigerator. For longer storage, add 2 tablespoons cider vinegar. You will know by the taste and color if it is losing its strength and flavor, as the vinegar takes over and the radish starts turning brown.

To serve fresh horseradish with roast beef or steak, try shaving it like wood with a vegetable peeler. Put little mounds of curly shavings around your roast, or a little bunch of them on each steak. They are simply delicious and look very intriguing.

---

*Do not use shredding disks. The root is quite fibrous and can cause damage; also, you don't want "shreds."

FRESH HORSERADISH SAUCE I

*Makes about 3½ cups*

2 tablespoons flour
2 tablespoons butter
3 cups (¾ liter) Basic Beef Broth (p. 5), or use 2 Knorr
  beef bouillon cubes dissolved in 3 cups water
3 tablespoons grated fresh horseradish (If using bottled,
  use a freshly opened 4-ounce jar and drain out most
  of the liquid, which is mainly vinegar.)
½ cup (1 deciliter) sour cream
Salt and sugar to taste

Cook the flour in the butter, stirring, until smooth. Add the beef stock
and cook until the sauce is smooth and thickened, stirring constantly. Add
the horseradish. Below the simmer, add the sour cream, mixing well. Season
to taste with salt and sugar.

FRESH HORSERADISH SAUCE II

*Makes about 2 cups*

This sauce is served cold and is delicious with cold meat but even better
perhaps with cold poached fish, a delicate smoked trout, or a fish mousse.

1 cup (¼ liter) whipping or heavy cream
Freshly grated horseradish to taste
Salt to taste

Chill the cream, beater, and bowl in the refrigerator for an hour or two.
Drain any vinegar from the horseradish if it is not freshly grated. Whip the
cream and add to it the horseradish, 1 tablespoon at a time, until desired
strength is reached—very much a matter of individual preference and the
potency of the radish. Add salt to taste.

## SAUCE AUX OEUFS DURS

*Serves 6*

This is a good, old-fashioned accompaniment for poached fish, and you might like it on cooked chopped spinach.

6 hard-boiled eggs, chopped
2 sticks (8 ounces or 225 grams) butter, melted
Salt and pepper to taste
1 tablespoon finely cut chives (optional)

Stir the chopped eggs into the melted butter, gently, without mashing them. Taste and season the sauce with salt and pepper. Stir in the chives, if you like, and serve warm.

### Variation: With Capers

Add ½ cup rinsed and drained capers, the small ones if available (if using the larger ones, chop them very slightly, taking care not to mash them). Mix the capers with the egg mixture and serve with any poached white fish.

# CARAMEL SAUCE
## WITH RAISINS AND ALMONDS

*Makes about 3 cups*

This is a medium brown sauce with a nice balance of sweet and sour flavors. I like to serve it with fresh beef tongue, and with ham.

   1 tablespoon flour
   1 tablespoon butter
   2 cups (½ liter) rich meat broth, from
      cooked tongue if possible (p. 211), or
      use 1½ Knorr beef bouillon cubes
      dissolved in 2 cups water
   5 tablespoons sugar
   2 tablespoons vinegar
   ½ cup (1 deciliter) white (pale yellow) raisins
   ½ cup (1 deciliter) skinned, slivered almonds

Cook the flour in the butter until thickened and smooth. Add the broth and cook, stirring, until it has thickened slightly and the flour no longer tastes raw. Caramelize the sugar; that is, melt it in a small, heavy pan, stirring constantly, until it has stopped bubbling and is a pale amber color. (Full details on caramelizing sugar are on page 66.) Add this immediately to the sauce. Pour in the vinegar gradually, tasting carefully, and add the raisins and almonds. Bring the sauce to a boil, stirring, and let it simmer a few minutes, until the raisins are soft and swollen.

# $\mathcal{N}$otions

This section contains some ideas that don't quite fit into other categories, and a few more detailed descriptions of odds and ends that come up in various recipes elsewhere in the book—caramelizing sugar, for instance. There are some suggestions for serving caviar, and, at the other extreme, an old and delicious home remedy for a sore throat. I hope you will find some novel or useful suggestions in these pages.

## CLARIFIED BUTTER

The main purpose of clarifying butter is to be able to use it at higher heat levels without its burning—it is the whey that burns more readily. Once clarified, and put in a covered jar in the refrigerator, it keeps up to three weeks.

Melt the butter very slowly. A white sediment, whey, will form on the bottom of the pan, and a froth on top. Skim off the froth, and carefully pour off the clear butter, leaving the whey at the bottom. Or strain the whole amount through a moistened paper towel. Cool before refrigerating.

## CLABBERED MILK
*(Kwaśne Mleko,* pronounced *kvahsh*-ne m*leh*-ko)

*Serves 4*

Cool, refreshing, and delicious, this is one of those hard-to-classify dishes that has been part of our family food forever. It is vaguely related to yogurt, but is not as sour-tasting, and has the consistency of a rennet custard. We have it daily in the summer, at the lighter meal, whether at noontime or evening. The proof of its universal appeal is that my six all-American grandchildren literally lap it up.

In the country, if you have access to "raw" milk, it is easiest to use that. Pasteurized milk works well with a bit more sour "starter." As we have it every day, we actually use a bit of one batch to start the next. In the days when milk was not homogenized, lovely thick cream would surface, and would be fought over by everyone not on a diet, or a greedy one would collect all the cream off the dieters' portions, leaving them with sinless skim.

Serve the clabbered milk in soup plates, and accompany it with Boiled Potatoes with Bacon and Onion (p. 279) on separate plates.

1 tablespoon sour cream, yogurt, or
   "starter" from previous batch
1 quart (1 liter) milk

In a bowl, stir sour cream or yogurt into milk, blend well, and leave milk, covered, undisturbed, at room temperature for 24 hours. Gently place it in the refrigerator and leave for about 4–6 hours before serving.

## BACON CUBES
### *(Skwarki,* pronounced sk*vah* r-kee)

To make *skwarki,* little pieces of slab bacon, a tiny bit bigger than ¼-inch cubes, are gently sautéed until they render some of their fat and become crisp and brown, not *burned.* Remove them with a slotted spoon. They are absolutely delicious sprinkled over boiled potatoes, *pierogi,* or diced cooked rutabaga.

If you like, chop onions medium-fine, and when the bacon is about half done, spoon some of the rendered fat into another skillet. Sauté until the onion is golden-brown, combine the two, and serve as above. If you are not worrying about calories, leave a bit of the warm bacon fat with the *skwarki* —in place of butter on the potatoes, for instance.

## GREEN CHEESE
### (Sapsago)

All my children, and grandchildren, insisted that I include a word or two about this little-known but delectable green cheese from Switzerland. We are all rather addicted to it. It is a hard cheese made of sage and skimmed milk, with a strong odor but wonderful taste. It is found here foil-wrapped and shaped like a cone with its point cut off, about 2½ inches tall.

In Switzerland, where it is fresh, it is fairly soft and can easily be "shaved" with a knife into lovely curls to press into sweet butter on a morning muffin or fresh bread. Here we grate it, and keep it in the refrigerator, preferably in a container shallow and wide enough to permit inverting a well-buttered muffin into it and removing it with as much cheese as adheres to the butter.

Caution: avoid sneezing when about to take a bite!

Grated "green cheese" can also be blended with sardines and butter, then mashed into a paste to make a canapé spread.

# CARAMEL

To caramelize sugar, heat it until some of its water content boils away and evaporates. It is no more trouble than browning bread crumbs or boiling an egg, but a lot of people are nervous about the procedure. Once you've done it, you'll laugh at me for going into all this detail. I do so to reassure you, because so many cookbooks are full of scary warnings.

Pour granulated sugar and half as much water—for example, ½ cup sugar and ¼ cup water—into a heavy, thick-walled pan. So that you can monitor the developing color, use a shiny pan or else a light-colored wooden or metal spoon. Turn the heat to medium-high, hotter than for browning meat. Almost at once the sugar will begin to melt and take on color, at the bottom and around the edges. Keep turning and stirring it steadily. It will make some tiny brown lumps at this stage, but if you move it constantly you will avoid large lumps that take too long to dissolve. If any of the sugar starts to turn dark brown, remove the pan from the heat, mix the sugar thoroughly, and return the pan to the heat. In a minute or two, when most of the sugar is colored, it will hiss and bubble. Don't worry; just keep stirring. In another minute, all the sugar will be a lovely pale amber color. Remove it from the heat. It will continue to cook and darken, so use it at once.

Do not pour liquid into the hot caramel at this point; if you pour the hot caramel into hot or tepid liquid, it will mix nicely. For caramel syrup, let the caramel cool for 2 minutes, then add to it boiling water, a very little at a time. As the sugar is still much hotter than boiling water, expect bubbles and steam. Keep adding water until the syrup has the consistency you want, bearing in mind that it will thicken slightly as it cools.

For a hard, shiny glaze (as in the Almond Mazurka, p. 337), pour very hot caramel onto a cool or tepid surface.

To color a sauce without sweetening it, cook the caramel until it is mahogany brown (only a minute or two longer than for the pale amber color). At this stage, most of the flavor is gone.

To clean your caramel pan, let it cool for a few minutes, then fill it with hot water and let it sit until the sugar glaze has dissolved.

## CAVIAR AND FISH ROE

A small amount of caviar, distributed in servings of good jellied soup (p. 10), makes an excellent and luxurious dish at a reasonable price. Several kinds of fish roe, although not exactly caviar, are sold salted and sometimes smoked; mixed with butter or cream cheese, the good ones make a nice spread for crackers. Pressed caviar—real sturgeon eggs, salted and packed down—is delicious, especially with blinis (p. 84).

In the days when good caviar, Beluga or Malossol, was not quite as prohibitively expensive as it is now, I would sometimes serve it to guests "straight" in one of two ways, both very simple. Before coming to the table, we would have small chilled glasses of Polish Wyborowa vodka right from the freezer (vodka doesn't freeze) and caviar canapés made with small (1½-inch or round) pieces of very good, *untoasted* white bread, cut thin and lightly buttered to the edges, sealing the surface. The caviar would be gently mounded on these, not spread too thinly or carefully. Another way, a little more luxurious, would be to pass the caviar, its original tin embedded in a bowl of ice, at the table (with the vodka, of course), accompanied only by thin slices of white toast. I have never liked the sieved egg, onion, or lemon garnishes one sometimes encounters—they seem to me to spoil or cover the real taste of the caviar.

There are two other highly unorthodox but absolutely delicious ways of eating caviar. One way is to serve it with French crêpes (p. 78), which can be made, stacked in advance, and kept warm covered in a large napkin; the caviar is passed separately and each person spreads a little on a crêpe and rolls it up. The other way, perhaps best, certainly easiest of all, is with simple baked potatoes and butter. My husband and I had it this simple way years ago at dinner for four given by Princess Beatrix and her husband.

## VARIATIONS ON ICE CREAM

Once in Marbella I lunched with the Guy de Rothschilds and had for dessert a delicious mint ice cream with chocolate sauce. Embarrassed to ask for the recipe, and as usual enjoying the challenge of trying it on my own, I bought in a local tea shop a "neutral" ice cream called *nata* (which simply means cream), softened it in the refrigerator, beat in some crème de menthe, and refroze it. I even added a touch of my own, blending in some chopped fresh mint leaves, and served it with chocolate sauce. Although *nata* is not available in the U.S., anyone who has an ice-cream maker of any sort can make it by following directions for vanilla ice cream, omitting the vanilla.

There can be many amusing variations on this, although one must be cautious to avoid a muddy confusion of flavors. Liqueurs, for instance: crème de menthe or peppermint liqueur in a chocolate ice cream, crème de noyau or amaretto in coffee ice cream. Preserved ginger (in minute quantities, very finely diced) and candied peels are good with fruit flavors like lemon or orange. With chocolate one must remember that it freezes harder than ice cream—one doesn't want chocolate gravel—but a little chocolate sauce may be swirled into vanilla or coffee ice cream.

## COFFEE

In my long, though unscientific experience, I have concluded that one sudden, violent, total drenching with furiously boiling water gets almost all the good out of coffee grains. After that, they seem to get tired. The best, and certainly the un-fussiest coffee maker I ever knew was our Spanish cook in Buenos Aires, in the thirties: she simply dumped freshly ground coffee into a saucepan, and then, holding the kettle high, poured on boiling water. She then let the infusion sit for a minute or two, and strained it through a cloth sieve into the pot, which was warmed beforehand.

About choosing coffees, I have two suggestions. If you use canned pre-ground coffee, buy it in small amounts, and change brands often. Like the first puff on a freshly lit cigar (I am told), the first cup of a different brand has its own charm. If you grind your own beans or have them ground at the supermarket, I suggest you try a blend of equal parts of Brazilian, "French roast," and Mocha.

## "COUGH MEDICINE": HONEY-BUTTER CANDY

My children insist that this book must include our family way of soothing a sore throat. Boil 2 parts honey to 1 part butter together over medium heat; don't let them get to the caramel stage, but start testing when the bubbles begin to look plump and crowded. (I just dribble a drop or two of the mixture onto a saucer and poke at it with a spoon.) If you stop the cooking when the drops remain elastic as they cool, you will have produced what used to be called an electuary: a soft, thick, comforting paste. If you cook it a little longer, to the point when the drops harden at once on a cool surface, you can make cough lozenges by distributing tablespoonfuls on a buttered baking sheet. (While "tasting," my daughter Eva, then nine, and I ate the whole amount, hot from the pot, with spoons. This is *not* recommended!)

## CRÈME FRAÎCHE

This is so good with fresh berries: a thick, semifermented, rich-flavored cream, available all over France. Nowadays you can buy *crème fraîche* in fancy American food shops, but at a price much too high to interest me. To make an excellent version at home, simply mix ½ cup sour cream with 1 cup heavy sweet cream and let the mixture stand with a piece of cheese-cloth over the top at room temperature for 6 hours. Then refrigerate it, covered; it will keep for a week or more.

## SPICED FRUIT COMPOTE
(Savory or Sweet)

*Serves 4*

I am very fond of sweet-sour accompaniments for game birds like guinea hen and pheasant, and the same applies to chicken cutlets and veal medal-lions. For game, lingonberries are traditional but they are quite expensive.

If you poach the fruit as a sweet compote, you have a good convenient dessert, which is nice served with heavy cream. If fresh fruit is unavailable, you can use canned fruits; boil down the liquid with a bit of lemon zest and perhaps a cinnamon stick until it is syrupy; immerse the fruit in it to steep in the refrigerator, and serve it chilled with cream.

THE HEAVY SYRUP (using 1 pound fruit)

> 1 cup (200 grams) sugar (use more sugar
>   to taste if fruit is very acid)
> ½ cup (1 deciliter) water
> Zest of 1 lemon, cut in large strips
> 2 sticks cinnamon
> 8 whole cloves
> ½ cup (1 deciliter) vinegar, or to taste
>   (omit for dessert compote)

Combine the sugar, water, lemon zest, cinnamon sticks, cloves, and vinegar in a heavy pot. Bring slowly to the boil, stirring, and simmer, uncovered, until the mixture reaches the consistency of heavy cream.

THE FRUIT

I have used plums, nectarines, apricots, pears, peaches, and sometimes apples in this manner, singly, or in any combination. If using plums or nectarines, prick the skins before cooking; peel apples, pears, and peaches. For a savory (or condiment) compote, which is eaten with white meat or fowl, cut the fruit in chunks. To serve savory compote, remove the fruit from the syrup and pass it in a bowl; if it is not all eaten, it can be kept in a jar in the syrup for at least a week. For a dessert compote, make larger segments, so that the slices suggest the original shape. Cooking time depends on the thickness of the slices and the ripeness of the fruit. Simply simmer the fruit slices in the syrup, uncovered, until they are soft but not mushy enough to lose their shape. Five minutes is often enough for ripe peaches; 15 minutes may not be too long for crisp apples. Chill the compote before serving.

## HERBS

You can get much more pleasure and savor from fresh herbs by cutting them according to the use you want to make of them. When you want their juice, as in an uncooked salad dressing, crush them in a mortar. But for a chopped herb garnish, I don't really "chop" at all. *Chopping* to me means pivoting a knife blade on its point, making very fast, rat-tat-tat cuts. This is efficient for mincing onions or mushrooms, for instance, but it usually bruises or shreds herbs. Herbs are better *cut,* with an extremely sharp knife, slowly and carefully making as few and as well-aimed cuts as possible. Mature (hollow-leaved) chives then look like minute, crisp-edged cylinders, parsley like infinitesimal crystals, and so on. As much moisture as possible stays in each little piece. This is, therefore, the way to cut herbs for freezing in small parcels: just make the parcels airtight. For a cooked mixture like a filling, where the herb specks attractively announce their contribution to the flavor, I cut them this way too.

*Fresh herbs:* Obviously these have more taste and are much more attractive. In parts of the country where they are not available year-round, one might also grow many of them in pots in a sunny window.

On the whole, I use herbs cautiously, in small amounts and simple combinations. Too much or too many can mask the main ingredients of a dish. However, one old-fashioned standard combination, "Italian seasoning," has its uses. And lately, since it has become widely available in America, I am using instead the delicious "Herbes de Provence," a mixture imported from France, where it is blended and sold by a company called quaintly Aux Anysetiers du Roy.

*Dried herbs:* A good rule of thumb is to use one-third the volume you would use of fresh herbs. If you are making Meat Loaf (p. 219), for instance, and have fresh marjoram, use three times the quantity specified for dried marjoram. You will have a superlative dish. If you find yours have gone stale on the shelf, which inevitably happens sometimes, don't increase the quantity given in the recipe, but try soaking the dried herbs in lemon juice for 15 minutes; you'll find very often the flavor comes back to life.

## SANGRÍA

*Makes 1 quart (1 liter)*

This pleasant punch, based on red wine, originated in Spain and has become popular almost everywhere in the world. Traditionally, it is made with brandy and spices as well as fruit and is allowed to steep for several hours. My own version is less robust and less alcoholic. Since one tastes the wine quite clearly, I use one that is at least good enough to be drunk for its own sake, and not too harsh.

In extremely hot weather, something cool always seems to me more refreshing than something cold. In blazing-hot Andalusia, the home of Sangría, the drink is served in a thick earthenware pitcher with a little dam across the pouring funnel to hold back the fruit pieces. This seems to me just the right container, better insulation than glass or metal would be, and properly rustic looking.

1 quart (1 liter) good dry red wine, Rioja,
   for instance
2 ripe peaches, diced
1 orange, sliced
1 lemon, sliced   } seeds and skins left on
1 ripe pear, sliced
½ cup (100 grams) sugar

Let the wine steep with the diced peaches, the sliced orange, lemon, and pear, and the sugar, in the refrigerator for an hour. Serve it with a separate bowl of ice cubes for those who prefer a milder drink.

Crêpes with Beef Filling
Crêpes with Chicken Filling
Crêpes with Calf's Brain Filling
Filled Crêpes, Sautéed
Filled Crêpes, Gratinéed
Blinis
Fritter Batter for Entrées or Desserts
Fish Fritters with Prune Compote
Cauliflower Fritters
Eggplant Fritters
French Dumplings
Pâte à Choux
Cheese Dumplings I (Serniki I)
Cheese Dumplings II (Serniki II)
Marrow and Matzo Dumplings
Noodle Dough
Angel's Hair
Fettucine
Lazanki with Mushrooms and Onions
Pasta with Fresh Basil
Dough for Pierogi, Kolduny, and Uszka
Cheese and Potato Filling for Pierogi and Uszka
Kolduny with Meat and Marrow Filling
Uszka with Mushroom Filling for Uszka or Pierożkis
Coulibiac with Cabbage and Mushroom Filling
Pierożki with Ham, Spinach, and Mushroom Filling
Quiche Polonaise
Kasha
Kasha with Mushrooms
Rice
Oeufs Farcis à la Polonaise
Eggs Mimosa
Hard-boiled Eggs in Curry Sauce
Tomato Eggs
Scrambled Eggs
Poached Eggs (or Eggs Mollet) Florentine
Tortilla Andalusa
Cheese Soufflé
Fish Soufflé

# Little Entrées

This chapter is fairly long, perhaps because it contains some of my favorite dishes, both to eat and, especially, to make. These are recipes based on ingredients I always have on hand—flour and grains, milk, cream, eggs, farmer cheese, and sour cream—and are among the most useful ones in my "repertoire." They are nearly all extremely adaptable and can appear at almost any meal: at brunch, at lunch with soup or a salad, as a light supper before or after a concert or the theater. Although the basic ingredients may strike you as somewhat rich, the dishes are so satisfying that one tends not to overdo—although some of us *have* been known to indulge in an occasional dumpling- or blinis-binge!

These are the dishes you are least likely to find in restaurants, and that benefit most from the home cook's personal touch, above all from the cook's ability to serve a dish almost straight from the oven or skillet—dumplings and fritters particularly don't wait around too well. Another attraction is that some of the recipes can involve a few extra hands (even quite young ones), and in our family, past, present, and into my grandchildren's generation, there has never been a want of eager apprentices, who often later became very good cooks themselves, and whose children in turn . . .

I hope you will enjoy these recipes, many of which are among my earliest memories from our kitchen in Lithuania. I am sure that as you become familiar with these basically easy techniques, the more often you'll want to do them and the easier they will be. And the more your own imagination will dream up new ways to use crêpes and quiches and dumplings.

# Crêpes and Pancakes

Crêpes, those thin French pancakes—of which nearly every country on earth has a version, and with good reason—rightfully lead off this chapter. I can't think of anything one can make in a kitchen that lends itself as easily to so many variations, that goes happily from a kitchen-table brunch or supper to a black-tie dinner party, or that can transform humble leftovers into a dish fit for guests. One's imagination is the only limit.

Crêpes, cooked, stacked, and wrapped, keep beautifully for days in the refrigerator, and perfectly in the freezer. They keep equally well when filled, rolled, folded, but not sauced, covered in plastic wrap in the refrigerator or freezer, and so are wonderful for party meals that must be made in advance.

Many fillings for crêpes are also suited to the pastries in this chapter. I have suggested a few favorites, but the possibilities are endless. (Dessert crêpes, made with a lighter batter, are on page 348, but there is nothing wrong with the ones described here, dabbed with sweet butter or jam and sugar, fresh from the pan onto the plate.)

## CRÊPES

*Makes twelve 7-inch crêpes*

Crêpe batter must sit for at least 30 minutes to let the flour absorb the liquid; so make it first and set it aside while you make a filling and attend to other things.

For making crêpes, use a shallow, flat-bottomed pan (or a regular crêpe pan) with a 7-inch diameter.

1 cup (140 grams) flour
1 cup (¼ liter) milk
¾ cup (1¾ deciliters) heavy cream
¼ teaspoon salt
2 eggs
About 3 tablespoons butter, softened

Beating vigorously, combine well the flour, milk, cream, and salt. Add the eggs, still beating. (For the blender: pour in the milk and cream first. Add the flour and salt, blend well, then add the eggs and blend again.) Let the batter rest for 30 minutes.

Arrange your crêpes setup efficiently: 1 or 2 crêpe pans on the stove top; next to them a pitcher or bowl of batter and a whisk, with a ¼-cup measure or a ladle; and a little softened butter with a pastry brush for filming the pan. Beside you, have a board (wood, plastic, whatever) or a large plate, on which to tip the crêpes when done.

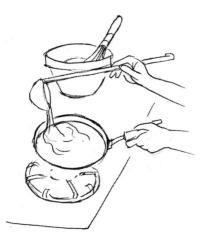

Set the pan or pans over high heat and film them with the butter. Whisk up the batter with two or three strokes, adding a little water if it seems too thick. For each 7-inch crêpe, allow a scant ¼ cup of batter.

Tilt the pan, rotating it, as you pour the batter in, so that the surface is all covered. Tip any excess batter back into the pitcher or bowl.

In about 30–45 seconds, the surface of the crêpe will go from pasty white to creamy, and the edges will begin to curl a bit. At this point flip or turn the crêpe over and very briefly cook the other side, which will not brown as much as the first.

Tip the finished crêpe onto the board or plate and start the next one. If the pan gets dry or the crêpe sticks, add a little butter. If the pan gets too hot, simply lift it off the heat for a moment.

Depending on how many pans you have, and whether you are an experienced crêpe maker, you can develop your own "production line" for efficiency. (This is a fine time to call in friendly helpers, but not at all necessary.) If you are making a stack of crepes for later use, just drop them on top of each other as they are done, on foil if they are to be refrigerated or frozen, on a plate if to be used the same day or the next. Let them cool and cover the stack with plastic wrap.

If you are making crêpes to be filled, your filling should be ready, not too hot or cold. Proceed this way: start one crêpe, as indicated above. When the second side is done, slide it onto your board. Start a second crêpe. While the first side is baking, fill the first one, and roll or fold it according to which recipe you are making (see crêpes gratinéed on p. 83 or crêpes sautéed on p. 82). By the time you have filled the first crêpe, the second should be ready to turn. Turn it, cook briefly, and slide it out. Start a third. Fill the second. Continue in this manner until all your crêpes are made and filled.

Never worry about crêpes lying on top of each other, warm or cool, if they are done faster than you can fill them. Just stack them, and when they are all done, gently peel the top one off the stack, put it on the board, fill it, set it aside, and do the next. It is all easier than it may seem written out, and *much* more fun.

## *Three Fillings for Crêpes, Choux, Pierogis, or Pierożkis*

BEEF FILLING

*Makes 2½ cups*

2 cups (½ liter) cooked beef, pot roast, boiled beef, etc.
½ pound (225 grams) mushrooms, minced very fine
2 medium onions, peeled and minced very fine
2 tablespoons finely cut parsley or dill (optional)
1 tablespoon butter
1 Knorr beef bouillon cube

Mince or grind the beef and set it aside. Sauté the mushrooms and onions and optional parsley or dill lightly in the butter. Break up the bouillon cube, add to the vegetables, and cover, so that the cube may dissolve in the juices.

Uncover the pan, stir the mixture well, and add the beef. You will probably not want salt, since the bouillon cube is salty.

This filling is excellent when you want to make a hearty dish with the crêpes. See Filled Crêpes, Gratinéed and Filled Crêpes, Sautéed on pages 82 and 83.


CHICKEN FILLING

*Makes 2½ cups*


2 cups (½ liter) cooked chicken, with plenty of
    dark meat for flavor
½ cup (1 deciliter) medium Béchamel Sauce (p. 48)
2 medium onions, peeled
2 tablespoons finely cut parsley or dill (optional)
1 tablespoon butter
1 Knorr chicken bouillon cube


Proceed as in preceding recipe for beef filling. As chicken is drier than beef, add the béchamel with the minced chicken. For the béchamel liquid, use ½ cup cream or milk or chicken broth.


CALF'S BRAIN FILLING (for crêpes, *choux,* or *pieroźkis*)

*Makes about 2 cups*

Another version of this preparation, Calves' Brains en Coquille, makes a nice gratin (p. 209).


1 calf's brain, about 1 pound (450 grams)
1 teaspoon salt
3 grinds black pepper
1 bay leaf
½ cup (1 deciliter) finely chopped onion
3 tablespoons butter
2 tablespoons sour cream
1 egg yolk
More salt and pepper to taste

It is not necessary to soak the brain, but pick it over carefully under cold running water, removing the coarse membranes and any traces of blood. Put the brain into a saucepan and cover with cold water. Add the 1 teaspoon salt, the 3 grinds black pepper, and the bay leaf, bring the liquid to a boil, and cook for 3 minutes. Drain and pat dry the brain. Cook the onion in the butter over low heat, until it is golden but not brown. Add the brain, breaking it up with a fork—not too finely—and stir while sautéing for 2 minutes. Off the heat, stir in the sour cream and egg yolk and mix well. Taste and season the mixture with more salt and pepper.

## FILLED CRÊPES, SAUTÉED

Crêpes wrapped around any of the above fillings, and sautéed, are a delicious complement to a strong clear soup, like *Clear Barszcz* (p. 18). They are served with the soup, on small separate plates, with forks. Sometimes for a light lunch I serve them, two or three per person, with a salad.

Make Crêpes (p. 78). While batter rests for 30 minutes, make filling; fill each finished crêpe as you are cooking the next one or add the filling when the whole batch is made (both methods described on pages 79–80).

In the middle of the best, first cooked side of each crêpe, place a lump of filling (about 1 tablespoon), then spread it thinly in the center, leaving a margin of about 2 inches all around. Bring two opposite edges of the crêpe up over the filling, overlapping them. Fold over the two remaining edges, making a soft oblong of about 2 inches by 3 inches.

Heat a sauté pan, preferably nonstick, as it requires less fat. Add 1 or 2 tablespoons fat, depending on the pan size. Clarified butter is ideal, as it does not burn over medium–high heat and adds a delicious flavor, but vegetable shortening or fresh vegetable oil will do. When the fat has bubbled but before it colors, add the crêpe parcels, seam side down (to seal the seams), and turn them gently until they are golden-brown on all sides.

You can make these ahead in large quantities for parties. They taste best right after sautéing, but can be sautéed and kept, lightly covered with foil, in a large ovenproof dish, then gently warmed in a 300°F (150°C) oven just to heat them through before serving.

## FILLED CRÊPES, GRATINÉED

These are best with the Beef Filling (page 80) or the Ham, Spinach, and Mushroom Filling (page 117), which hold their own against the blander crêpes and béchamel sauce.

Make Crêpes (p. 78). Make Beef Filling while batter rests for 30 minutes.

Make 2 cups medium Béchamel Sauce (p. 48). Add to it 4 ounces grated cheese (imported or domestic Gruyère or Appenzell), stirring until the cheese melts. Taste sauce for seasoning.

Make crêpes according to instructions on pages 79–80. Or make all the crêpes first, stacking them, and fill them afterward.

Preheat the oven to 350°F (180°C). Butter lightly the bottom and sides of a low ovenproof dish or gratin dish. Put a sausage-shaped lump of filling (about ¼ cup) on the first, more cooked side of each crêpe. Roll up the crêpes and set them close together in the dish, seam side down. Warm the béchamel sauce, stirring constantly, and pour it evenly over the crêpes,

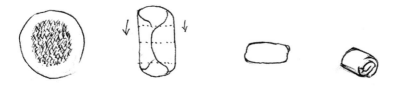

covering them completely. It is nice to sprinkle on a little freshly grated Parmesan cheese and a few dots of butter. Heat the dish in the oven (about 15 minutes). Then slide it under the broiler until the crêpes brown slightly and sizzle on top; serve them at once.

# BLINIS

*Makes thirty-six 4-inch blinis*

These are small raised pancakes, 4 inches in diameter, traditionally eaten with caviar or with a quickly made mixture of Salt Herring and Eggs (p. 170). They are often served for a festive occasion, but are wonderful for an elegant brunch, or indeed any other time. I am rather particular about them; the usual kind, made with part buckwheat flour, seem to me too strong tasting. I like the distinctive whiff of yeast and a simple white-flour batter. Though their inside is fluffy, blinis should be quite thin, and dry—not greasy at all. They are best when freshly made and piping hot. (In Paris one can buy, expensively, ready-made blinis to be reheated in foil. They aren't bad; and I have successfully reheated my blinis, stacked and wrapped in foil, in a moderate oven.)

Serve your blinis with sour cream and melted butter to accompany the caviar or herring (or both), and chilled glasses of vodka straight from the freezer. This makes a substantial main course for lunch. If you serve blinis as a first course for a copious dinner, follow them with a Clear *Barszcz* (p. 18) or madrilène, and/or a very simple, unsauced roast.

STARTER

> 1 package active dry yeast
> ½ teaspoon sugar
> Dash of salt
> ½ cup (1 deciliter) warm water (maximum 100°F/38°C)

BATTER

> 4 eggs, separated
> 2 cups (280 grams) flour
> 1½ cups (3½ deciliters) warm milk
> 6 tablespoons butter, melted
> 1 teaspoon sugar
> ¼ teaspoon salt

In a small bowl, dissolve the yeast, sugar, and salt in the warm water. Let the mixture stand while you mix the other ingredients (about 10 minutes); it will foam and expand somewhat.

Beat the egg whites. (If you are using an electric mixer, use the largest bowl, then slide the beaten whites into another bowl—you can then mix the other ingredients in the first bowl and need not wash the beaters.)

Put the flour into the large mixer bowl. Pour the warm milk into it, with the mixer first on low, then on medium speed; add the egg yolks, butter, sugar, and salt. Add the yeast mixture, which should by now have become foamy. Mix thoroughly. Fold in the egg whites as thoroughly as possible. (The mixture should not have little "clouds" of egg white.) Cover the bowl with a dishcloth and let the mixture rise until doubled, about 3½ hours. (The time will depend somewhat on the temperature of the room.) *Don't* put the bowl near a heater or the stove.

Spoon up about 2 tablespoonfuls of batter and bake on a lightly buttered griddle or skillet (so you can do several at a time) over medium-high heat. They will spread to about 4 inches across and will look rather like flapjacks.

# Fritters

It is not always necessary to deep-fry fritters, and I do so rarely, as deep-frying uses so much fat. Instead, I sauté them. One may improvise with all kinds of fish, shellfish, vegetables, or, for dessert, fruit. The recipes here are only illustrations of the general principle.

When you improvise with fritters, bear in mind that the batter envelope is fragile. Do not use large pieces, or the batter will burn before they cook through. For a golden, crisp fritter with a juicy interior, use a ½-inch slice —no thicker—of zucchini, or apple, or whatever, or a medium-size shrimp. And be sure each slice is well dried before you dip it in batter.

Sautéing, as compared with deep-frying, will give a little of the batter time to ooze downward, so that each fritter has a small plaque of "fry" on one side. It may not look perfectly elegant, but the extra bit of crunch is delicious.

## FRITTER BATTER FOR ENTRÉES OR DESSERTS

*Makes about 2½ cups*

½ cup (70 grams) flour
½ cup (1 deciliter) heavy cream
¼ cup (½ deciliter) milk
2 eggs, separated
¼ teaspoon salt
Small pinch of baking soda

Beat well together the flour, cream, milk, egg yolks, and salt. Let them stand 15 minutes. Beat the egg whites until they hold together in soft peaks. Stir the baking soda into the flour mixture and fold in the egg whites.

## FISH FRITTERS WITH PRUNE COMPOTE

*Serves 6*

Here is a most unusual dish, which was served in my parents' home. It might seem odd to serve the fish with compote of prunes but, believe me, it is very good. I remembered it from my childhood and have since tried it on many refined gourmets, who, having at first raised their eyebrows, after tasting it were quite delighted.

1½ pounds (675 grams) fillets of white, firm fish
    like monkfish, cusk, or tilefish (avoid strong-tasting
    fish like mackerel or salmon)
1 recipe Fritter Batter (preceding recipe)
Solid vegetable shortening and/or vegetable oil,
    for frying

Cut fish into pieces or slices about 1 by 2 inches, and ½ inch thick. Lay them on paper or dish towels and pat with towels before dipping in the batter, which clings better to a dry surface.

Use a heavy sauté pan with a perfectly flat bottom. Choose a fat that will not burn over quite high heat and is not expensive (since one uses a good deal). Solid vegetable shortening is ideal, but you can use vegetable oil, or half oil and half vegetable shortening.

The fat should be ½ inch deep in the pan. Heat it slowly until a little speck of batter dropped in the hot fat sizzles and turns golden.

With a long fork, immerse each piece of fish in the batter and, without shaking off the excess, transfer it at once to the fat. To avoid cooling the fat, don't crowd the pieces (do 2 or 3 batches, if necessary); keep them warm in a slow oven. The fritters are done when golden and crisp on both sides. Remove them with a skimmer, drain on paper towels, and serve at once with the prune compote.

PRUNE COMPOTE

*Serves 6 as a condiment*

18 pitted prunes
Zest of ½ lemon, in large pieces
Sugar to taste (optional)

Use a heavy, covered pot, a small one so that you won't need much water. Place in it the prunes and lemon zest. Cover, just barely, with water, and let the prunes soak for an hour or more to blend flavors. Then simmer slowly until the prunes are soft (see package directions, as prunes vary). Taste the compote for sweetness and cautiously add sugar, if necessary. Serve warm.

# CAULIFLOWER FRITTERS

*Serves 6*

These are good with ham or with such full-flavored meats as Roast Pork Shoulder (p. 205).

1 small cauliflower
1 recipe Fritter Batter (p. 86)
Solid vegetable shortening and/or vegetable oil, for frying

Break or cut the cauliflower into florets, or pieces about ½ inch thick. (Discard any bits that crumble off.) Cook them in a steamer, covered, for about 5 minutes after the water boils. As soon as the pieces are just done, not crunchy but firm to the bite, drain them and let them cool. Pat them dry carefully. Coat with batter and fry them as directed in recipe for Fish Fritters (p. 86).

*For the pressure cooker:* Cook the florets in ½ cup cold water for 2 minutes after pressure is reached, then cool and uncover the pot. Proceed as above.

## EGGPLANT FRITTERS

*Serves 6*

In contrast to cauliflower and root vegetables like carrots, eggplants are watery and should be lightly macerated in a little salt before being batter-fried. I do this with the summer squash family as well: zucchini, yellow crookneck squash, etc. Additionally, eggplants have a slight bitterness, which drains away with the excess moisture after salting.

1½ pounds (675 grams) eggplant
1½ teaspoons salt
1 recipe Fritter Batter (p. 86)
Solid vegetable shortening and/or vegetable oil, for frying
2 teaspoons finely cut basil (optional)

If your eggplants are small and young, you can slice them crosswise, ½ inch thick, and leave the skin on. Larger ones are best peeled and cut into sticks ½ inch thick.

In a small bowl, gently toss the eggplant pieces or slices with the salt. Let them sit, tossing occasionally, for 30 minutes. First spread the pieces on paper towels to drain, then weight them: On a folded dish towel, arrange the pieces in a single layer. Cover this with another folded dish towel, and cover this with a baking sheet, on which you set weights (several 8-ounce cans, for instance). Let this arrangement sit for 15 minutes or so, or until some moisture has exuded. Pat the eggplant pieces dry, then coat with batter and fry as directed in recipe for Fish Fritters (p. 86).

Before serving eggplant fritters, I like to sprinkle them with a little finely cut fresh basil, when available.

# Four/Five Dumplings

Here are several dumplings—one made with a buttery batter, really a *choux* (cream puff) paste, and served in soup; then two made with farmer cheese; and finally a rich marrow dumpling, served traditionally in Poland with tripe (p. 96).

## FRENCH DUMPLINGS

*Serves 6*

The flavor of these pale ivory ovals is mild and buttery; the texture is light and so smooth it glides on the tongue. They are based on that adaptable substance, *choux* paste. (See the end of the recipe for more ideas on using this.)

The shape must be a plump, smooth oval, with no ignominious little tatters or tails. Once you have the trick, these become so quick and easy that I often make myself a few as I might scramble myself an egg. Please read the recipe carefully the first time; the second time, I promise, you will be able to skip most of the instructions.

> 1 cup (¼ liter) water
> 4 tablespoons (60 grams) butter
> ½ teaspoon salt
> ½ cup (70 grams) flour
> 2 eggs (large or extralarge; use 3 if small)
> 2 quarts poaching liquid

In a small saucepan (the small size is important), heat together the water, butter, and salt until the butter melts. Bring them to a boil. Remove the pot from the heat and immediately add all the flour, blending with a stiff whisk. When the mixture is smooth, beat in the eggs, one at a time, thoroughly incorporating the first before adding the second.

Set the saucepan aside, uncovered, for 15 minutes at least. Prop up (with a folded towel, perhaps) the saucepan so that it will remain tilted, helping to mass the *choux* paste for shaping. First resting the dough, and then always keeping the mass plump and convex during shaping, are two of my three Great Dumpling Secrets.

The third is to have the poaching liquid just below the simmer in a big wide pot (the wider the better—depth is less important) so as to give the dumplings room to expand without crowding each other and spoiling each other's shape.

For shaping, use a thin, rather pointed dessert spoon. An iced-tea spoon is perfect. First dip the bowl of the spoon into the hot poaching liquid, then, using the tip and one side of the bowl, take up a plump, convex lump of paste. (As the bowl of the spoon shapes the bottom of the dumpling, the curve of the dough mass supplies the rounded top.) Clean off the near edge of the spoon by drawing it upward, slantwise, against the saucepan wall. Now plunge the spoon point down into the simmering liquid, immersing the dumpling. It should fall in—if it doesn't, tap the spoon on the bottom of the soup pot.

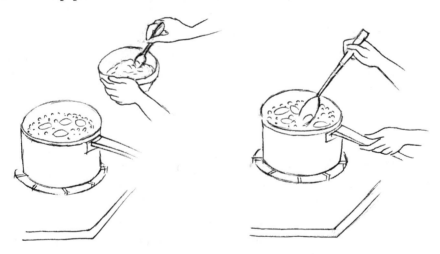

Mass up the dough again, dip the bowl of the spoon in the poaching liquid, and continue. Do this for each dumpling. Work briskly so no dumplings get overcooked. When all are in the cooking liquid, cover the pot. After 2 minutes, uncover the pot for a quick check. Dumplings are done when they have risen to the surface and have expanded to twice their original size. It may take up to 4 minutes.

Now stop the simmer by adding cold water or an ice cube to the liquid. Serve the dumplings with the broth as soon as possible.

*Variation: Tiny French dumplings as garnish for consommé*

These are the same dumplings, but made very small, with just the tip of the spoon's bowl (like half a demitasse spoon). A bowl of rich consommé with six dumplings or so floating in it makes an elegant garnish for a dinner party and of course is not so filling before a more elaborate meal.

These dumplings, cooked, will be about the size of small lima beans and take a very short time (about 1 minute) to cook and swell to double their original size. Watch them carefully.

## PÂTE À CHOUX
### (for gnocchi, for deep-frying and baking, for quenelles)

If you add an egg and 2 tablespoons flour (or an egg and 4 tablespoons freshly boiled potato, mashed or riced) to the French Dumpling recipe, you can make a dumpling firm enough to be served gratinéed after poaching, like gnocchi.

Filbert-size bits of this stiffer paste can be deep-fried; they expand enormously, into crisp golden balloons.

Or you can make the paste into tiny *choux* (delicious for a cocktail party when the cooked *choux* are filled with something savory like the calf's brains recipe on page 81), or big ones to be served as cream puffs.* *Choux* are baked. In a preheated 425°F (220°C) oven, bake 1-inch *choux* for about 8 minutes. Slit the tops with a very sharp knife to let steam escape, and keep them warm so they will become dry inside and stay crisp. The larger puffs should be baked at 425°F (220°C) for 5 minutes, then at 375°F (190°C) until done, about 10–12 minutes more. Slit them, or cut the tops right off, and keep them warm. You may have to spoon out a little unbaked dough from the insides.

Fish, processed raw until very soft and smooth, almost a purée, and lightly

---

*For cream puffs, the eggs and flour addition is recommended.

seasoned, may be added to this stiffer *choux* dough, about half and half, to make quenelles. Form them into 1½-inch-long egg shapes between 2 soup-spoons, or roll them quickly in the floured palm of your hand. Chill them for about 30 minutes so they will hold their shape, then poach them in broth or salted water, and serve them with a creamy sauce.

In our family, we use this stiffer *choux* dough for a funny-looking cookie we call *schmoor* (p. 346).

## CHEESE DUMPLINGS I
### (Serniki I)

*Serves 4 as a main course*

These are quite firm and easy to shape, and they can be made in advance and reheated in a steamer. They look like white, plump, diamond-shaped cushions and can be served with buttered crumbs as a light entrée. Or you can sprinkle them with sugar, then buttered crumbs, and serve them with sour cream for dessert. I prefer them hot, but others like them lukewarm.

Begin by tasting the cheese, to find out how much salt to use.

½ pound (225 grams) farmer cheese or pressed cottage cheese*
2 eggs
Salt to taste (½ teaspoon or so)
½–¾ cup (70–105 grams) flour

Combine the cheese, eggs, and salt thoroughly, then mix in ½ cup flour. The total amount of flour varies with the dryness of the cheese and also with the weather. When you have cooked a sample dumpling, you will know how much more to add.

---

*Farmer cheese recently has become available in most supermarkets. Some markets make their own, fresh and almost unsalted. If you can't find farmer cheese, you can easily make it by pressing small-curd cottage cheese to force the moisture out: Make a pouch of cheesecloth (2 or 3 layers thick), rinse it with cold water, and fill it with cottage cheese. Hang the full pouch over the sink to drip for 12 hours. Then weight the pouchful with a brick or a heavy can, set in or a board slanting into the sink or pan, and leave it for 6 hours longer.

Let the dough rest for 30 minutes or longer. (If you don't have the time, skip it—in this case the dumplings will taste just as good.)

On a lightly floured board, place 1 tablespoon of the dough and try shaping it with floured fingers into a little sausage. Fan out your fingers and very lightly roll the dough back and forth. If it will shape up at all, it is ready. If not, return it to the bowl, add a little more flour to the dough, mix, and try again. Add more flour to the board only if necessary for forming. The dough should have about the consistency of *choux* paste; if you drop a spoonful softly onto the board, it should hold its shape.

Now make your second test. In a wide pot, with at least 2 inches of simmering water, poach a bit of the dough to see if it stays together. If not, add a bit more flour to the dough bowl, mix well, and try again.

Having made sure that the dough can be formed and poached without disintegrating, put all the mixture on the floured board. With fanned-out fingers, roll the dough back and forth into long sausages about ¾ inch in diameter. With a sharp, wide-bladed knife, lightly flatten the top of each sausage, then crosshatch it closely with shallow cuts. This is not just for looks; it helps the dumplings to cohere.

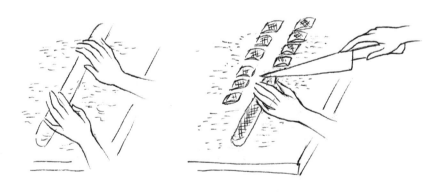

Cut the sausages diagonally into diamond shapes about 1¼ inches across at the widest place. Use the tip of the knife and pull it away quickly after each cut. Slip the dumplings into a wide pot with at least 2 inches simmering water and poach uncovered. They will sink at first. After about 5 minutes they will rise to the surface, a sign that they are done. Remove them with a slotted spoon, drain them for a moment on a folded towel, and serve.

## CHEESE DUMPLINGS II
### (Serniki II)

*Serves 6 as a side dish*

This recipe for smooth and extra-delicate dumplings was given me by a brilliant cook, my old friend Fela Krance. They are nice with bread crumbs fried in butter or, for dessert, with cinnamon, sugar, and sour cream.

½ pound (225 grams) farmer cheese or pressed cottage cheese
   (see preceding recipe note)
3 eggs, separated
½ cup (70 grams) flour
½ teaspoon salt

In the bowl of a mixer, processor, or blender, put the cheese, egg yolks, flour, and salt, and mix or blend until smooth. Let it rest for 15 minutes or more. Beat the egg whites and fold them into the mixture.

For full details on testing and poaching dumplings, see the preceding recipe. Briefly, test a spoonful of the dough in simmering salted water and add flour if necessary to make a coherent dough.

Form the dumplings as you would French Dumplings (p. 90), slightly larger, with the tip and lower side of a dessert spoon, and slide them into the water. The pot should be covered. The dumplings will sink; they are done in 4–5 minutes, when they rise to the surface. Drain them well and serve at once.

## MARROW AND MATZO DUMPLINGS

*Serves 6 as a garnish*

These are easy to manage because they are coated with flour before poaching. I like them served in the soup plate with Tripes à la Varsovienne (p. 212) or other well-seasoned ragouts, such as goulash. In Germany and Austria, dumplings of this type are shaped as big as baseballs and served in soup, one for each plate. This I don't like. For details about marrow, see *Kolduny,* page 108.

¼ pound (115 grams) veal suet (preferably kidney fat)
   or marrow, or half and half (you can substitute
   vegetable shortening)
1 cup (225 grams) matzo meal or *unseasoned* bread crumbs
2 eggs, separated
2 tablespoons finely cut dill or parsley
Salt and pepper to taste
3 tablespoons flour, for forming

Grind or finely cut the suet or marrow (don't use the processor or blender) into the matzo meal as if making pastry. If you are using vegetable shortening, just rub it in with the fingertips. Mix in the egg yolks, dill or parsley, and salt and pepper. Add the egg whites, beaten stiff: you can't really fold them in, but mix them in lightly. Shape the mixture into walnut-size balls and roll them in the flour. Simmer them, covered, in salted water for 40 minutes or until the dumplings rise to the surface. Remove them with a slotted spoon and serve a few in each soup plate.

# $\mathcal{P}asta$

Of all culinary pleasures, the mixing, kneading, and rolling of dough for egg pasta are the most rewarding. So of course I make noodles whenever the urge overtakes me; during our touring days I sometimes made them on a card table in our hotel room if there wasn't space in the kitchenette, or even on a hard-topped suitcase! Everybody loves tender, mellow-flavored fresh pasta, but the trouble is most people make too big a project of it. Often I hear busy young working people say, "We're saving up for a pasta machine so we can make our own." Don't wait, I want to say. I like machines myself, and I am busy too, but noodles are not only better, but also more quickly made, by hand.

I find them better, because the slight irregularities of hand cutting add a dimension to the flavor, with every mouthful seeming a bit different; also, the machine compresses the dough too fiercely—I prefer the tender hand-kneaded texture. And, yes, they are made more quickly. You won't believe this until you have done it a couple of times, but it is true. This very "live" dough is so responsive to the rolling pin that you learn to sense just the right next move. Fifteen minutes' working time, plus one 15-minute rest for the dough, and you're all done, with only a board, a knife, and a pin to tidy up.

## NOODLE DOUGH

You will soon get in the habit of thinking, "Six persons, therefore three eggs, and as much flour as they will take," and you will automatically increase the proportions if noodles are the main dish. But here is a general formula for your first try. (As always in these recipes, I have in mind U.S. extra-large eggs and plain all-purpose flour.)

2½ cups (350 grams) flour, with more available
3 eggs, lightly beaten
¾ teaspoon salt
1 tablespoon oil
1 tablespoon water, with more available

On any clean, smooth working surface 2 feet square or so (kitchen table, counter top, pastry board), mound the flour, and in the middle make a well about 6 inches across. Into this pour the beaten eggs, damming any rivulets with some of the flour. Add the salt and oil. Working from the outside inward, with the edge of your cupped hand push flour into the eggs. (Don't worry about sticky hands—all the goo comes off hands and board as you knead.) When the eggs are absorbed into the flour, gather the mass together and roll it around the board to incorporate any crumbly bits.

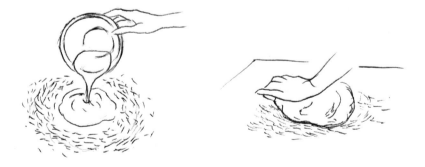

To make the mass more elastic, pat it flat and, with the heel of your hand, smear sections of dough along the board; then gather up the mass. Now it will be much easier to knead. Flour your hands. Gather the dough into one lump, press into it and forward with the heels of both hands, give it a quarter-turn, gather it, and press again; lean on it with stiff elbows, so that the dough gets the force of your weight.

If, after a few shoves, the dough remains sticky, sprinkle the board with a little flour. Incorporate this, then use more if you need to. About 10 minutes of vigorous kneading is usually enough. The dough should respond actively but resistantly to your hand, and when you stretch it, it will shrink right back. At this point the surface feels literally silky.

Now ball it up and rest it 15 minutes under an inverted bowl. Divide the dough in half, leaving half the dough under the bowl. (If you have a little experience and enough space, you roll out the whole amount at once.) Flatten the dough into a round cake about an inch thick and begin rolling in short, firm strokes from the center outward, one toward you, one away. Turn it after every few strokes. (Sprinkle additional flour, as needed, on your working surface and your rolling pin.) Now and then turn the dough over. If you tear the dough, cut a piece from the edge, lay it over the tear, and roll it in.

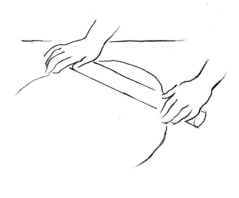

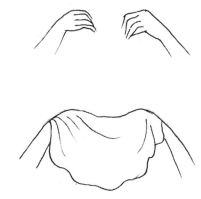

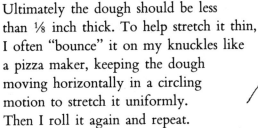

Ultimately the dough should be less than ⅛ inch thick. To help stretch it thin, I often "bounce" it on my knuckles like a pizza maker, keeping the dough moving horizontally in a circling motion to stretch it uniformly. Then I roll it again and repeat.

When the dough is uniformly thin, let it sit 5 minutes to stiffen very slightly, so cutting is easier. (But don't let it sit longer, or it will get brittle.)

At this point you are ready to decide what kind, or kinds, of noodles you are going to make: *lazanki* (square noodles, served with chopped onions and mushrooms); fettucine; or fine noodles (angel's hair) for soup—or, if you like, some of each.

## CUTTING NOODLE DOUGH

This is a fine time to recruit even very young hands; they might learn to do the cutting and certainly will enjoy uncurling the soft strips of dough.

*To cut the dough for lazanki:* Cut the sheet of dough into squares about 1½ inches, and lay the squares on a floured surface (a large tray is perfect) to dry for a few minutes.

*To cut the dough for fettucine:* Flour the surface of the rolled-out dough liberally, then fold it, to a depth of 4 inches, and fold over and over until you have used up all the dough. Then with a sharp knife (a French chef's knife is good) cut the dough crosswise into ¼-inch slices. Every few cuts, take the folded strips, unfold them gently, and lay them on a floured surface to dry.

*To cut the dough for very fine noodles (angel's hair) for soup:* Follow the procedure above exactly, except cut the strips very, very fine, about ⅛ inch.

*Note:* If you mean to refrigerate or freeze cut noodle dough, toss the pieces lightly in flour (which will shake right off later) to prevent sticking and tie them up in plastic bags. Cook them without first bringing them to room temperature.

Homemade noodle dough cooks very fast. Add 1 tablespoon oil and 1 tablespoon salt to a big potful of boiling water, throw in the noodle pieces, and start tasting for doneness after 4 minutes. Then drain well.

## ANGEL'S HAIR

Some of the Noodle Dough (p. 98), cut for Angel's Hair (p. 100)

Cook the noodles carefully, and briefly, in boiling water, drain, then add to soup. Do not cook them *in* the soup as too much of it may evaporate.

## FETTUCINE

*Serves 6 as a side dish*

1 recipe Noodle Dough (p. 98), cut for Fettucine (p. 100)
Butter to taste

Boil the noodles in salted water. When they are done, drain well, return to the pot, and add butter to taste. These are delicious served with almost any kind of veal and with Beef Stroganoff (p. 186).

## LAZANKI WITH MUSHROOMS
## AND ONIONS

*Serves 6 as a side dish*

This combination is a great favorite with the whole family, is easy to make, and is especially good for large parties, as it improves with being kept warm. It is a perfect accompaniment for Chicken Cutlets (p. 237). (If you want to have *lazanki* without making the dough yourself, you can of course buy very wide egg noodles and break them into squares before cooking, then boil *al dente.*)

2 medium onions, chopped very fine
1 tablespoon butter
½ pound (225 grams) mushrooms, chopped very fine
Dash of Maggi extract
Pinch of salt
1 recipe Noodle Dough (p. 98), cut for *lazanki* (p. 101),
    and cooked *al dente*

Sauté the onions in butter until they are soft and golden, then add mushrooms. Continue to cook until the juices evaporate. Add the Maggi extract, taste, and add salt, cautiously, if you like.

In a casserole or thick-walled serving dish, combine the cooked *lazanki* with the mushroom mixture. Cover and keep warm for 10 minutes, or longer, before serving. The brief wait seems to unite the bland noodle taste with the mushrooms' richness.

## PASTA WITH FRESH BASIL

*Serves 4–6*

Here is another of those wonderful, satisfying, and slightly unusual dishes that can be served at any time of day or night, for one or for a crowd, in a matter of minutes (with the heaviest labor being the cutting of the basil). Increasingly one can find tortellini and cappelletti (small meat-filled pastries shaped something like a tiny doughnut) in either dry or frozen form. With this sauce, and a green salad on the side, they make a complete lunch or dinner. A lighter version of pasta, spaghettini or elbow macaroni, can be served alone as brunch or supper, or with a not too saucy meat entrée such as breaded veal scallops (p. 193).

1½ pounds (675 grams) tortellini, cappelletti, spaghettini
    (thin spaghetti), or elbow macaroni
2–3 tablespoons butter
2 large cloves garlic
1½ cups crisp fresh basil leaves,
    lightly pressed down
1 cup (¼ liter) sour cream
1 cup (¼ liter) heavy cream
6 tablespoons freshly grated Parmesan cheese,
    with more to pass separately

In a large pot of vigorously boiling salted water, with 1 tablespoon oil added (to prevent the pasta from sticking), boil the pasta, uncovered, for about 7 minutes, or to your taste.

Meanwhile put the garlic cloves through a garlic press. Cut the basil leaves very fine with a knife and mix with the garlic. The mixture must have a moist and leafy texture; it must *not* be a mush.

Drain the pasta well, and return to the pot with the butter. Toss so that each piece is coated with the butter. Then add the basil-and-garlic mixture and toss again. Mix the sour cream and heavy cream and add this to the pasta. Heat carefully, tossing. Add the Parmesan and toss again.

Serve with a little bowl of additional grated Parmesan.

# Pierogi, Kolduny, and Uszka

*Pierogi* are small, filled, poached pastries, very like wontons or ravioli, except that Polish cooks shape them in little half-moons, and often fill them with something sweet and serve them for dessert. *Kolduny* are a specialty: small (extra-thin-skinned) *pierogi* with an elegant meat and marrow filling. *Uszka,* little noodle pastries filled with a chopped mushroom mixture, are traditionally served in a meatless *barszcz.*

A thin skin is important for all poached pastries, since the sealed edges are doubled anyway, and each bite should have a nice balance between dough and filling.

Using the assembly-line method I have developed, it is scarcely more work to make these pastries for eighteen people than for six. Moreover, the formed but uncooked pastries freeze well, so they are practical for parties. Although *kolduny* and *uszka* are made only with the specific filling given, *pierogis* can be made with a number of others equally well—the Cabbage and Mushroom, for *Coulibiac* (p. 113), or the Meat Filling (p. 80). Your own invention and inspiration will surely suggest still other tasty combinations.

One makes the filling beforehand, or while the dough is resting, since it must cool to room temperature before the pastries are formed. The Cheese and Potato Filling (p. 108) will not be warm.

## DOUGH FOR PIEROGI, KOLDUNY, AND USZKA

*Makes about 40 pieces*

2 cups (280 grams) flour, with more available
½ teaspoon salt
1 egg, beaten
⅔ cup (1½ deciliters) *lukewarm* water,
   with more available
1 tablespoon oil

Thoroughly flour a large board. Mix the salt into the flour, mound it on the board, and make a well in the mound. Pour the beaten egg into the well, and work in as much flour as possible. Add the water, about 3 tablespoons at a time, working it in thoroughly, and add the oil with the last addition of water. The dough at this point should be very stiff, but if it is too stiff to blend, add a little more water. If the dough is too soft, add a little flour. The proportions vary a bit, depending on your brand of flour and the humidity of the day.

When the dough begins to clear the board (that is, to feel uniform and to take up all the scattered flour), it is ready to knead. Knead it just as you would noodle dough. That is, push down and forward into the mass with the heels of your hands, applying your weight; double over the pad of dough, give it a quarter-turn, and repeat. Knead it thoroughly, for 10 minutes or more, until the dough feels elastic and silky. Shape it into a ball and let it rest under a small overturned bowl. It will relax and soften in about 15 minutes. If you must leave it longer, cover it first with plastic wrap to prevent forming a skin, but do not refrigerate it.

If you have not yet made the filling, now is a good time.

After this pause, flour the rolling pin and reflour the board. Pat the dough into a flat cake, and roll from the center in all directions, using a good deal of pressure. If the dough becomes at all sticky, sprinkle it with additional flour. As you work it, it will become elastic: the edges will visibly retract when you lift the pin.

Cut the dough sheet in half and lay a dampened dish towel over one half, to prevent its drying out. Drape the other half over the backs of your hands, held close together in loose fists, and move your hands gently up and apart, tossing the sheet of dough upward and a little sideways with each motion. Repeat several times, continuously. The middle will thin out rather more than the edges. Put the dough on the refloured board, and roll again to make the outside edges the same thickness as the center. (As the dough is by now elastic and retracts somewhat stubbornly, I sometimes literally weigh one edge down with a heavy pot while I roll and thin out another.) Eventually

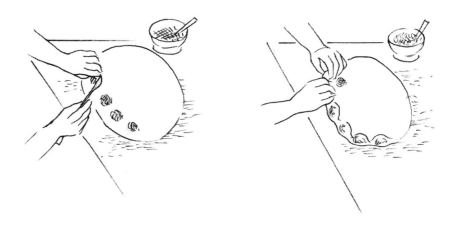

you will have an oval or circle (it doesn't matter) with roughly an 18-inch diameter and a surface that feels like suede. It is thin, but not so thin as strudel or phyllo dough.

Here is the quickest way to form *pierogis*. Have ready a floured tray. Two inches inside the edge of the dough, all the way around, space little mounds of filling, about 1 teaspoon each. Fold the edge of the dough over the row of mounds, press down with cupped hands leaving ½ inch around each mound to seal, then cut half-circles, using a glass or a cookie cutter or a pizza wheel. *Make sure each pastry is well sealed* (if you like, press the edges together with your fingertips). Put the pastries on the floured tray. Cut off and reserve the dough scraps between the pastries. Repeat the process until the sheet of dough is used up, then lightly dampen and reroll the scraps into a smaller sheet, to fill and form pastries as before. Don't worry if you cannot use up all the dough. The scraps may get too dry to be worth saving.

Then roll out the other half of the dough (which has been resting under the bowl) and repeat the procedure exactly.

Poach the *pierogis* in a large quantity of simmering salted water. Cover the pot when the water returns to the simmer. In about 8 minutes (depending on their size), the *pierogis* will rise to the surface, and then they are done.

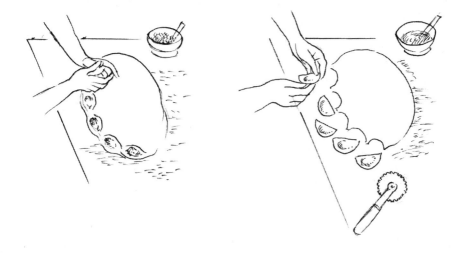

(Taste one, to be sure the dough is cooked.) Drain them and serve at once, or they can wait for a while; keep them warm, buttered to prevent sticking, in a covered dish. They are wonderful sprinkled with diced fried bacon and onions, *Skwarki* (p. 65).

CHEESE AND POTATO FILLING (for *pierogi* and *uszka*)

1 large baking potato
¼ cup (½ deciliter) finely chopped onion
1 tablespoon butter
1 clove garlic (optional)
12 ounces (340 grams) farmer cheese
2 tablespoons finely cut chives or fine tender scallion greens,
    with a bit of the white part
½ teaspoon salt
6–8 grinds pepper

Bake the potato. Cut it open, scoop out the interior, and mash it with a fork until smooth. Cool. Sauté the chopped onion in the butter. If you are using the garlic clove, press it through a garlic press into the onions and stir. Put the farmer cheese into a bowl, add the mashed potato, and mix together well; the mixture should be smooth and creamy. Add the sautéed onion and garlic, the chives, and salt and pepper. This filling improves with time and is best done the day before, if possible. Taste it again, before using, at room temperature. Add salt or pepper if necessary.

## KOLDUNY
(pronounced kohl-*doon*-ih)

*Makes about 36 pieces*

This dish is one of the supreme delicacies of the old, "high" Polish cuisine. In large American cities with a Polish population, one can often find a chef or caterer who specializes in *kolduny* and will make them for private parties.

*Kolduny* are one of my earliest memories, and it was only at home that I could ever eat my fill of them. Years later, at the Polish restaurant Ognisko in London, I would order two servings of *kolduny* at once, knowing that one order would consist of *only* ten!

The nature of the filling dictates the shape of the pastries, and also the manner of eating them (which takes a bit of dexterity). They are filled with fine, lean, *raw* lamb and beef, so the dough envelope must be very thin, otherwise it will still be tough when the filling is cooked. Marrow enriches the meat; as it cooks, the marrow melts. Therefore each pastry must be small, for it is eaten in one bite so that the marrow neither congeals nor leaks out. As your teeth puncture the tender skin, the marrow squirts in a hot succulent trickle against the palate. It is delicious! The traditional thing is to pour a small amount of strong consommé into a hot soup plate, dab a little grated horseradish on the rim, and fill up the plate with *kolduny*. I prefer to eat the *kolduny* in a soup plate with just a bit of broth to keep them from sticking, with the consommé in a cup on the side. This, for me, is a meal in itself.

The dough for *kolduny* is just like *pierogi* dough (p. 105), but it is rolled out thinner.

Follow the directions for mixing, kneading, rolling, filling, and cutting given on pages 105–107. But here, for convenience, is a summary.

On a large floured board, mix the flour and salt. Sprinkle with water, about 3 tablespoons at a time, working it in well, and add the oil with the last addition of water. Add flour or water as needed.

Knead the dough for 10 minutes, or until it is smooth and elastic (though it will be very resistant). Rest it for 15 minutes, under an inverted bowl.

During this pause, you can make the filling; it should be at room temperature, like the dough.

MEAT AND MARROW FILLING

½ pound (225 grams) lamb steak from the leg,
  carefully trimmed of all fat (or use a well-trimmed
  loin lamb chop)
½ pound (225 grams) beef fillet, carefully trimmed
½ pound (225 grams) beef marrow* or veal kidney fat
2 teaspoons dried leaf marjoram
6 grinds pepper
1 teaspoon finely grated onion, with its juice

---

*If you can't get marrow, use veal kidney fat. To extract marrow, ask your butcher to split the bones with his saw, lengthwise. Otherwise scrape out their contents with a knife. Include any red bits, along with the white. Keep or freeze the bones for stock or soup.

Finely grind the meats and marrow together, but not to a purée. (Do not use the processor.) They should have a seed-pearl grain. Thoroughly combine the mixture with the marjoram, pepper, and onion. The filling should be at room temperature when you fill the dough.

Cut the dough in half, leaving half under the bowl. On a floured board, roll the dough as thin as you can to less than ⅛ inch if possible.

Follow the instructions for rolling out the dough and for forming *pierogi* (p. 125), except roll it thinner. Use both halves of the dough. You should have pastries (resembling little turnovers) about 2 inches across. Be especially careful when forming the *kolduny* to leave about ⅓ inch of space around the mound of filling for the marrow to melt in.

Do not stack the formed pastries, or they will stick and tear when separated. If marrow fat gets on your fingers, rinse and dry them as you handle the pastries. Form them just before poaching, if possible, and keep them carefully covered and well chilled if they must wait. They can be frozen before poaching.

Cook the *kolduny* in a large pot of *simmering* salted water, for about 5–6 minutes, always tasting one to be sure the dough is done. Remove the *kolduny* with a slotted spoon very carefully so as not to break them and put them into a warm tureen. Serve them in hot soup plates with a little hot beef consommé poured over them and sprinkled liberally with fresh cut parsley; then serve the rest of the consommé in cups on the side. Or serve the *kolduny* just floating in the soup. Grated horseradish is passed separately.

## USZKA
### (pronounced *oosh*-kah)

*Makes about 36 pieces*

*Uszka,* which means "little ears" in Polish, are little filled pastries very similar to Italian tortellini. Traditionally, they are made with a mushroom filling and are eaten in meatless *barszcz,* as one of the many satisfying dishes invented over the years by Catholic Poles for their frequent, and rather lengthy, periods of fasting—Lent, Advent, and meatless Fridays, all of which were strictly observed. Of course, *uszka* can also be made with a Beef Filling (p. 80).

The dough for *uszka* is just like *pierogi* dough (p. 105). Follow the directions for mixing, kneading, and rolling given on pages 105–107. When you have your dough rolled out, cut a 3-inch square, put a little mound (about 1 teaspoon) of filling in the center, and fold the dough over it, making a triangle. Seal the edges well. Bring together, and pinch to join, the two points of the long side—you will have a little pointed "ear" with a hole in the middle. Cut and fill one pastry at a time, so the dough doesn't dry. Cook as for *Kolduny* (pp. 108–110), then drain the *uszka* well on paper towels, and serve as soon as possible, in hot *barszcz*.

MUSHROOM FILLING (for *uszka* or *pierożkis*)

*Makes about 1½ cups*

½ cup (1 deciliter) finely chopped onion
2 tablespoons butter
1 pound (450 grams) mushrooms, chopped fine
¼ teaspoon salt
6–8 grinds pepper
1 egg yolk

Sauté the onion in the butter until it is translucent. Add the chopped mushrooms and the salt, and cook, stirring, until all liquid has exuded. Add the pepper and cool the mixture. When it is cool, stir in the egg yolk. Refrigerate for 30 minutes before filling the pastries.

# Coulibiac and Pierożkis

I use a special dough made with cream cheese for these filled baked pastries. The original recipe (made with sour cream) was given me years ago by Mrs. Sergei Rachmaninoff, who was given it by her chef (who had been the chef of the last czar). I later learned that made with cream cheese the dough shrank less and was more flaky when baked. It makes delicious pastry that stays crisp when filled and has an unusual and lively flavor due to the slight fermentation of the cheese.

Made with this dough, baked filled pastries freeze very well. Of course, you can chill or freeze the unbaked dough by itself. I have not given directions for making it with the processor; this dough is better made by hand, since you can precisely control its flakiness; besides, it is so quickly done that it is not worth the time it takes to wash the machine.

## COULIBIAC

*Serves 6*

I make this nice plump pastry in a roll; for a large party, I double or triple the quantities and make several rolls. It is a simple dish, which I often serve as an entrée, hot, with a sauce—for instance, Mushroom Sauce (p. 57) or Dill Sauce (p. 49), or as an accompaniment to *barszcz. Coulibiac* is ideal for a buffet, as it is delicious hot, warm, or cold (it can be reheated in foil most successfully), so it has always been one of my faithful "standbys" and is a great favorite with both family and friends.

The quantity in this recipe is based on half a standard 8-ounce package of commercial cream cheese. For a *coulibiac* serving 6, you might have a bit left over (nice for the cookies on page 345, or you can just bake it in squares to serve with cocktails or soup).

1 cup (140 grams) flour
¼ teaspoon salt, or to taste
1 teaspoon sugar
1 stick (4 ounces or 115 grams) butter, well chilled
4 ounces (115 grams) cream cheese, well chilled
1 egg for glaze

Combine the flour, salt, and sugar, and cut in the butter, to rice-grain size. I like to use a "demilune," a single-blade cutter, in a small wooden bowl. Blend in the cheese, very roughly, with the fingertips, until the dough looks "marbleized" with broad white streaks. Bear in mind that when the dough is rolled, the cheese will be further blended in. Mass the dough quickly into a thick flat cake, wrap it closely, and refrigerate it for about 2 hours, before you roll it. (If your butter and cheese are fresh from the refrigerator and you work quickly, you don't need to chill it.) While the dough is chilling, you can make and cool the filling (see following recipe), or make it the day before, wrap it closely, and chill it. As always with filled pastries, dough and filling should be at about the same temperature when you combine them.

Preheat the oven to 450°F (230°C). Place the cake of chilled dough on a lightly floured baking sheet. If the dough seems too cold to roll, leave it out just long enough to be malleable. If, as you are rolling, the dough begins to soften and stick, chill it again for a few minutes, then continue. Sprinkle on extra flour as needed to prevent stickiness.

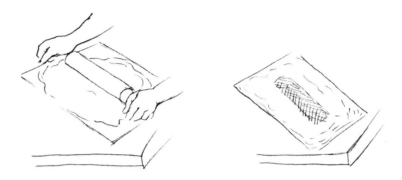

With a floured rolling pin, make one stroke from the center of the dough toward each edge. Lightly flour the surface of the dough and roll again, making a rectangle about 9 or 10 inches by 12 or 13 inches and about ⅛ inch thick. You can use your fingertips to even out edges. Lay the filling down the middle of the pastry in a fat oblong, leaving enough pastry to meet at the top and overlap slightly, about an inch. Pull the ends up, and cut off any excess pastry, by pinching together lightly; and seal. Make sure the pastry envelope is well sealed.

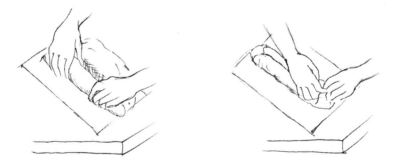

Beat the egg with 1 tablespoon water. With a pastry brush gently glaze the entire surface of the pastry. Cut 2 small slits in the top.

Slide the baking sheet into the preheated oven, on the middle rack, and turn the oven down to 375° (190°C). Baking time will be 25–30 minutes, or until the crust is golden-brown all over.

CABBAGE AND MUSHROOM FILLING (especially for *coulibiac,* but can be used in *pierogis, uszka,* and *pierożkis*)

*Makes about 2 cups*

I have always used the classic wooden chopping bowl and demilune for chopping the hard-boiled eggs, the mushrooms, and the cabbage (after cooking). It helps me to control the texture of the various ingredients, which should remain identifiable. This is sometimes difficult with the processor, which runs at such devilish speed that one needs to be skilled not to turn onions and mushrooms into mush, and egg to paste! A bowl is also almost indispensable for combining the ingredients.

> 1 small head Savoy (frilly) or hard green cabbage,
> cored and shredded; a 1-pound (450-gram) head
> yields about 5 cups (1¼ liters) of shreds,
> pressed down
> Piece of lemon zest, including white pith,
> about 1 by 2 inches
> 5 tablespoons butter (2 tablespoons may be
> vegetable shortening instead)
> Salt and pepper to taste
> 2 medium onions, chopped fine
> 1 pound (450 grams) mushrooms,
> in coarse ⅓-inch dice
> 2 hard-boiled eggs (for *coulibiac* only)
> 3 tablespoons finely cut dill or parsley
> Maggi extract to taste, or ½ Knorr beef
> bouillon cube, crumbled (optional)
> ¼ teaspoon grated fresh nutmeg

In a large quantity of boiling water, blanch the cabbage shreds, uncovered, with the lemon zest, for 5 minutes. Drain them and discard the zest.

In a large pan, place 3 tablespoons of the butter, the cabbage, 1½ teaspoons salt, 5 grinds of pepper, and cook slowly, covered, until the cabbage is soft but not quite limp. (Keep tasting!)

In another large pan, sauté the onions in the remaining 2 tablespoons of butter or in 2 tablespoons vegetable shortening until they are a deep golden color and quite soft. Add the diced mushrooms and cook together slowly until the mushroom juice has exuded and evaporated. Season the mixture with ¼ teaspoon salt and 6 grinds of pepper.

Drain the cooked cabbage shreds in a colander, put the cabbage into a wooden bowl, and chop the shreds into slightly smaller pieces. Add the hard-boiled eggs and chop them together with the cabbage until everything is *minced* but *not mushed.* (The egg yolks drink up the butter and the juice of the cabbage.) Now add this to the mushroom-onion mixture, add the dill or parsley, mix thoroughly, and cook, stirring, for a few minutes. *Taste.* Add Maggi extract or crumbled bouillon cube, if necessary, or salt and pepper to taste, and the grated nutmeg. Let the mixture stand until cool, stirring occasionally. Like most cabbage mixtures, it will develop more flavor if it stands for an hour or more. Cool the filling thoroughly and chill it briefly before filling the pastries.

# PIEROŻKI

*Serves 6*

These are little baked turnovers, traditional in Poland and Russia. Tiny ones, to eat with the fingers, are nice for cocktail parties; 3-inch ones can be served on a separate plate with soup—delicious with a clear *barszcz!* Other good fillings are Cabbage and Mushroom (p. 115) and Mushroom (p. 111); for dessert *pierożkis,* use the sweet fillings on pages 350 and 351.

1 recipe *Coulibiac* (cream cheese) dough (p. 113)

Follow the *Coulibiac* recipe and instructions exactly, including refrigeration time. If you have a marble pastry slab and/or rolling pin, use these when rolling out the dough. If you don't, and if you have space in the refrigerator, chill your pastry board and pin! While the dough chills, you can make your filling, and let it cool to room temperature. Preheat your oven to 375°F (190°C). Bring the dough to about normal room temperature. Flour your chilled board or marble slab, your rolling pin, and your hands. Roll out the dough, in all directions, from the center, until it is about ⅛ inch thick. Put a rounded teaspoon of filling about 2 inches from the edge of the dough sheet, and gently fold the edge over it. Follow directions for *Pierogi* (pp. 105–107), cutting out the pastry with a 3-inch glass dipped in flour. Seal the edges carefully, perhaps with the tines of a fork.

Because the pastry dough made with cream cheese is very "short," it should be handled as little as possible, so the shortening does not begin to melt. Therefore it is a good idea to form the little pastries one at a time and put them on a large floured plate in the refrigerator as they are made until they are all done and ready to be baked. (Be sure to mass up the "scraps" of dough after cutting out the *pierożkis*. You can reroll the dough and make a few more, or refrigerate or freeze, or reserve it perhaps for a sweet filling.)

Put the formed *pierożkis* on a baking sheet (no need to butter it) and brush over them the egg beaten with 1 tablespoon water. Bake them for about 15 minutes, or until they are golden-brown all over. Serve hot or warm. (*Pierożkis* can be eaten cool as well, or reheated easily in foil.)

HAM, SPINACH, AND MUSHROOM FILLING
(for *pierogis, crêpes, choux,* and *pierożkis*)

*Makes about 2¾ cups*

The meat filling I like best for crêpes is the Beef Filling (page 80), but this combination of ham, spinach, and mushrooms is also delicious for crêpes as well as *pierogis,* choux, and *pierożkis*. If crêpes are to be stuffed with this filling, they will be more delicious covered with a Béchamel Sauce and gratinéed as described on page 83. In this case, use ½ cup of the béchamel you will be making to bind the filling (add cheese only to the top to gratinée), then the remaining 1¾ cup béchamel, thinned with a little cream, should be sufficient to cover 8 to 10 rolled crepes. If you need to make only the ½ cup béchamel prescribed below for the filling, use 1 tablespoon butter and 1 tablespoon flour to ⅓ to ½ cup milk; it should be quite thick.

¾ cup cooked, chopped spinach (about
   1 pound fresh or 1 package frozen)
¼ pound mushrooms, finely chopped
1 tablespoon butter
2 minced scallions
2 cups finely chopped ham (may be done
   in the processor)
½ cup Béchamel Sauce (page 48)
Salt and freshly ground pepper to taste

Sauté the mushrooms in the butter with the minced scallions for a few minutes until they have exuded most of their juice. Squeeze the spinach to extract the water. Mix the mushroom mixture with the spinach, ham, and cream sauce. Add pepper and taste to see if it needs salt; if the ham is very salty, it may not need any more. Cool the filling before using.

## QUICHE POLONAISE

Every cookbook tells you how to make quiches, and the classical formula is delicious. I call this version "Polish" because the filling is flavored with dill. The pastry dough is my variation on the classical *pâte brisée:* I use a whole egg and only butter as shortening. It is perfect for tart shells. (For shapes requiring a more flexible, foldable dough, I prefer the *Coulibiac* dough on page 113.)

THE PASTRY

*Makes enough for a 10-inch tart shell*

1¼ cups (175 grams) flour
1 stick (4 ounces or 115 grams) butter
1 egg
½ teaspoon salt

Put the flour in a large bowl. Cut the butter into the flour until you have pieces the size of fat rice. Lightly beat the egg with the salt, pour it into the flour mixture, and mix well with your fingertips. If it does not cohere, gradually add another tablespoon or two of flour. As soon as you can roughly mass it, pack it into a rough cake. Wrap it in plastic and chill it for an hour.

Preheat the oven to 400°F (205°C). Place the chilled dough cake in the center of your tart mold or a flan ring set on a baking sheet, which does not need to be buttered or floured. It is easier to form this dough with your fingertips than to roll it. (See the recipe on page 329 for *Pâte Sablée,* the dessert version, for full details.) With a quick stabbing gesture of your fingertips, press the dough downward and outward, so that a deeply dimpled surface spreads out to the edges and up the sides of the mold. It should be about ⅛ inch thick. Trim the edge; you may have a small handful of extra dough.

Bake the shell for about 10 minutes in the preheated oven. It should begin to color, and the dimples will have halfway flattened out. Remove the shell and reduce the oven temperature to 350°F (180°C). Let the shell cool while you make the filling.

THE FILLING

5 strips bacon
5 ounces (140 grams) genuine Swiss cheese,
    like Emmenthal or Appenzell
3 eggs
1½ cups (3½ deciliters) half-and-half
2 tablespoons finely cut dill, or 1 tablespoon
    finely cut parsley
2 thin slices boiled ham, chopped fine
Dash of grated nutmeg

Cook the bacon until not quite done; drain, and chop fine.

Cut the cheese into ¼-inch dice, in hopes that it will melt not quite completely into the custard. Combine, in the blender if you like, the eggs, half-and-half, and dill or parsley.

Scatter the ham, bacon bits, and cheese dice over the bottom of the tart shell. Place the shell in the lower rack of the oven and pull the rack out halfway, so that the shell sits level but is easy to get at. Pour in the custard mixture, to a level just a hairline below the edge of the pastry shell. Sprinkle with nutmeg. (During the baking, the custard will puff a little. It must not overflow. Jiggle the rack gently to settle the custard mixture evenly.)

Bake in a preheated 350°F (150°C) oven for about 35–40 minutes. The custard will be slightly puffed and an even golden-brown.

## KASHA (BUCKWHEAT)

*Serves 6*

Buckwheat "groats" (grains) are a traditional accompaniment in Eastern Europe to dishes like Beef Stroganoff (p. 186), and I like them especially with Swiss steak, goulash, and stuffed cabbage rolls or simply with mushroom sauce as a main dish. Moreover, it is a great source of protein, which perhaps explains why kasha is so satisfying.

Groats are available whole or cracked. This recipe is for the whole ones, but adjust your cooking time to the package directions, depending on which kind you are using. The whole groats have a texture I find more pleasing, but either way the taste is the same.

2 cups (½ liter) buckwheat groats
2 eggs, well beaten
3 cups (¾ liter) boiling water (but check package
    directions for cracked, milled groats)
2–3 tablespoons butter
Salt to taste (optional)

Set a heavy frying pan over low heat. Spread the buckwheat groats (or milled groats) evenly over the pan surface and let them warm through. They won't stick. Pour on the eggs and stir vigorously with a fork until each bit of buckwheat is coated. Some of the egg will stick to the pan; don't worry. Immediately stir in the boiling water, which will pick up and distribute all the egg bits in almost invisible shreds among the grains. Add the butter. Cover the pan and cook slowly, tasting after 10 minutes, until the grains are cooked and the water has been absorbed. Each grain should be distinct and unsticky, and, with whole grains, each should show a fleck of white where it has opened up.

Kasha can also be made in a heavy, covered oven casserole, cooked on the stove top until you add the butter, then baked, covered, for about 30 minutes in a slow 300°F (150°C) oven.

When the kasha is done, taste it. Add salt if necessary. If it seems dry, you can add a tablespoon or so of water, stir well, cover, and let cook for a moment longer.

## KASHA WITH MUSHROOMS

One of my favorite ways of making kasha, this makes a rich and filling main dish. Serve with Mushroom Sauce (p. 57).

¾ pound (340 grams) mushrooms, sliced
2 tablespoons butter, or a mixture of butter and vegetable oil
1 recipe Kasha (preceding recipe), cooked

Sauté the mushrooms in the butter, or vegetable oil and butter, in a fairly large skillet. Stir and turn them over medium-high heat (not allowing the fat to burn), in order to seal in the juices. If the juices exude, let them evaporate. Then mix the mushrooms into the cooked kasha.

# RICE

I don't think that I ever really understood rice until our cook Kamiko taught me her Oriental method, which makes the grains just sticky enough to eat with chopsticks, but certainly not glutinous. Kamiko cooked for us in California at the beginning of World War II, which after Pearl Harbor became such a wretched time for many patriotic Americans of Japanese origin—including charming Kamiko, who had been much loved and appreciated by us. She always washed rice, and, contrary to the directions on modern packages, I still do.

2 cups (½ liter) long-grain white rice
4 cups (1 liter) cold water
2 tablespoons fresh peanut or vegetable oil
3 teaspoons salt

Wash the rice in the heavy pot you will use for cooking. When the water runs clear, drain the rice, and put it back in the pot. Add the cold water, oil, and salt, cover the pot, and bring it to the simmer. Cooking time is exactly 19 minutes after the pot comes to the simmer. Simmer gently and don't uncover the pot, or steam will be lost.

The rice is now ready to serve, but you can keep it warm, covered, in a very low oven, a double boiler or bain-marie, or a steamer (over hot but not boiling water). It will keep perfectly for at least an hour.

# $\mathcal{E}ggs$

Like most people I cook eggs in all kinds of familiar ways: just as everybody else does. This small collection of egg dishes is chosen for you in the hope that you may find a surprise or two, that you may even recover a lost memory, and that you may find useful one or two minor hints I can offer.

## OEUFS FARCIS À LA POLONAISE

*Serves 6 as a garnish*

These are nothing like the stuffed eggs one takes on picnics or serves for a cold lunch. Polish stuffed eggs are *hot,* just not too hot to touch, and they are my favorite accompaniment to a delicately sour soup like Sorrel (p. 26). Since eggs in the shell do roll around, I serve them propped on a lettuce leaf or a few sprigs of watercress, on a small side plate for each person, with a teaspoon. It affords a contrast in tempo: one takes a big spoonful of the savory soup, puts down that spoon, takes up the smaller one, and nibbles at the finely chopped egg coated with buttered crumbs.

For a light entrée, I serve each person two eggs, that is, four halves.

6 eggs
3 tablespoons butter, softened
3 teaspoons finely cut chives or scallions
Salt and pepper to taste
3 tablespoons bread crumbs

Do not use leftover hard-boiled eggs for this dish. Boil them freshly: prick the shells at the large end, ⅜ inch deep, to prevent their cracking. Immerse the eggs in a large potful of simmering water, and cook them for 14 minutes after the water returns to the simmer. Immediately cool the eggs in a bowlful of cold water. Dry them and cut them in half, shell and all, with a sharp, thin-bladed knife. (Loose bits of shell, at the edges, can be

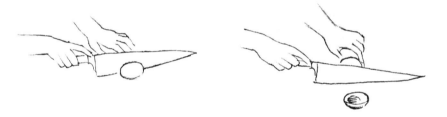

trimmed off with small scissors. Irregular edges, however, will be hidden by the topping, and the egg's inner membrane prevents them from coming away in the spoon; don't worry.) Empty the half shells of their contents.

Finely chop the cooked eggs, or crush them with a table fork, mixing in 2 tablespoons of the soft butter, the chives, and salt and pepper. As you will eat them rewarmed, be cautious with the salt. Replace the egg mixture in the half shells, and coat the uncovered tops with bread crumbs.

Now heat the eggs through and brown the
crumbed tops in a nonstick pan with the
remaining tablespoon of butter. Put the egg halves
very gently crumbs down in the pan. Cover
and heat for a few minutes. Serve immediately.

## EGGS MIMOSA

*Serves 6, lightly*

I am told that all American cookbooks of a generation ago included this
simple dish, the weekend breakfast delight of my younger children. I might
never have known it but for Kate, who was part of our California household
for eighteen years, and my beloved friend. This is one of the many good
American recipes she gave me.

6 hard-boiled eggs
6 thick slices good bread, toasted

THE BÉCHAMEL

5 tablespoons butter
5 tablespoons flour
1 cup (¼ liter) heavy cream
2 cups (½ liter) milk
Pinch of salt

Carefully scoop the yolks out of the eggs and chop the whites very coarse;
reserve both whites and yolks. Cut off the crusts of the toast, and cut each
piece into 2 triangular halves. To make the béchamel, melt the butter in a
saucepan, stir in the flour, and cook together a few minutes, stirring constantly, until the mixture is smooth and thick and the flour no longer tastes
raw. Add the cream, milk, and salt, and cook, stirring, as it slowly reaches
the boil; simmer for a few minutes. Add the very coarsely chopped egg

whites and allow them to warm in the sauce. Taste the sauce. You may want a few grains more salt.

Pour the sauce over the toast, then put the egg yolks through a sieve, distributing them over the servings of toast and sauce. Serve at once.

## HARD-BOILED EGGS IN CURRY SAUCE

*Serves 6*

Served over boiled white rice, this makes a pleasant luncheon dish, something like the classic Oeufs à la Tripe. The sauce is not the usual French *"sauce au cari,"* or *"à l'indienne,"* meaning a béchamel or velouté mildly accented with curry powder; it is quite spicy, and best made in the pressure cooker, which brings out the good onion and celery flavors.

½ cup (1 deciliter) finely chopped onion
5 tablespoons butter
6 tablespoons finely chopped celery
2 cups (½ liter) Chicken Broth (p. 8)
  or Basic Beef Broth (p. 5), or use
  1 Knorr chicken or beef bouillon cube
  dissolved in 2 cups water
3 tablespoons flour
2½ tablespoons curry powder, or more to taste
12 hard-boiled eggs, quartered and reserved
1 recipe Rice (p. 122)

In the open pressure cooker, sauté the onion in 1 tablespoon of the butter, until it colors slightly. Add the celery and continue to cook until the vegetables are soft. Add the broth, cover the pressure cooker, and let cook for 2 minutes after pressure is reached.

In a separate pan, melt the remaining 4 tablespoons butter, stir in the flour, and cook them together slowly, stirring constantly, for several minutes, until the mixture is smooth and the flour no longer tastes raw. Add the curry powder and stir it in well. Let the mixture cook for several minutes to develop the flavor. Then add the celery and onions and their liquid, stirring constantly, and bring the mixture to a boil, stirring as it thickens. Let it boil 1 minute, to thicken completely, and taste it. Depending on your brand of curry powder, you may want a little more. If you do, add it cautiously, and let the sauce cook a moment longer. Arrange the reserved egg quarters on the rice, and pour the sauce over.

If you have no pressure cooker, of course use any reasonably heavy, covered saucepan. The usual rule of thumb is that 1 minute in the pressure cooker (after pressure is reached) is like 3 minutes in a covered pot. For this dish, you need longer, I don't know why: about 20 minutes' simmering.

As above, sauté the vegetables, first the onion, then the celery with it. Add the broth, cover the pot, simmer gently for a good 20 minutes, and taste for full flavor. Make the butter and flour roux in a separate pan, stir in the curry powder and cook it, add the vegetables and liquid, and cook until thickened. Taste, adding curry powder if you want more, and pour it over the reserved eggs arranged on the rice.

## TOMATO EGGS

*Serves 2*

2 very ripe tomatoes,
   peeled, seeded, and sliced
2 tablespoons butter
3 eggs
1 tablespoon heavy cream
Salt and pepper to taste

In a nonstick pan, cook the tomatoes in the butter over a medium fire, until they exude a mellow fragrance (about 5 minutes). With a plastic spatula, mix in the eggs and heavy cream. Push them around from side to side with a scooping movement; don't scramble them, though. The whites and yolks should be a bit streaky. Cook for 2 or 3 minutes until the eggs are only just set. Season with a pinch of salt and a few grinds of pepper.

# SCRAMBLED EGGS

*Serves 2*

By my method you really cannot scramble more than 3 eggs at a time. It is so quick, however, that you can serve 4, or even 6, people in much less time than it takes them to eat the eggs.

3 eggs
Salt and pepper to taste
1 tablespoon heavy cream
1 teaspoon finely cut chives or scallions
   (using only the tender green parts,
   not the white)
1 tablespoon butter

Beat the eggs with a fork, only until the whites and yolks are well blended, and stir in the salt, pepper, cream, and chives or scallions. Set a small skillet (the ideal is an aluminum nonstick pan) over high heat and let it get *hot.* Add the butter. The moment it foams, before it has a chance to color, add the eggs all at once. Stir the eggs very fast with a spoon, constantly turning them and cleaning the pan surface. In a matter of a few seconds the eggs will begin to set. Remove the pan immediately from the heat and keep stirring in the same manner for a second or two until the eggs become creamy. This is the way I like them, so I turn them out immediately onto a warm plate. But if someone else prefers them a little more done, return the pan to the heat for a couple of seconds, always stirring.

# POACHED EGGS (OR EGGS MOLLET) FLORENTINE

*Serves 6*

This is a lovely dish of fresh chopped spinach as a bed for poached eggs (or eggs mollet), the whole covered with a well-seasoned, cheese-flavored sauce. The perfection of the eggs is everything. They must make nice little domes under the sauce, and certainly must not be flat and ragged-edged. I always test one of my batch of eggs before poaching any; that is, I break it into a saucer, and if the yolk is nicely convex and the white clings to it closely, I go ahead and make poached eggs, for the first step. But if my test egg looks flat and limp, I will use it for some other purpose, and I will cook the remaining eggs mollet.

## THE SAUCE

This is simply a medium-thick béchamel enriched with cheese and cream and enlivened with Maggi extract.

3 tablespoons butter
3 tablespoons flour
1½ cups (3½ deciliters) milk
4 tablespoons heavy cream
Maggi extract
½ cup (1 deciliter) grated or shredded Swiss cheese,
  like Le Comté, Appenzell, or Gruyère

Melt the butter over low heat, stir in the flour, and let them cook, stirring constantly, until the mixture is smooth and the flour no longer tastes raw. Add the milk and cream, stirring constantly until the sauce has thickened. Add about 10 shakes of Maggi extract and taste. Add the Swiss cheese, stirring constantly until it has melted. Do not let the sauce boil after adding the cheese.

THE SPINACH

4 cups (1 liter) cooked chopped spinach:
   (3 pounds [1350 grams] fresh spinach, or
   4 packages frozen chopped spinach)
Dash of sugar

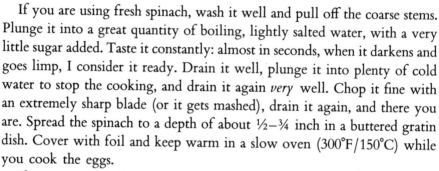

If you are using fresh spinach, wash it well and pull off the coarse stems. Plunge it into a great quantity of boiling, lightly salted water, with a very little sugar added. Taste it constantly: almost in seconds, when it darkens and goes limp, I consider it ready. Drain it well, plunge it into plenty of cold water to stop the cooking, and drain it again *very* well. Chop it fine with an extremely sharp blade (or it gets mashed), drain it again, and there you are. Spread the spinach to a depth of about ½–¾ inch in a buttered gratin dish. Cover with foil and keep warm in a slow oven (300°F/150°C) while you cook the eggs.

If you are using frozen chopped spinach, thaw it first (in water if you are hurried) for more even cooking. Squeeze out almost all the juice and turn it quickly in a buttered frying pan over heat. Then spread in a gratin dish and proceed as instructed for fresh chopped spinach.

THE EGGS

12 eggs
Salt
2 teaspoons vinegar

For the fullest possible discussion of poached eggs (and a way of dealing with not perfectly fresh ones), I refer you to *Julia Child & Company* (New York: Knopf, 1978). I simply put water into a skillet, bring it to the simmer, add salt and vinegar. Then I open a cracked egg as close as possible to the surface of the simmering water, wait 3 minutes, take it out with a skimmer, drain it well on paper towels, and cook another egg. With fresh eggs and a large pan, I can do as many as 3–4 eggs at once.

For an egg mollet, prick (⅜ inch deep) the large end of the shell, put it in a large pot of boiling water, turn off the heat, cover the pan, and wait 5 minutes, then cool off the egg and shell it at once. For many eggs mollet, I lower them into the pot in a frying basket, so the heat seizes them all simultaneously, and wait until the water returns to the boil before turning off the heat. Eggs mollet are cooked all the way through, but the yolk remains soft. They are extremely good just by themselves, with a bit of toast perhaps. I often serve them (shelled, of course) on a deep dish of tomato sauce, with fluffy white rice on the side.

COMPLETING THE GRATIN

4 tablespoons freshly grated Parmesan cheese

Preheat the broiler. Drain the eggs and pat them dry with a paper towel, then place them on the spinach. Pour the sauce over, and sprinkle the top with the Parmesan cheese. Return the dish to the oven for 5 minutes, then slide it under the broiler for just long enough to brown (lightly) the cheese on top. Serve at once.

## TORTILLA ANDALUSA

*Serves 1 or 2*

This is not the tortilla of Mexican cooking; rather it is a close relative to the omelette, a dish common to many countries (in Italy it's a frittata, and in China it's—almost—egg foo yung). I learned it in Spain from my great friend and helper Pepa. You can make this concoction with all kinds of cooked vegetable substitutes for potatoes. It can also be served at room temperature, cut bite-size: nice with cocktails.

2 tablespoons good olive oil
1 small onion, chopped medium-fine
1 cup (¼ liter) very finely diced raw potato
2 eggs, beaten in a good-size bowl

In the olive oil fry the onion until lightly colored. Add the potato dice and cook over medium heat until they are a pale golden-brown and taste just barely done: about 5 minutes if the dice are really fine. Remove the pan from the heat. With a slotted spoon, shaking each spoonful to return the oil to the pan, remove and drain the onion and potato. Add them to the beaten eggs in the bowl.

Since the oil was never hot enough to burn (good Spanish cooks are most careful about this), return the pan to the heat. Let the oil get only medium-hot. A test: drop in a tiny speck of butter. You will see it melt before it disappears.

Pour in the egg-onion-potato mixture and cook it over medium-high heat for 1 or 2 minutes, or until the bottom is golden-brown. Turn the tortilla and cook until the second side is golden-brown. Pepa did this by covering the pan with a big plate or a flat pot lid, reversing the tortilla onto it, returning the pan to the fire, and sliding the tortilla back in, with the browned side now on top.

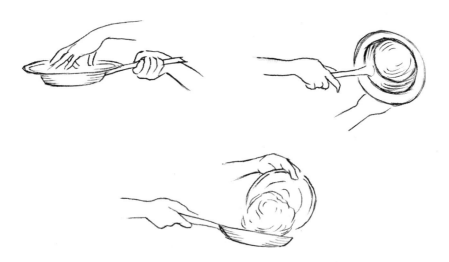

When the bottom is brown (in another 2 minutes or so) slide the tortilla onto a warm serving plate, cut into wedges, and serve immediately.

## CHEESE SOUFFLÉ

*Serves 4*

Soufflés are much easier to make than most people think. I have recently discovered that they can even be prepared several hours ahead, refrigerated in their baking dish, and put in the oven 20 minutes before serving (of course first allowing a little time for the cold soufflé dish to come to room temperature so it does not crack). It will still rise beautifully. A few times I even refrigerated it overnight, and it was fine! So you could make a soufflé in the morning before going to work and have it ready to bake for dinner.

3 tablespoons butter
3 tablespoons flour
1 cup (¼ liter) milk
3 ounces (90 grams) coarsely grated Appenzell or
    Swiss Gruyère cheese
3 tablespoons freshly grated Parmesan cheese
4 eggs, separated
Dash of Maggi extract
Dash of nutmeg
Cayenne pepper (or a few drops of A-1 Steak Sauce
    or Worcestershire Sauce)
Salt to taste

Cook the butter and flour over low heat, stirring for 2 or 3 minutes. Add the milk, whisking, to make a very thick béchamel. Bring just to the boil, stirring constantly, and remove from heat. Add the Swiss cheese and all but 1 tablespoon of the Parmesan, stirring until they are melted. Let the mixture cool for a minute or two, then add the egg yolks, 1 by 1, blending thoroughly after each addition. Add a few drops of Maggi extract, the nutmeg, and a pinch of cayenne pepper (or one of the substitutes). Taste mixture for salt; you may find there is enough from the Maggi extract and cheese.

Preheat the oven to 375°F (190°C). Butter and flour a 1½-quart soufflé dish. Beat the egg whites until they form peaks but are not dry. Fold them into the cheese mixture. Pour it into the baking dish; it should be about three-quarters full. At this point it can be refrigerated and baked later. Sprinkle the remaining 1 tablespoon Parmesan over the top. Place the dish on the middle rack. Bake about 20 minutes, until the soufflé has risen 1½–2 inches and the top is lightly above the rim of the dish and browned (ovens vary). Serve at once.

## FISH SOUFFLÉ

*Serves 6*

This is a delicately flavored, light soufflé that is delicious served with a mushroom sauce. Use the one on page 57 but omit the onion because you do not need the extra flavor with this subtle soufflé. When making the sauce, it would be good to use a fish rather than a beef or chicken broth; reserve the liquid you will have left over after poaching the fish, adding additional fish broth if neccessary.

¾ pound (350 grams) white fish,
    such as flounder, sole, halibut, etc.
1 tablespoon chopped parsley
2 tablespoons chopped chives
2 tablespoons chopped dill
2 teaspoons grated onion
4 tablespoons butter
3 tablespoons flour
1½ cups (3½ deciliters) milk
Salt to taste
White pepper to taste
Dash of cayenne
¼ teaspoon nutmeg
5 eggs, separated
2–3 tablespoons breadcrumbs
Mushroom Sauce (p. 57)

Poach the fish in water to cover for just a few minutes until it begins to separate. Remove, reserving the liquid, and drain on paper towels. Put the fish in the food processor, adding the parsley, chives, dill, and onion, and purée.

Cook the butter and flour over low heat, stirring for 2 or 3 minutes. Add the milk and bring to a boil, whisking constantly. When thick, remove from the heat. Stir the sauce into the fish mixture. Add salt, pepper, cayenne to taste, and the nutmeg. Beat the egg yolks until fluffy and stir them into the fish mixture.

Preheat the oven to 375°F (190° C). Butter a 2-quart soufflé dish, then sprinkle lightly with bread crumbs. Beat the egg whites until they form peaks (but don't let them become dry), then fold them into the fish mixture. Place the soufflé in a bain-marie—a larger pan of hot water that will come about one third of the way up the soufflé dish—and bake about 20 minutes. Meanwhile prepare the sauce so it will be ready when the soufflé comes out of the oven, and serve immediately.

Fish Stew with Refrito
Crayfish Ragout
Crayfish Bisque with Crayfish-Butter Dumplings
Shrimp Marinière
Shrimp with Dill and Sherry
Small Shrimp in Jelly with Green and Pink Mayonnaise
Fried Fish, Spanish Style
Flounder Fried in Its Skin
Fish Cutlets
Baked Carp
Carp in Jelly
Poached Carp with Caramel and Raisin Sauce
Cold Poached Striped Bass
Monkfish Baked with Tomatoes and Shallots
Smelts
Sole with Mushrooms
Soles aux Petits Légumes
Smoked Haddock
Salt Herring and Eggs
Salt Herring Salad
Fish Salad with Potato and Egg
Paella de Carmela

# Seafood

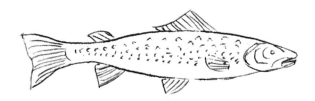

Fish is without question one of my favorite foods, on condition that it be absolutely fresh; so for most of my life, wherever I was, I was usually inspired to cook local varieties. Frozen fish seemed to me quite inadmissible; but recently this prejudice of mine has dissolved. Since transport has improved, and now that ocean fish are often frozen right on the high seas as soon as caught, I have found that one can really use them very successfully. Not only are they perfectly adaptable to many recipes, especially those calling for fillets, but they are often safer than "fresh" fish which may have been lingering a day too long at the market. And as prices for truly fresh fish have risen so much lately, the frozen ones allow us to enjoy many dishes, even out of season or far from their source, with little or no compromise in quality or taste.

The recipes in this chapter (note also the one for fish fritters on page 86) were gathered from Lithuania to Los Angeles, from Warsaw to Wisconsin, from London's Savoy Grill to a fishing village in southern Spain, then freely adapted. And a few I invented. There are not many recipes: one can cook so many kinds of fish in the same ways, and in general I like them best very simply prepared. I did put a little emphasis on some particular fish I love, which need special treatment: carp and crayfish, for example, not well known everywhere in the United States, but certainly cultivated here—perhaps these recipes will tempt you to ask for them at your fish store; and then, salt herring and smoked haddock, exceptions to my insistence on fresh fish—so easy to prepare, so inexpensive, and yet so good. But, of course, with such a wonderful variety available here from two oceans, from many rivers, and from innumerable lakes of all types, no cookbook could ever deal with the whole range of American fish. These are just a few tested and true favorites among my recipes, and I am sure you will add to them or adapt them to your own favorite fish.

## FISH STEW WITH REFRITO

*Serves 6*

I like this even better than its French cousin, bouillabaise. You taste the fish more and the flavor in general is more delicate.

Use at least two kinds of fish for flavor and variety of texture; you might choose among monkfish, cod, tilefish, halibut, shrimp, sole, and flounder. You want the pieces of fish chunky, so they won't disintegrate in the cooking. If you use thin fillets (as of sole or flounder), they must have only about 2 minutes' cooking. This is true of most shellfish as well. Monkfish has a rather special texture and needs to be cooked half again as long as the others.

This recipe assumes that all the fish are skinned and boned. (If you can get scraps, add them to the fish stock, cook them for a few minutes, and strain it.) Since it is served with rice, start cooking that first so it will be ready.

4 cups (1 liter) fresh Fish Broth (p. 41)
2 pounds (900 grams) fresh fish, at least 2 kinds (see above)
2 cups (½ liter) warmed *Refrito* (p. 52)
GARNISH: about 1½ cups (3½ deciliters) steamed Rice (p. 122)

Bring the fish stock to the simmer, and plan on a total cooking time of 10 minutes. Drop the chunkier pieces of fish into the stock first, for longer cooking (about 7 minutes for 1-inch cubes), and the thin bits last, for 2 minutes' cooking or even 1 minute. After 7 minutes, either lift out the fish or strain the stock and reserve the fish. Mix the warm *refrito* with the stock, and return the fish. (You remove the fish while mixing so that the pieces won't flake.)

Taste the stew. The *refrito* alone should supply enough seasoning, but make sure. Serve in a big, hot tureen, with a small bowl of the rice so that each person may stir in a spoonful.

*This stew cannot be made successfully in the pressure cooker.*

# Crayfish

Crayfish, which look exactly like miniature lobsters, are considered a great (and expensive!) delicacy in some parts of the world—Paris, for instance. Elsewhere they are fairly common (Sweden, Louisiana); they are exported by Poland and Turkey, but in some places (Los Angeles in the fifties, luckily for us) they are, or were, almost unknown. A friend, the actress Anna Q. Nilsson, who had seen small boys using crayfish as bait, told us that these little creatures lurked in the muddy banks of the Los Angeles River (which I understand has since been paved over). She gave us directions, in great secret, to an unprepossessing vacant lot, at the back of which was a narrow and fairly shallow bit of the river, obscured by trees and bushes.

Rising at dawn, on a morning when school holidays had begun and the whole family was home, we dressed in our oldest clothes—which for one member of the family meant an elegant outfit worn at daytime rehearsals in the hot summer for outdoor concerts. This included a fine Panama hat, a carnation boutonnière, and his pearl stickpin. Armed with a jar of bait (horse liver bought at an odd little market) and a motley assemblage of buckets, string, sticks, sieves, strainers, and one real fish net, the adult and teenage members of the household drove off over the hills into the valley.

The system for catching (not fishing, really) the elusive crayfish was perfectly simple, requiring nothing much more than infinite patience and almost total silence. One took a piece of the bait and tied a 5-foot piece of string to it. Choosing a shady and reasonably comfortable place on the bank, one would gently lower the bait into the water near the shore, holding on to the other end of the string. Then the waiting would begin. The idea was simply to wait for a little tug on the string, which would (usually) mean a crayfish was munching on the bait. With breath suspended, and with motion so slow as to be nearly imperceptible, one would very, very smoothly pull the string in, with, one hoped, the crayfish attached to the bait; but as the creature was "hooked" on nothing more than its own greed, more often than not it would let go and, with astounding speed, literally flipping itself into reverse with its lobsterlike tail, it would vanish into the less-than-limpid water. But if one had kept the crayfish attached and the creature was now pulled into sight, the next challenge was to scoop it up with a sieve or strainer tied to a stick—difficult, as the sieves were shallow, and metal, and the clever creature would sometimes leap out just as we thought he was caught.

Competition was in the air, and jealousy over each crayfish brought in and "pailed" made us change places often and tug too nervously on our strings. There was the added pressure of time, as the crayfish would venture from their homes along the shady banks only in the cool of the morning, and by ten o'clock of a California day in spring or summer it was far too hot and sunny for them, and for us.

Arthur, being comfortably placed on the best rock in the shadiest spot, and having the steadiest hands (and the only proper net), invariably caught twice as many crayfish as anyone else. In a few hours the six or seven of us once caught about 450, enough for a real feast, which would have cost a fortune anywhere in the world—and all for the price of a few pounds of horse liver!

Hot, dusty, and hungry for a real breakfast, we would drive home. Afterward the gentlemen in the party, more interested in the sport and the dinner to come, would vanish mysteriously, and the rest of us would begin the somewhat messy, but delightful, process of transforming our morning's catch into a perfectly marvelous meal: a crayfish bisque, with little dumplings (some of them stuffed into reproachful-looking head shells) full of crayfish butter and dill; then a *potrawka,* a "ragout" of the meats of the tails and the larger claws in a sauce also based on the rich, reddish orange butter, with dill, of course, and served over hot rice.

The recipe for the ragout is given first (p. 145), as you have to cook the crayfish in order to make either dish, and refrigerating the tail and claw meats changes the texture somewhat. And since the broth and the butter, both made by extracting the flavor from the ground crayfish shells, can be frozen, you can always make the Crayfish Bisque (p. 146) some other day. Making these dishes in New York recently, I was dazzled again by what short work a blender and/or processor makes of such things as grinding the shells, a task that in the old days required turn-taking—and a strong arm —on a manual meat grinder.

Absolutely *nothing* about these dishes is difficult or tricky—so don't be discouraged by the length of the recipe. It is a bit time-consuming, but easy, fun, and unbelievably delicious.

## Washing and cooking

4 pounds (1800 grams) live crayfish
Salt to taste
2 bunches fresh dill

As the size of the crayfish will vary, one cannot give a number per person, but count about 2 pounds for 3 people. *Crayfish must be alive,* caught or bought.

Depending on their provenance (a local fishmonger vs. a local stream or river), you may need to give your crayfish a good rinse before cooking; do this with cool running water—easiest outdoors, of course, where possible, with hose and bucket. Remember you will be using the shells, so make sure there is no mud anywhere; the water should finally run very clear.

Bring to a boil a large kettle, or two, of water, with a little salt and a dozen or more stalks of dill, stems, sprigs and all, tied in a piece of rinsed cheesecloth (for easy removal later).

Just before cooking, check that all the crayfish are alive. Plunge them into the boiling water. If your pot is large enough, the water will return to the boil faster. Cook the crayfish for 6 minutes after the water boils again. They go from greenish-black to red, like lobsters. Drain them well, discarding the dill and water.

## Shelling and cleaning

As soon as they are cool enough to handle, pull the tails off the crayfish and remove the small amount of precious meat from the shells. Reserve the shells and put the tail meats in a bowl. If the larger crayfish have claws that look meaty, crack them and remove as much meat as possible, adding it to the tail meats. Cover and reserve all the meats. Pull the legs off each crayfish, all at once, which nearly empties the head shell, and add the legs and whatever adheres to them to your shell pile. Now, with a spoon, clean out the insides of the head shells, discard any sac and tissue near the front, and add the head shells to the rest. (Traditionally, when making the bisque, some of the head shells are kept and filled with the dumpling mixture. If you wish to do this, keep out 2 large head shells per person and store them in a plastic bag in the freezer.)

## Grinding the shells

In a processor fitted with the steel blade, or in a blender, grind the accumulated shells into small pieces. Do it in several batches. Spread the shell fragments on large, flat baking trays or on heavy foil. Put them in a slow oven, about 200°F (95°C). (If you have an electric oven, set to warm, and if your timing permits, let the shells dry overnight. If this means refrigerating the meats, make sure they are *very* closely covered.)

## Making the crayfish butter and broth

4 sticks (1 pound or 450 grams) butter
2 quarts (2 liters) water, Fish Broth (p. 41), or broth
    made with 4 Knorr fish or chicken bouillon cubes
    dissolved in 2 quarts water

When the shells are really dry (their red color will intensify also during oven drying), put the partly ground shells in the processor or blender again, and this time grind to the consistency of raw oatmeal. Again, do it in 2 or 3 batches. Melt the butter slowly in a very large skillet or sauté pan, wok, or large but fairly shallow saucepan (the pan must accommodate the shells plus 2 quarts liquid—and the broth should reach the top to facilitate skimming). Add the ground shells, and stir to make a mushy mixture, for about 5 minutes. Bring the fish broth to a boil and pour it over the shell mixture.

Stirring the whole mass occasionally, then pressing it down with a big cooking spoon, begin skimming off the orange-colored butter as it rises to the surface. Reserve it in a bowl and refrigerate it long enough to congeal the butter and separate it from any of the fish broth. This whole process will take about an hour (you don't have to stand over it every minute). When you have skimmed off as much butter as seems to be forthcoming, begin spooning off and reserving the remaining broth. (Don't worry about its grayish color—it *tastes* good.) When as much of the liquid as possible has been spooned off, strain the mass of ground shells through a rinsed and wrung-out washcloth placed in a colander, pressing down to extract as much liquid as you can. Don't forget to also add whatever broth has separated from the refrigerated butter.

## CRAYFISH RAGOUT
(*"Potrawka Rakowa,"* pronounced Pot-*rahv*-ka Rah-*koh*-vah)

*Serves 6*

4 tablespoons Crayfish Butter (see opposite)
4 tablespoons flour
3 cups (¾ liter) Crayfish Broth (see above; if too mild,
    add ½ Knorr fish or chicken bouillon cube)
3 tablespoons finely cut dill
1 tablespoon brandy
Reserved meats from tails (and claws) of cooked crayfish
    (see above)
Salt to taste
5 grinds white pepper
Boiled Rice (p. 122)

Make a roux with the butter and flour, cooking for a minute or two until the flour does not taste raw. Add the crayfish broth, stirring or whisking continuously. Bring it gently to the boil, and simmer, stirring, for about 2 minutes. Add and mix in the dill, brandy, and the reserved meats of the crayfish tails (and claws, if any). Add salt and white pepper. Simmer just until the crayfish meats are heated through—do not cook longer or they may toughen. Serve immediately, with boiled rice.

# CRAYFISH BISQUE WITH
# CRAYFISH-BUTTER DUMPLINGS

*Serves 6*

THE BISQUE

4 tablespoons Crayfish Butter (p. 144)
4 tablespoons flour
6 cups (1½ liters) Crayfish Broth (p. 144),
 or broth augmented or fortified with
 fish stock or Knorr fish bouillon cubes
Salt, if necessary

Make a roux with the butter and flour, stirring for a few minutes until the flour no longer tastes raw. Add the broth, whisking well. Bring to a boil, stirring, and simmer for a few minutes. Taste for salt and strength of broth. Correct seasonings.

THE DUMPLINGS

1 stick (4 ounces or 115 grams) Crayfish Butter (p. 144)
1 cup (¼ liter) unseasoned bread crumbs
1 tablespoon finely cut dill
3 eggs, separated
Salt to taste
White pepper to taste

Cream together the butter and bread crumbs. Add the dill and the egg yolks. Blend together thoroughly, then add the salt and pepper to taste. Beat the egg whites until they are stiff but not dry; stir one-third of them into the bread-crumb mixture, then fold in the rest.

Flour your hands, and make little balls about ¾ inch in diameter, rolling between your palms lightly. If you have reserved the crayfish head shells for this, spoon some of the mixture into them, lightly, as it will swell.

FINISHING THE BISQUE AND DUMPLINGS

Bring the soup to the simmer. Put in the dumplings and the stuffed shells, if any. Cover the pot, and simmer for 5 minutes (you can take a peek to make sure the soup is not boiling). The dumplings are done when they float to the surface and have at least doubled in size.

Serve in soup plates, distributing the dumplings and laying the shells red side up, "swimming" in the broth.

*Note:* If you should have any of the crayfish butter left after all this, by all means freeze it! It will make a splendid base for any sauce for fish, especially something delicate such as quenelles (p. 92), or Fish Cutlets (p. 154).

# Shrimp

As shrimp have become quite expensive recently, it is important to buy them, and cook them, with care. The best way to be sure of the freshest shrimp possible is to get them from a reliable fishmonger. Avoid packaged "fresh" shrimp covered in plastic. Above all, do not overcook shrimp, and remember that long refrigeration is apt to change their texture.

## SHRIMP MARINIÈRE

*Serves 6 as a first course or 3 as a main course*

24 medium shrimp
4 tablespoons butter
2 tablespoons finely minced shallots or onion
½ cup (1 deciliter) dry white wine
½ cup (1 deciliter) Hollandaise Sauce (p. 55) or sour cream

Shell the shrimp, split them lengthwise, and devein them, if necessary. Sauté the shrimp halves quickly in the butter with the minced shallots or onion. Remove the shrimp and keep warm. Deglaze the pan with the white wine and boil up for a moment to reduce the liquid by half. Mix in the Hollandaise or sour cream, and serve hot on individual small plates with toast as a first course or with rice as a main course.

## SHRIMP WITH DILL AND SHERRY

*Serves 6*

This recipe is based on one in Craig Claiborne's first *New York Times Cook Book,* and has become a great favorite of ours in this form as well as in the original. It is a dish that benefits from going directly from skillet to table, so the shrimp do not toughen by being kept warm after cooking. (If you want to make "seconds," it takes only 3 minutes to make a fresh batch.)

1 stick (4 ounces or 115 grams) butter
2 pounds (900 grams) medium shrimp, shelled and deveined
Juice of 1 lemon
½ cup (1 deciliter) medium-dry sherry
2 tablespoons finely cut dill
Rice (p. 122)

In a skillet large enough to hold all the shrimp in 1 layer, heat the butter over a medium fire. When it begins to bubble, add the shrimp, and cook them on one side for about 1½ minutes; turn them and cook the other side another 1½ minutes. Both sides should be opaque and pink. If you are using larger or smaller shrimp, adjust the time a little, but be careful not to overcook them—they should be cooked through but remain absolutely moist and tender. (To test, you can cut one in its thickest part; if the inside is grayish, it isn't done; if white, it is.)

Sprinkle the lemon juice, sherry, and dill over the shrimp in the skillet, stir everything together, and serve immediately, with boiled rice.

## SMALL SHRIMP IN JELLY

*Serves 6*

This is an easy and attractive dish for a first course at dinner or a main course at a summer lunch. I love the taste, and I don't mind using ready-made consommé. The slight sweetness of canned beef consommé or madrilène, curiously, suits shrimp very well; and the two dishes of mildly doctored mayonnaise taste delicious.

36 small or medium shrimp
1 bay leaf
Black peppercorns
Two 11-ounce (315-gram) cans beef consommé, or madrilène*
½ cup (1 deciliter) good dry sherry
Salt and white pepper to taste
1 tablespoon (1 envelope) unflavored gelatin
   (if not using jellied consommé)
GARNISH: 1 lemon, sliced thin; parsley; one additional
   11-ounce can consommé or madrilène (optional)†

---

*If you use the condensed canned consommé, to which one adds water, use only one can; if you use canned jellied consommé, you need no additional gelatin. In fact, you should add a little water or beef broth, because the jelly should be quite soft, and not rubbery.

†If you are going to use the extra consommé for decoration, it must be jelled in advance for about 3 hours, or preferably overnight.

Drop the shrimp into boiling water, with a bay leaf and a few peppercorns. Simmer gently, 5 minutes for medium shrimp and 4 minutes for small. Let them cool in the liquid. Peel and devein them if necessary. Do not refrigerate the shrimp unless you are boiling them hours ahead; they are apt to toughen.

Heat the consommé and flavor it with the sherry and salt and white pepper to taste. (Be careful: some canned soups are quite salty.) Chill for 10 minutes. If you are using gelatin, dissolve it first in the sherry, then add to heated consommé; let it cool and chill for 10 minutes. Arrange the shrimp in a shallow serving dish and cover with the consommé. Chill the dish for at least 2 hours.

### GREEN MAYONNAISE

1 cup (¼ liter) homemade or commercial mayonnaise
1 tablespoon finely cut fresh chives
1 tablespoon finely cut fresh tarragon (when available)
1 tablespoon finely cut fresh dill
½ teaspoon sugar
Prepared English mustard to taste

Mix all ingredients thoroughly. The taste improves if done ahead.

### PINK MAYONNAISE

1 cup (¼ liter) homemade or commercial mayonnaise
2 tablespoons tomato ketchup
½ teaspoon sugar
Few drops Tabasco or other hot pepper sauce

Mix all ingredients thoroughly.

Serve the finished dish decorated with thin slices of lemon and small bunches of parsley, and accompanied by the two bowls of mayonnaise, one green and one pink. If you want to use the extra consommé for decoration, empty the previously jelled extra can into a bowl, stir with a fork to froth slightly, and arrange little mounds alternately with the lemon and parsley.

# Fried Fish

"Fried" usually means deep-fried, which is an extravagance because it uses so much oil. I do very little deep-frying, though it is a good way to treat small pieces of fish, but in general I prefer to shallow-fry. And it is so very quick.

## FRIED FISH, SPANISH STYLE

*Serves 6*

Our first Andalusian cook, when we came to Marbella, was, like most of her people, very thrifty. But she insisted on pure olive oil, which, even though it was made locally, was not cheap, and she seemed to be using it in petrifying quantities. Then I noticed that she never allowed it to burn and that she kept it in a special bottle and used it several times. She even kept the excess flour, patted off the fish just before frying, in a special packet for reuse. Her recipe for fried fish is simple indeed, but one must be precise about it to have it come out her way.

Serve the fish hot, lukewarm, or cool (not cold), with steamed potatoes and a little mayonnaise, or just a piece of lemon.

Pinch of salt
1 cup (140 grams) flour
2 pounds (900 grams) almost any kind of fish, in pieces
    ½ inch thick and 2½ inches square*
Oil for frying (part olive and part vegetable oil)

Mix the salt with the flour on a large plate. Pat the flour thickly over all the fish surfaces and let it sit for 10 minutes. As the fish sits, it exudes a little moisture that mixes with the nearest flour and starts crusting; the hot oil immediately seals the crust, browns it, and keeps the fish inside very tender.

Use enough oil to fill your sauté pan ½ inch deep. You use a lot, so that it will not cool off when the fish goes in and so that the pieces are almost covered. Bring the oil to medium-high heat. When the surface of the oil begins to dimple faintly and create a little haze, it is ready.

Carefully pat the excess flour off the fish. Lay the pieces in the oil, not crowding them. (Do 2 batches if necessary.) Fry them skin side down until the top surface is almost opaque, then turn them. The skin side should now be pale gold. After a minute, start testing the fish for doneness with the flat of a fork. When done the pieces should feel firm but slightly resilient.

*If you have a strong-tasting fish, like bluefish or mackeral, soak it in milk for 10 minutes before you dry and flour it.

## FLOUNDER FRIED IN ITS SKIN

*Serves 4*

I had this utterly simple but simply delicious version of flounder in the restaurant Casa Nicolasa in San Sebastián, Spain—prepared by Nicolasa herself.

Vegetable oil, or half vegetable and half olive oil
4 small flounders, about 9–10 inches long, whole and
    with their skins on
Lemon wedges

In a large skillet, or two if possible, heat enough oil to have it about 1 inch deep. (If you use only one skillet and therefore do only one fish at a time, put paper toweling on a large platter or on foil in the oven, turned to *warm,* and put each fish there as it is done.) Transfer them to a serving platter when all are ready. When it is hot enough, a small cube of bread will sizzle and toast. Carefully place the flounder, "eyes-side" down, in the oil. Cook about 2 minutes, turn them over carefully, and cook 2 minutes more. Drain for a few moments on paper toweling, and serve immediately, with lemon wedges. Salt and pepper are added at the table by each individual, to taste. (One doesn't eat the skin, but it looks better to serve the fish whole.)

## FISH CUTLETS

*Serves 4–6*

This is a very easy and delicious way to use fish fillets, and a perfect recipe to adapt for frozen fillets. The "cutlets" are made almost exactly the same way as Chicken Cutlets (p. 237), give or take a few ingredients, and they look identical. They are good for parties, can be made ahead, and are both tasty and attractive with Tomato Sauce (p. 54) to which finely cut fresh dill has been added. They can also be served cold, in slices, with a mayonnaise.

2 pounds (900 grams) any white fish fillets,
or thawed frozen fillets, cut in 2-inch pieces
(if you cut frozen fillets, they thaw almost
immediately)
1 stick (4 ounces or 115 grams) butter
¾ cup (1¾ deciliters) Fish Broth (p. 41), or
use ½ Knorr fish bouillon cube dissolved
in ¾ cup water
2 slices crustless white bread
2 tablespoons grated onion
2 eggs, beaten
2 tablespoons finely cut dill or parsley
Salt to taste
10 grinds white pepper
Grating or pinch of nutmeg
Flour for coating
2–3 tablespoons butter or vegetable shortening
for sautéing

Grind the fish pieces *once* through the larger grinding disc, or process them very carefully, in short bursts, so as to keep some texture and not make a mush. Melt the butter in the broth, crumble the bread into the liquid, add the onion, beaten eggs, dill or parsley, salt and pepper, and nutmeg, and mix thoroughly. Cool the mixture, then add the ground fish, and refrigerate, covered closely with plastic wrap, for about an hour.

Form the mixture into oval cutlets, just slightly over 2 inches by 3 inches, and about 1¼ inches thick. As you form them, roll them lightly in flour, patting off the excess. Sauté them in butter or vegetable shortening over medium-high heat until they are light golden-brown on both sides.

The cutlets may be formed and floured, then refrigerated, covered lightly, until you are ready to cook them. They also may be sautéed, then slightly before they are cooked through put into a baking dish, covered, in a very slow oven. They can then wait for 30 minutes or so.

# Carp

In Europe, these lovely pearly-scaled fish are kept in very pure water to make them ready for cooking. In Israel, you see many carp ponds from which the fish are brought in special tank cars. In Poland, where carp for Christmas is a tradition, city people buy their carp a day or two early and keep them in the bathtub. In New York, as in many cities with a large Jewish population, it can often be found alive and swimming in tanks, or even cut into chunks at supermarkets.

The flesh has a light brown color and a very rich, full, almost meaty taste, so that you may prefer to serve it with red wine instead of white. Under the skin lies a heavy layer of fat, but the rest of the fish is fairly lean—leaner than mackerel or salmon, for instance. Therefore the following way of baking carp, which may look to you rather rich, in fact works beautifully.

## BAKED CARP

These fish can be enormous, and if you can't find a whole one small enough for this dish, buy a chunk with the skin on, as you would buy a piece of swordfish. The quantity may seem large, but the carp's thick skin accounts for that.

I like to serve this with steamed potatoes sprinkled with chopped chives, or with noodles.

10 strips bacon, uncooked
3–4 pounds (1350–1800 grams) fresh carp
1 teaspoon salt
5 grinds pepper
2½ tablespoons flour
1¼ cups (3 deciliters) sour cream
⅓ cup (¾ deciliter) grated Swiss cheese

Preheat the oven to 350°F (180°C). Line the bottom of a baking dish with 5 strips of bacon. On this place the fish, and rub it with salt and pepper. Cover the fish with the remaining bacon, and bake for about 30 minutes, depending on the shape of the fish. If it is a thick, chunky cut, it may take longer. Test it by probing it right down to the bone with two knives and pulling the cut apart. Right at the center, it should still look just a bit red and gelatinous. If you have an "instant" meat thermometer, the temperature, just short of the bone, should be 130°F (54°C).

Now raise the oven temperature to 400°F (205°C). Remove the bacon from under the fish but not the top. Mix the flour with the sour cream and pour it over the fish. Sprinkle it with the cheese and bake the fish for about 10 minutes more.

# CARP IN JELLY

This is something I learned from Barbarka at home in Lithuania, and it has always been a great favorite with children and grandchildren. Our Christmas Eve dinner, although not meatless as in Catholic Polish tradition, invariably began with this dish. It is, like many other dishes in this book, easily adaptable from very casual to very elegant presentations; it can be made right on the serving platter, or in a classic fish mold, or even to unmold in Pyrex custard cups as individual little portions. Pass separately grated horseradish, and a *Sauce verte* mayonnaise (p. 295), into which you might blend or process some watercress leaves, washed, dried, and lightly salted. This adds a beautiful color and a very pleasant "bite" to the mayonnaise— no food coloring needed.

### THE COURT BOUILLON

1 pound (450 grams) fish "frames," skin, bones,
   and/or trimmings, and the head of the carp
   (or other fish)
5 onions, chopped coarse
5 carrots: 3 chopped coarse, 2 left whole
   for slicing and decorating
2 tablespoons sugar
3–4 cups (¾–1 liter) water*

6 carp steaks or a small whole carp,
   about 3 pounds (1350 grams)
8 grinds white pepper
Salt to taste
1 tablespoon (1 envelope) gelatin, if necessary;
   more, if none in broth

---

*If you cannot make the court bouillon, you may use fish stock and/or Knorr fish or chicken bouillon cubes dissolved in water.

Put into a soup pot the fish head, frames, trimmings, etc., the chopped onions and carrots, the whole carrots, and the sugar. Add 3–4 cups (¾–1 liter) water, enough to cover all the ingredients. Simmer for 30 minutes. Carefully remove the whole carrots and reserve. Strain the broth through a very fine sieve, or through rinsed cheesecloth; reserve the broth, and discard the remaining vegetables.

Put the carp steaks, or carp, into a fish poacher or a skillet. Pour over the carp the reserved broth. Cover, bring to the simmer, and poach for about 10 minutes if using steaks or 10 minutes per inch at the thickest end of a whole fish. Let the fish cool in the broth, with the cover off.

With a skimmer remove the carp from the broth onto a dish. Scrape off the skin and remove larger bones from the fish, then return the skins and bones to the broth. Simmer it gently again for 15 minutes. While the broth cooks again with the larger bones, carefully remove all remaining bones from the poached carp, *by hand.* (Messy but fun. Steal a bite now and then!) Strain the broth as before, discarding all solids and reserving the broth. Taste. Add the pepper and salt if necessary. Slice the reserved whole carrots into rounds for decorating. If the carp is to be unmolded for serving, arrange the carrots at the bottom of the mold or molds. (If making it on the serving platter, put the carrots on top of the fish.)

If you have made the court bouillon in this recipe, you should have no trouble jelling it. Test by putting a teaspoonful into a saucer and refrigerating it for 10 minutes. It should be firm but *not* rubbery. If you have had to make the broth some other way, combining liquids and/or fish or chicken bouillon cubes containing *no* gelatin, you will need some. Test first. If necessary, soften 1 envelope gelatin (for each 2 cups broth) in a little cooled broth. Reheat the rest of the broth and dissolve in it the gelatin mixture. Cool it. Remember not to add salt too soon, especially if using Knorr cubes.

Distribute the boneless pieces of carp as nicely as possible (better boneless than beautiful) over your serving platter, or on top of the sliced carrots in the mold. Pour over the fish the strained, cooled broth, and refrigerate for about 4 hours, or until it is set. In a shallow platter it will jell faster than in a deeper mold.

# POACHED CARP WITH CARAMEL
## AND RAISIN SAUCE

*Serves 6*

Here is another extremely easy way of serving this rich and tasty fish. Serve with boiled potatoes.

### THE COURT BOUILLON

6 cups (1½ liters) water
2 medium carrots, chopped coarse
2 medium onions, chopped coarse
2 stalks celery, chopped coarse
2 bay leaves
2 tablespoons sugar
1 teaspoon salt
8–10 black peppercorns

3 pounds (1350 grams) carp steaks, or a small whole carp
1 recipe Caramel Sauce with Raisins and Almonds (p. 62)

In a soup pot, combine all ingredients for the court bouillon. Bring to the boil, then simmer for 30 minutes. Cool. Strain if you wish, or leave the vegetables in to cook with the fish.

Place the cool court bouillon in a fish poacher (or other appropriate pan with a cover), with the steaks or whole fish, and gently poach, covered, for 10 minutes for steaks or 10 minutes for each inch at the thickest point of a whole fish. If you wrap the fish in cheesecloth, with extra-long ends, it will be easier to remove from the court bouillon. Serve the fish immediately with Caramel Sauce with Raisins and Almonds, *omitting the vinegar* and adding ¼ cup of Malaga or other sweet red wine. Spoon a little sauce over each carp steak, or over the whole fish, and pass the rest separately.

## COLD POACHED STRIPED BASS

*Serves 6*

Here is a very simple and delicate recipe for this beautiful ocean fish. Bass is so flavorful, you hardly need a sauce, but a few slices of lemon, or a little mayonnaise, might be nice. If you prefer to serve the dish warm, make a Mousseline Sauce or Hollandaise Sauce (p. 55) to go with it. Cold, it is ideal for a summer lunch, or a buffet anytime.

1 whole striped bass, about 3 pounds (1350 grams)
Enough milk to cover the fish in the poaching pan;
    approximately 1½ quarts (1½ liters), depending
    on your pan
½ teaspoon salt
4 slightly cracked (not crushed) peppercorns

Put the cleaned, scaled fish, head intact, in your pan; the ideal one is a long covered fish poacher with a removable rack. If you don't own one, it is wise to wrap the fish in cheesecloth or a towel, leaving 2 long ends to help you lift it out. Pour the milk over the fish until it is completely covered by ½ inch. Add salt and pepper.

Remove the fish and heat the milk to just below the simmer. Replace the fish in the pan and raise the heat. Skin will form on the simmering milk, but, ½ inch above the fish, it won't touch (or stick to) the skin or fins.

Cover the pan and simmer the fish for about 15 minutes. (For poaching, I use James Beard's rule: 10 minutes' cooking for each inch of the fish's thickness at its thickest place.) With a skimmer, remove any skin that formed on the milk. Remove, drain, and cool the fish. You can chill it, but I like it at room temperature or just a little cooler. And the milk? Reserve it, if you like, to make a chowder.

## MONKFISH BAKED WITH TOMATOES
## AND SHALLOTS

*Serves 4*

I remember this delicious and simple dish made for me years ago by Casimir Krance, the husband of my oldest friend, Fela Krance, whose drawings illustrate this book.

3 large ripe tomatoes*
1 cup (¼ liter) finely chopped shallots or onions
2 tablespoons butter, softened
½ cup (1 deciliter) good dry white wine
2 pounds (900 grams) monkfish, or other firm-fleshed white fish
Salt and pepper to taste
Rice (p. 122)

Peel, seed, and coarsely chop the tomatoes.

Sauté the shallots in the butter for a few minutes, then add the tomatoes. Cook them together until the liquid from the tomatoes has exuded and reduced to about one-third its volume. Add the wine and reduce again by about half.

Preheat the oven to 350°F (180°C). Butter a baking dish. Dry the fish; butter, salt, and pepper it on both sides and lay it in the dish. Pour over it the tomato mixture.

Bake the fish for about 30 minutes, if it is monkfish, basting it several times with the liquid in the dish. Another kind of fish may bake faster; check it after 20 minutes with a fork—it should flake but still be very moist.

Serve the fish with boiled rice or steamed potatoes with cut fresh dill or parsley.

---

*It is better to use an equal volume of canned plum tomatoes than pale winter ones.

## SMELTS

*Serves 6*

You may think the combination of fish with sugared sauerkraut is odd, but please try it. Like my recipe for Fish Fritters with Prune Compote (p. 86), this brings out something in the taste of fish that is obscured in most dishes. The elegant, inexpensive, silvery little smelt has a rich flavor, for which sauerkraut is just right as a condiment.

    18 smelts
    ½ cup (70 grams) flour
    3–4 tablespoons oil
    1 pound (450 grams) canned sauerkraut
    2 tablespoons sugar

Dry the smelts well, sprinkle them with flour, and sauté them whole in the oil. It takes only about 5 minutes. With them serve the sauerkraut, just as it comes from the can, cold with all its juice, and mixed with the sugar.

*Variations:* You can also bone the smelts. (This is very easy: pinch the spine at the neck end between finger and thumb and pull. It comes out with all the bones attached. If any bones do remain, they are so hair fine you can just eat them.) Flatten the fish and sauté them in butter, about 1 minute on each side. Or you can dredge smelts (boned or unboned) with flour, dip them in beaten egg, coat them with crumbs, and deep-fry them.

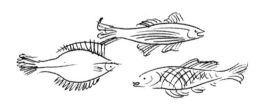

# $\mathcal{S}ole$

The following recipes are suited to any fillets of lean, white-fleshed ocean fish and would therefore include very young specimens of such fish as cod and halibut (usually, indiscriminately called "scrod" when young), which are sold in fillets when young, in steaks when older and larger.

# SOLE WITH MUSHROOMS

*Serves 6*

I love the flavors of fish and mushrooms combined, and this dish is particularly rich and smooth. Though one must be careful about timing, so that the fish is not overcooked, it is quite practical to prepare and cool the components, then assemble them, all in advance. It can then be baked at the last minute. I like to serve this dish with steamed potatoes.

THE STOCK

 1 pound (450 grams) fish skins and bones
 2 medium carrots, chopped
 2 small onions, chopped
 2 small bay leaves
 ½ cup (1 deciliter) dry white wine
 1½ cups (3½ deciliters) water

THE FISH AND VEGETABLES

 2 pounds (900 grams) fillets of sole,
  or other lean white fish
 1 pound (450 grams) mushrooms
 2 tablespoons grated onion
 2 tablespoons butter
 3 tablespoons flour
 Salt and pepper to taste
 3 egg yolks
 ¾ cup (1¾ deciliters) heavy cream

Simmer the fish skins and bones, the chopped carrots and onions, and the bay leaves in the wine and water for 30 minutes. Strain the broth, and pour it into a fish steamer or a large frying pan. For easy removal of the fish after poaching, set a rack in the pan: a pressure cooker rack will do for the frying pan. Or wrap the fillets in one fold of rinsed cheesecloth. Add the fillets to the stock and poach them, covered, until they are just done. Depending on their thickness and whether they are layered in the pan, this can take from 3 to 10 minutes. They should look opaque and feel as though a firm prod from your fingertip would flake them apart.

Remove and reserve the fish. Boil the broth rapidly, uncovered, until it has reduced to 1½ cups.

Chop the mushrooms fine or put through a grinder. Mix in the grated onion. The texture should have a little grain. Cook the mushroom mixture in the butter until the juices have exuded but not quite evaporated. Sprinkle on 1 tablespoon of the flour and cook until the mixture has thickened. Season it to taste with salt and pepper.

Beat the egg yolks with the cream; beat into this the remaining 2 tablespoons flour, and beat in a little fish broth. Add this mixture to the remaining fish broth. Heat this sauce slowly, stirring, until it will coat a spoon.

In a buttered baking dish, make a layer of the mushroom mixture, place the fillets on it, pour on the sauce, and bake at 350°F (180°C) until the dish is heated through, about 10 minutes. Put it under the broiler very briefly until lightly golden on top.


## SOLES AUX PETITS LÉGUMES

*Serves 6*

There is nothing unusual about serving sole, or any fine lean white fish, in a cream sauce enriched with egg yolk and flavored with aromatic vegetables. But this recipe is a little different because the fish is cut in strips and blanched, and the tiny crisp vegetables make a nice contrast.

I must underline the importance of buying very crisp and colorful vegetables and of cutting them nicely. To make superfine juliennes, it is better to use a knife than a processor. Work quite deliberately, controlling the knife with a finger on top of the blade, sharpening it often, making each stroke count.

As for the fish, try to buy fairly thick fillets. If you use one of the less flavorful fish like cod or, especially, monkfish, add 2 tablespoons minced shallots and a glass of white wine to your stock before simmering it. Keep tasting as you proceed: the fish and vegetables must not overcook.

THE STOCK

   1½ pounds (675 grams) fish skins and bones
   3 medium carrots, chopped
   Green top of 1 leek, chopped
   6 ribs celery, chopped
   1 large onion, chopped
   1 teaspoon salt
   8 white peppercorns

Place all these ingredients in the pressure cooker in water to cover for 5 minutes, or simmer them in an ordinary pot for 20 minutes. Strain, and discard the solids.

THE FISH AND VEGETABLES

   2 pounds (900 grams) fillets of lean white fish
   ½ cup (1 deciliter) dry white wine
   3 very green ribs celery (about 6 inches long)
   White part of 1 leek
   1 medium carrot
   3 egg yolks
   ½ cup (1 deciliter) heavy cream
   1 teaspoon white pepper

Slice the fillets diagonally into ½-inch-wide strips. Simmer them for 3 minutes in the fish stock and the wine. They will stiffen and curl slightly. Drain them and set them aside. Cut the vegetables into the finest julienne. The celery and leek should be sliced not into slivers but into very thin rings, crosswise. (Don't try to wash the inner surfaces of the leek before you cut it. Cut it, then separate the little rings, and briefly rinse them.) Simmer the finely cut carrot, celery, and leek in the fish stock until barely done and still crisp: start tasting for doneness after a minute. Drain the vegetables well, and reserve them.

Beat the egg yolks with the cream to blend them thoroughly, add white pepper, and mix in a little hot fish stock; reserve the mixture.

Measure the remaining fish stock. You want quite a lot of sauce, about 2 cups in all. Into about 1⅓ cups fish stock, pour the egg-cream-stock mixture, and heat the sauce slowly, stirring, until it has thickened enough to coat a spoon. Don't let it boil. Add the reserved fish, stirring carefully so that the strips don't break, and let it heat through. Serve the fish in its sauce in a deep, heated platter, with the "little vegetables" scattered over the top.

*Variations:* The sauce can easily be adapted to serve with a Fish Cutlet (p. 154), fish quenelles, or a fish soufflé. Make the stock stronger with additional fish bones and skins (one can often buy fish skeletons that have been filleted but still have lots of flesh). Make the sauce thicker by adding 5 egg yolks to the 1⅓ cups of stock plus ½ cup of cream. And use a little more pepper.

If you have leftover fish, sauce, and vegetables, you can make a fine soup by reheating them all together, to the barest simmer, with a bit more liquid (fish stock, Knorr fish bouillon cubes dissolved in water, or milk, or light cream). Taste carefully for seasoning; you might need a pinch of salt. This soup is good with rounds of hard (baked) toast.

## SMOKED HADDOCK

*Serves 6*

This is a version of a dish I always liked at the Savoy Hotel in London. It is the easiest fish dish I can imagine, and extremely savory: nice for a quiet supper on a cold night.

2½ pounds (1125 grams) smoked haddock, in 1 piece
1½ cups (3½ deciliters) heavy cream
4 tablespoons tomato paste
Pepper to taste

Soak the fish in warm water for an hour, changing the water twice. Put it in a good-size baking dish (the reason for this is that the sauce will reduce better: you want it quite thick). Pour the heavy cream over the fish and bake it at 350°F (180°C) for 10 minutes. Then put the tomato paste in spoonfuls down the middle of the fish and continue baking for 10 minutes more. Baste occasionally; this will make the tomato paste run streakily into the cream, which will condense into a rich and luxurious sauce. Smoked fish provides more than enough salt, but a few grinds of pepper might be nice.

# Salt Herring

I learned to love salt herring during the long Warsaw winters, when there was not much fresh fish after the Baltic froze.

Here, especially in large cities, salt herring is often available in different forms. Some delicatessens catering to a Jewish clientele will have it "from the barrel," which means whole "schmaltz" (fat) herrings in brine—these must be soaked, in several changes of cold water, for 24 hours, more or less. (You may use milk for the final 8 hours.) They need not be refrigerated during this time. These days some delicatessens sell herrings, whole or filleted, that have been desalted and are ready to use. Be sure to ask which kind you are getting. Soaking a previously desalted herring destroys its flavor, while trying to eat a briny one is not recommended! If you can obtain desalted fillets, you have almost no work to do.

If you must fillet salt herring, proceed as follows:

Pull off the skin. The bones run vertically. With a sharp, pointed knife, cut along the center of the back from head to tail, with the knife tip scraping along the bones. Lift one fillet off, turn the herring, and remove the fillet from the other side. Refrigerate the fillets in vegetable oil to cover, until you are ready to use them. (Wipe most of the oil off before using.)

To enjoy plain salt herring, cut the fillets crosswise into 1-inch slices and serve them as is, or with sour cream and sliced onion.

## SALT HERRING AND EGGS

*Serves 6*

This simple herring mixture, served with Blinis (p. 84), is almost as good as caviar, and of course is not expensive at all. I like it with chilled glasses of the best Polish vodka, which should be put in the freezer one day in advance and kept icy. (It will not freeze. I store my vodka permanently in the freezer.) It is also very nice as a canapé with cocktails or a glass of cold beer.

1–1½ pounds (450–675 grams) desalted fillets of salt herring
    (2 medium herrings)
4 hard-boiled eggs
GARNISH: sour cream and minced onion

Grind or thoroughly chop together the desalted fillets with the eggs. Serve the mixture in a bowl, with smaller bowls of sour cream and minced raw sweet onion, to accompany piping hot blinis and your favorite drink.

## SALT HERRING SALAD

*Serves 6*

If my children, or *their* children, are around when I am making this, and they are offering opinions while "tasting"—a bit more apple, a bit more onion—often there is little left to serve!

This salad can be an hors d'oeuvre, on rounds of fresh rye bread; a first course; or a light supper or lunch dish, served with baked potatoes. It has a mild sweet-sour flavor, which the garnish enhances pleasantly.

1 pound (450 grams) desalted fillets of salt herring
2 small onions, peeled
2 apples, peeled and cored
2 large slices crustless rye bread, made into crumbs

GARNISH

Pickled Mushrooms (p. 276)
Pickled beets
Cherry tomatoes
Finely cut parsley
Thin onion slices, blanched for 1 minute in equal parts
    water and wine vinegar, just enough to cover,
    and drained afterward

Grind or process together the herring, onions, and apples. Stir in the rye bread crumbs. (Either the blender or processor makes crumbs.) Let the mixture stand until the crumbs have absorbed all the juices. Shape it attractively on a serving plate (like a fish, perhaps), and garnish it.

## FISH SALAD WITH POTATO AND EGG

*Serves 6*

This is a delicious way to serve fish in the summer. It is also perfect for any buffet, and a fine way to use leftover poached, or even baked, fish, as long as it has not been sauced. The fish may be poached in a court bouillon as in Poached Carp with Caramel and Raisin Sauce (p. 160) or simply in lightly salted water to cover. Remember to allow time for all the ingredients to cool to room temperature before mixing and refrigerating the salad.

1 pound (450 grams) any firm-fleshed white fish
(steaks, or in a chunk), like bass, hake, sea trout, or cod
1 recipe Court Bouillon (p. 160), or 6 cups (1½ liters)
lightly salted water with 1 bay leaf and 5 peppercorns
1½ cups (3½ deciliters) cooked diced potatoes
(2 medium potatoes, boiled in their skins, cooled,
and peeled)
½ cup (1 deciliter) very finely cut celery hearts
(use only the tender centers)
½ cup (1 deciliter) very finely chopped onion,
or the white part only of 6–8 scallions
¾ cup (1¾ deciliters) mayonnaise
1 teaspoon Dijon-type mustard
3 hard-boiled eggs: 2 coarsely chopped and 1 sliced
for decoration
Salt to taste
6 grinds pepper, or to taste
Boston lettuce leaves or watercress
GARNISH: black olives, halved and pitted; red pimiento
strips

Poach the fish in the court bouillon or the seasoned water according to the instructions on page 160, for 10 minutes for steaks or for 10 minutes for each inch at the thickest point of a chunk. Cool the fish in the broth.

Remove it, take the meat off the bones, and flake it gently into a bowl. Cover and reserve it.

In another bowl, toss the potatoes, celery, and onion together. Mix the mayonnaise and mustard, add them to the vegetables, and mix well. To this mixture add the 2 chopped hard-boiled eggs, toss lightly, then add the fish. Toss the whole salad thoroughly but lightly, with 2 forks, adding salt and pepper.

Line a salad bowl, or a platter, with Boston lettuce leaves, or watercress. Heap the fish salad in it and decorate with the sliced hard-boiled egg, olives, and pimiento strips.

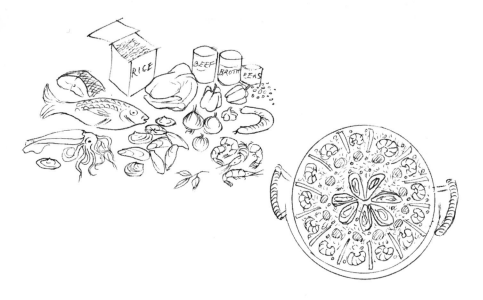

## PAELLA DE CARMELA

*Serves 10*

Paella, that wonderful, typically Spanish, and truly spectacular dish, has almost as many versions as there are provinces in Spain. The most famous is of course the Paella Valenciana, but many of the others are equally delicious.

Based on rice cooked with a variety of fish, shellfish, meat, chicken, and vegetables, paella is quite a filling dish; if hard to make for fewer than eight to ten people, it is easy to increase the recipe for a larger group. It is a party dish par excellence, and although a bit time-consuming, it is certainly not difficult to make—and well worth the effort.

It is useful to have a real paella pan, but a very large skillet with an ovenproof handle might do. More important is that you use *only* the plump, short-grained Spanish or Italian rice, which behaves quite differently from the long-grained variety, and will not make a mush.

This recipe, inspired by my cook Carmela, is my favorite version of paella. As accompaniment, it needs nothing more than a bowl of crisp green salad and pitchers of iced Sangría.

¾ pound (340 grams) pork shoulder
Two 2½-pound (1125-gram) chickens, cut into
    8 pieces each
3 spicy chorizos (approximately 4 inches each),
    or ½ Italian pepperoni sausage
1 green pepper
2 onions
2 cloves garlic
2 ripe tomatoes
1 dozen clams
30 medium shrimp
Peppercorns
¾ pound (340 grams) monkfish
1½ pounds (675 grams) squid
4–4½ cups (1–1¼ liters) liquid reserved from
    cooking the clams, fish, shrimp, etc.
Salt to taste
1½–2 cups (3½ deciliters–½ liter) strong Fish Broth
    (p. 41), or use 1 Knorr fish or chicken bouillon
    cube dissolved in 1½–2 cups water
⅔ cup (1½ deciliters) olive oil
3 cups (¾ liter) uncooked short-grain rice
½ teaspoon saffron powder
¼ teaspoon finely ground pepper
1 cup (¼ liter) green peas, fresh or frozen
20 mussels (3½ deciliters–½ liter), scrubbed and
    debearded
1 small can red pimiento strips for decoration

Cut the pork into slices about 1 inch wide and ⅜ inch thick. Bone the chicken; cut the meat of each breast into 3 pieces, and each leg into 2. Slice the chorizos into ¼-inch rounds. Reserve a few slices for decoration. Cut the pepper in half, seed, and cut into very small pieces. Chop the onions very fine. Crush the garlic. Peel and seed the tomatoes, then cut them into pieces.

Now, wash and steam the clams in ½ cup (1 deciliter) water. Wash and boil the shrimp in 2 cups (½ liter) lightly salted water with a few peppercorns for about 5 minutes. Poach the fish and the squid together in 2 cups (½ liter) lightly salted water for 15 minutes; then cut the squid into strips, the fish into chunks. Take the clams out of their shells, reserving the meats. Reserve all the liquid from boiling and steaming and add to it 1½–2 cups strong fish stock or make a broth with 1 Knorr fish or chicken bouillon cube and 1½–2 cups of water. There should be 6 cups of liquid in all. Taste for salt and strength.

Sauté the pork in the paella pan in 2–3 tablespoons of the oil, and after 6–7 minutes add the chicken pieces; sauté until the chicken begins to color. Then add the tomatoes, pepper, onions, and garlic. Add more oil if necessary. Cook until the meat is tender, about 10 minutes. Remove and keep covered all these ingredients. Put the rice into the paella pan and fry it for a few minutes in 3 more tablespoons of oil, stirring constantly to coat all over.

Now comes the moment of putting all the ingredients together. Bring the reserved liquid to a boil, and add the saffron and ground pepper. To the mixture in the paella pan add the meats, chorizo (reserving 10 slices), peas, fish, squid, clam meats, and the shrimp (reserving 10). Mix everything together a little and add 4 cups of the reserved liquid, boiling hot.

Preheat the oven to 350°F (180°C). Place the pan over a slow fire, stirring occasionally, and wait until the liquid is absorbed, about 10 minutes; then add *gradually* the rest of the fish liquid. Taste the rice; it should not be too soft and mushy. When nearly all the liquid is absorbed, cover the pan lightly with foil (if it has no cover) and put it in the oven for 10–15 minutes. During the last 10 minutes of cooking, steam open the mussels in a separate pot.

At the last moment, decorate with the reserved shrimp, slices of chorizo, strips of red pimiento, and the mussels on the half shell.

## MEAT

New York Cut (Shell Sirloin)
and Rib Eye Steaks
Tenderloin Steaks, or Filets Mignons
Cube Steaks, Pot Roast Style
Beef Tenderloin, Roasted,
with Smothered Onions
Beef Cutlets, Spanish Style
Beef Stroganoff
Boiled Beef with Horseradish Sauce
Pot Roast
Goulash with Caraway Seeds
Veal Piccata
Breaded Veal Escalopes
Veal Émincé
Veal Cutlets
Roast Leg of Lamb
Shashlik
Lamb Cutlets
Navarin of Lamb
Roast Pork Loin with Baked Apples
Roast Pork Shoulder
Ham Steaks
Aniela's Pork Fillet Medallions
Calves' Liver Veneziana
Calves' Brains en Coquille
Veal Kidneys
Fresh Beef Tongue
Tripes à la Varsovienne
Cabbage Rolls
Pâté Barbarka
Meat Loaf
Bigos

## FOWL

Chicken with Prunes
Roast Cornish Hens Polonaise
Chicken with Orange
Chicken Fricassee, Andalusian Style
Lemon Chicken
Lemon Chicken en Chaud-froid
Deviled Chicken Legs
Chicken Medallions
Chicken Cutlets
Chicken Liver and Egg Pâté
Chicken Liver Pâté in Aspic
Roast Turkey
Roast Duck à l'Orange
Plain Roast Duck
Roast Duck with Apples
Guinea Hen
Pheasant
Pheasant Smothered in Cabbage
Squabs with Grapes and Raisins

# Meat and Fowl

As I never attended any sort of cooking school, some of my best teachers were the butchers who taught me how to choose and even cook various meats and birds.

When I go to market for everyday meals, I quite often have only a general idea of a menu based on meat, fowl, or fish, but if I see something unexpected or especially appetizing, I am apt to change all my plans on the spot. What I finally will choose of course depends also on who is to eat it and under what circumstances. If it is a family reunion with children and grandchildren, their favorites take precedence. A small party for Polish friends nostalgic for a taste of home or a formal dinner with extra help— when I cannot be in the kitchen—will obviously affect my choice of the main course.

Although meat is usually central to my menus, it often will appear in forms such as filling for crêpes, cabbage rolls, *pierogi,* stuffed peppers or tomatoes, and of course *bigos,* where meat is only one of many harmonious ingredients.

Many of these recipes are wonderful "stretchers" when meat is expensive and were a real lifesaver during the meat-rationing days of World War II. Be sure to check the index for other entrées where meat plays only second fiddle, but plays it very well.

# Beef

Beef in America is so good that I have often been tempted to take some to Europe with me and "show off" to my Parisian butcher! Although because of recent regulations beef is now considerably leaner here than it used to be, it is still much fatter than European beef, and that, together with the fact that it is also hung longer, accounts for its superior flavor and tenderness.

I am particularly fond of American roast beef, the size and quality of which can't be matched anywhere, and the "New York cut," or shell, steaks, which are my own as well as my children's absolute favorite.

The only beef I have ever encountered that might be more tender is produced by cattle specially raised in Kobe, Japan, where (I hear) the animals are actually *massaged* to tenderize their tissues. The meat melts in your mouth, of course, but so does the money in your pocket.

## NEW YORK CUT (SHELL SIRLOIN) AND RIB EYE STEAKS

*Serves 6*

I buy the U.S. "Prime" grade, about ¾ inch thick and well marbled with fat, but trim off all the exterior fat. Nick the edges at 1-inch intervals, so that the steaks will lie perfectly flat in the pan. Pan-broiling, done preferably in a nonstick pan, is better than grilling because the meat is more quickly seared, yet does not develop a crust.

    2 cloves garlic, chopped
    2 teaspoons Herbes de Provence
    4 tablespoons olive oil
    16 grinds black pepper
    2¼ pounds (1000 grams), *after* trimming, shell sirloin
        or rib eye steaks, not more than ¾ inch thick

Mash together in a small mortar (or use a little bowl and the back of a soupspoon) the chopped garlic, herbs, oil, and pepper. Rub this well into all the surfaces of the meat, and leave the meat at room temperature for 15–20 minutes. Turn it once or twice in the interval before cooking.

Set a nonstick or cast-iron skillet over medium-high heat. A test: in the pan, a drop of water will slide and sizzle for just a moment before disappearing. A nonstick pan will need no fat. Brush an iron pan with oil. Lay the steaks in the skillet. When the undersides are browned, turn them over and cook the second side. It takes about 2–3 minutes per side to cook a ¾-inch steak rare, but not too wet and red. Serve steaks at once, as they continue to cook if allowed to sit. Be sure not to salt the meat until ready to serve.

## TENDERLOIN STEAKS, OR FILETS MIGNONS

*Serves 6*

If possible, buy a 2-pound (900-gram) piece of the whole tenderloin toward the smaller end and cut it into six ¾-inch-thick slices. Or ask the butcher to do this.

You can marinate them exactly like New York cut or rib eye steaks, but my favorite method is to pan-broil them 2 minutes on each side and serve them with Smothered Onions (p. 278). Do not salt the meat until ready to serve.

## CUBE STEAKS, POT ROAST STYLE

*Serves 6*

I use a pressure cooker for this and purée the vegetables to make a succulent light brown sauce, which may be enriched with sour cream.

It is important how you cut the vegetables for quick, even cooking.

1 ounce (30 grams) dried cèpes (optional)
2 medium onions, peeled and chopped coarse
½ cup (1 deciliter) peeled and chopped or
    finely julienned carrots
4 ounces (115 grams) sliced mushrooms
½ cup (1 deciliter) water or beef broth
2 tablespoons oil
2¼ pounds (1000 grams) cube steaks
6 grinds black pepper
1 bay leaf
½ cup (1 deciliter) sour cream (optional)
Salt to taste

Soak the dried cèpes, if you have them, for 1 hour if whole—30 minutes if sliced—in ½ cup (1 deciliter), water or beef broth and cut them in fine strips. You will be using the tasty soaking water for the sauce. Cut the vegetables carefully. The different cuts have a reason: you want all the vegetables to be quite soft at exactly the same time, and their water contents are all different.

Heat the oil in the open pressure cooker. Nick each slice of cube steak at 1-inch intervals, all around, so each will lie flat and brown evenly. Brown them on both sides over medium-high heat.

Add the dried cèpes and their juice, the onions, carrots, and mushrooms, the pepper, and bay leaf. Cook them, turning often, in the oil that remains in the pressure cooker, for about 3 minutes, over medium heat.

Cover and weight the pressure cooker, and cook for 3 minutes after pressure is reached. At once cool the pot under cold running water. Uncover the pressure cooker, remove the meat, and cover to keep it warm while you make the sauce: purée or blend the vegetables and their juices. Taste carefully. Mix in the sour cream if you are using it, taste again, and add salt if you need it. Pour the sauce around the meat on a serving dish, and serve.

*Variation:* Kate, our housekeeper in California, used to do cube steaks very simply in a covered skillet. She would flour them first, sauté them over quite high heat until well browned, and deglaze the pan with water. Then she added a little marjoram and a few dashes of Maggi extract, covered the pan, cooked the meat about 10 minutes over low heat, and completed the sauce by stirring a little cream into the pan.

# BEEF TENDERLOIN, ROASTED

*Serves 6*

Years ago, the chef at the Lucerne Palace Hotel in Switzerland let me watch as he prepared four whole beef tenderloins for roasting. I find his recipe delicious, even though I have shortened the length of time for the marinade.

Smothered Onions (following recipe) and a little freshly "shaved" horseradish make a perfect garnish for this simple, if luxurious, dish.

2-pound (900-gram) piece beef tenderloin
   from the large end of the fillet
1 large onion, sliced thin
2 lemons, sliced thin
6 grinds black pepper
½ cup (1 deciliter) vegetable oil
1½ tablespoons dry English mustard (Colman's,
   for instance)
1 teaspoon honey
GARNISH: Smothered Onions (following recipe)
   and Horseradish (p. 59)

Trim the meat of fat if necessary. Tie it with string, loosely, just so it keeps its shape. Take a dish only a little larger and deeper than the meat, and strew half the sliced onion and lemons over the bottom. Lay in the meat and strew the top with the remaining onion and lemons. Sprinkle the top with 6 grinds of black pepper, and pour the oil over it. Let the dish sit in a cool place for 6 hours, or even overnight, during which you turn the meat 2 or 3 times.

Preheat the oven to 400°F (205°C). Discard the marinade and pat the meat dry. Mix the mustard and honey with 1 teaspoon hot water and "massage" it into the meat. In a nonstick pan, or a heavy pan filmed with a little oil, brown all the meat surfaces, just enough to seal in the juices. Place the meat on a rack in a roasting pan on the middle rack of the oven. After 10 minutes, turn the oven temperature down to 350°F (180°C). To have the beef rare, roast for 25 minutes, or until a meat thermometer registers 140°F (60°C). Let the roast stand for 5 minutes at room temperature before slicing it into ¼-inch-thick slices. During the roasting time, prepare the Smothered Onions.

Garnish the meat platter with the smothered onions and small mounds of shaved fresh horseradish.

SMOTHERED ONIONS

2 large onions, sliced thin
2 tablespoons butter
Salt and pepper to taste

Slowly cook the sliced onions, covered, in the butter and a very little salt and pepper.

## BEEF CUTLETS, SPANISH STYLE
### (Ground meat)

*Serves 6*

A few words here about my "terminology" in referring to cuts of meat. I call these beef cutlets, rather than hamburgers or beef patties, because "cutlets" to me, translating directly from the Polish *kotletki,* mean plump little cushions of ground meat, whether they are beef, veal, lamb, or chicken, or even fish. For the thin slices of solid meat, which in America we call cutlets, I have here used "medallions," but very thin medallions of veal I call "piccata." I think these terms are really more descriptive of what you are making, so I am sticking to them.

Despite the difficulty of cooking ground meat perfectly, I love it, and have included four recipes for cutlets. I hope you will find my method helpful.

2 pounds (900 grams) ground round beef steak,
    about 25 percent fat*
2 small onions, minced fine
2 cloves garlic, minced fine
3 eggs, lightly beaten
Salt and pepper to taste
5 tablespoons flour
2 tablespoons olive oil

Mix the ground meat, onions, garlic, lightly beaten eggs, and salt and
pepper (about 1½ teaspoons salt and 8 grinds of pepper, for my taste). Form
the cutlets, not packing them too closely. They should have lots of center
and not too much surface to be juicy, so I use a large spoon to make rounds
or fat ovals about 3 inches across and ¾ inch thick.

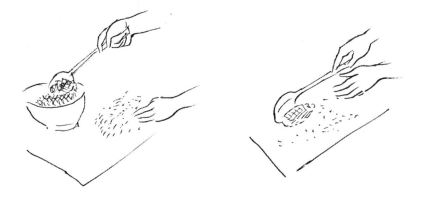

To get a good seal, which helps prevent juices from escaping, pat the
cutlets with flour just before cooking, and brush off all the excess flour.
    Sauté them in the oil, over medium-high heat, in a nonstick pan.
    Approximately 4 minutes' sautéing on each side is about right, but it is
hard to be precise. With experience, one can tell when cutlets are done by
poking them with the fingertips. The cutlet should be slightly resistant. Take
the pan off the heat, cover it closely, and leave it for no more than 2 minutes.
This causes the juices, which have shrunk back into the center, to redistribute
themselves through each cutlet. Now the cutlets are ready to serve, with the
pan juices poured over them.

---

*Meat that is fatter lets too much melt away during cooking; leaner is less tasty.

## BEEF STROGANOFF

This dish was originally created for a Count Stroganoff, who was famed as a gourmet during the reign of Czar Alexander III. Rumored to have owned nearly one hundred thousand serfs, he probably had no misgivings about the price of the best available beef.

The recipe given here is for the classic version, which, although made with tenderloin, presents the meat in such a simple way that every bite is a treat. The version calling for mushrooms and a lot of sour cream probably came from attempts to "stretch" the meat, but succeeds only in camouflaging the real taste of the beef and creating an entirely different dish, which should really have another name.

Beef Stroganoff is extremely easy and quick to make. It is ideal for chafing-dish, at-the-table cooking, as it must be eaten the moment it is ready. Serve it with boiled potatoes, boiled Rice (p. 122), or wide noodles.

2 pounds (900 grams) beef tenderloin
About 3 tablespoons flour for dredging
3 tablespoons clarified butter, oil, or
   vegetable shortening
1½ cups (3½ deciliters) Basic Beef Broth
   (p. 5), or use 1 Knorr beef bouillon cube
   dissolved in 1½ cups water
1 small onion
1 teaspoon paprika
¼ cup (½ deciliter) sour cream
2 tablespoons brandy

Cut the beef tenderloin into finger-size pieces; this is most easily done when it is well chilled. Dredge them with flour and shake off the excess. Sauté the pieces very quickly in the butter, oil, or vegetable shortening; they should remain bright red inside. Deglaze the pan by pouring in hot beef broth, as you turn the pieces and scrape up any brown bits; it instantly forms a thin brown sauce. Grate over the pan the onion, catching all the juices. Add the paprika and the sour cream. Turn the beef once more, just to mix well. Warm the brandy, ignite it, and pour it over the beef, distributing it quickly. Serve at once.

## BOILED BEEF WITH HORSERADISH SAUCE

*Serves 6*

There are reasons to use the pressure cooker for this dish: you get a more intensely flavored broth, the fat renders better out of the meat, and, of course, cooking time is much shorter. I like best the slightly fat but very tasty short ribs. After cooking, the meat is not too fat and very succulent, and the time gained by pressure cooking is ample for chilling and thoroughly defatting the delicious broth.

I use part of the broth to make the savory sauce. A little more broth is added to the meat dish, to keep each portion hot and moist. The remaining broth makes a fine soup to serve another day, perhaps with dumplings or small filled pastries.

    4 pounds (1800 grams) beef short ribs
        (the meatiest, chunkiest ones you can find)*
    2 large or 3 medium carrots, chopped coarse
    3 ribs celery, chopped coarse
    1 leek, sliced crosswise
    1 large or 2 medium onions, halved
    2 bay leaves
    10 peppercorns
    4 cups (1 liter) Basic Beef Broth (p. 5),
        or use 2 Knorr beef bouillon cubes
        dissolved in 4 cups water
    Salt, if necessary

In the pressure cooker, brown the short ribs in their own fat, until all surfaces are sealed. Do this in the open pot, over medium-high heat. Add

*You may also use beef brisket.

the carrots, celery, leek, onion, bay leaves, and peppercorns. Cover and weight the pot. For big, chunky pieces of meat, cook for 20 minutes after pressure is reached. Smaller and less compact pieces will take less time, about 15 minutes. (If using beef brisket, cook 50 minutes.) Cool and uncover the pressure cooker. Drain off 2 cups of the broth to use in the sauce. Degrease it: The quickest way is to pour it into a large, shallow dish and put it in the freezer. As the fat congeals, it rises to the surface and is easily removed.

Meanwhile, remove the meat from the pressure cooker and discard the vegetables. Slice the meat neatly, and return it to the pot to await reheating after the sauce (following recipe) is made.

Once the sauce is flavored to your liking, reheat the open pot of sliced meat, vegetables, and broth. Put the vegetables, and the meat with a little broth, into 2 warm serving dishes, and serve with the sauce in a separate bowl. The remaining broth can be defatted at your leisure.

*For the ordinary pot:* If you decide on short ribs, allow 1–1½ hours' cooking time, depending on the size of the pieces. If you choose a beef brisket, 3 pounds of meat will amply serve 6, and, if you cook it in 1 chunk, cooking time will be about 2 hours. For an ordinary pot, I would double the quantity of vegetables, and would quarter them rather than chop them.

HORSERADISH SAUCE

General recipes for Horseradish Sauce appear on pages 59 and 60.

*Makes 2 cups*

3 tablespoons butter
3 tablespoons flour
2 cups (½ liter) defatted broth from the pot
4 ounces (115 grams) bottled or fresh grated horseradish (p. 59)
Salt to taste
About 3 tablespoons heavy cream
About 1 teaspoon sugar, or to taste

Melt the butter, add the flour, and cook until thickened and well blended. Add the broth and cook, stirring constantly, until the mixture has thickened and the flour no longer tastes raw. Drain the grated horseradish (about four-fifths of the standard bottle), pressing out all the vinegary juice you can. Add the pulp to the broth.

Let the sauce rest for about 10 minutes or so. This wait will make it slightly thicker and will "marry" and mellow the flavors. Then taste it. Add very small amounts of salt, cream, and sugar, tasting repeatedly. This sauce is not as strongly flavored as you might expect, since you have eliminated the vinegary sharpness of the bottled horseradish.

## POT ROAST

*Serves 6–8*

I like to make pot roast for a number of reasons. It is very popular, it is economical, and, perhaps above all, such good things can be made with the leftovers—for instance, fillings for crêpes (p. 80) or stuffing for tomatoes or green peppers. This is certainly one of the dishes I cook often, not only because I like it, but because I am already planning another meal.

3 pounds (1350 grams) beef pot roast
2 tablespoons oil or vegetable shortening
1 cup (¼ liter) chopped celery with some leaves
1 cup (¼ liter) peeled and sliced carrots
1 cup (¼ liter) leeks, sliced in rounds
2 bay leaves
10 crushed peppercorns
2 ounces (60 grams) dried cèpes, not soaked, cut in strips
1 cup (¼ liter) very strong Basic Beef Broth (p. 5),
    or use 2 Knorr beef bouillon cubes dissolved
    in 1 cup water
Salt, if necessary
2 tablespoons sour cream

Trim the meat of excess fat and dry it well with paper towels. Brown it in oil or shortening over medium-high heat, making sure that every bit of surface gets browned. Line the bottom of a heavy pot or Dutch oven, small for a close fit, with the celery, carrots, and leeks. Put the meat on them, and add the bay leaves and peppercorns, cèpes, and broth. Cover and simmer for about 2 or 3 hours or until tender.

Transfer the meat to a hot serving dish, taste the sauce for seasoning, and either serve it as is or purée it in a blender. Mix into it the sour cream.

*For the pressure cooker:* Soak the dried cèpes in a little hot water for 30 minutes before proceeding. Cut them in strips and reserve the water. Brown the meat in the open cooker in 2 tablespoons oil or shortening. Sprinkle it with the peppercorns, the chopped celery, carrots, and leeks, and the soaked cèpes and their liquid. Add 1 beef bouillon cube and ½ cup water. Cook for 30 minutes after pressure is reached, then cool and uncover the pot and test the meat for tenderness. Cook it a little longer if necessary. When it is tender, purée the vegetables and their juices, and taste the sauce for saltiness. Blend in the sour cream, and serve.

## GOULASH WITH CARAWAY SEEDS

*Serves 6*

There are so many versions of goulash that it would be difficult to call any one typical and authentic. My favorite is one I learned from an Austrian, who cooked for us years ago in Los Angeles and whose happy notion it was to add caraway seeds.

The tempting reddish brown color of goulash is achieved first by almost caramelizing the onions, then by the addition of tomato paste, and third by including paprika, which should be thoroughly cooked in.

I much prefer to make this in the pressure cooker, but of course an ordinary pot will do. Goulash will keep after being cooked and so is good for make-ahead meals. Serve it with steamed or boiled potatoes, or noodles, and a green salad.

2 cups (450 grams) very finely chopped onions
6–7 tablespoons vegetable shortening
1–1½ tablespoons paprika*
3 pounds (1350 grams) beef, in 1¼-inch cubes
   (beef shoulder, which is well marbled,
   is a good choice)
3 tablespoons flour
1 tablespoon caraway seeds
6 grinds pepper
1 cup (¼ liter) strong Basic Beef Broth (p. 5),
   or use 1 Knorr beef bouillon cube
   dissolved in 1 cup water
1 tablespoon tomato paste
Salt, if necessary

In the open pressure cooker, turn the onions in 4–5 tablespoons of the shortening. Add the paprika, 1 tablespoon to begin with, and mix it in well. Sauté the onions slowly until they are a good deep brown, though not burned, then taste them, and add more paprika if you need it. Remove the onions from the pot, add 2 tablespoons more shortening, and raise the heat to medium-high. Brown the pieces of beef on all sides; golden-brown is dark enough.

    Lower the heat again. Sprinkle the meat with the flour, return the onions to the pot, add the caraway seeds and the pepper, and mix in the beef broth. Cover and cook for 15 minutes after pressure is reached. Cool and open the cooker, and test the meat for doneness. (It may need a few more minutes, depending on the quality of the meat.) Add the tomato paste, and let the goulash simmer slowly for 10 minutes. Taste it, add a little more tomato paste if you like, salt lightly if you wish, and serve.

*For the ordinary pot:* Proceed exactly as above, but, after you have added the beef broth, simmer the goulash, covered, for about 1½ hours or until the meat is tender. Check, during the cooking, to be sure the liquid has not evaporated, and add more broth as needed.

*If possible, get good Hungarian sweet paprika and keep it tightly covered in the refrigerator to preserve its flavor.

# Veal

## VEAL PICCATA

*Serves 4*

For this delicate dish, you really must have veal cut from the loin. It is much more tender than the leg, and the little slices are just the right size and shape. Although it is rather expensive, there is absolutely no waste—the same is true of Veal Émincé (p. 194). A nice accompaniment is *Lazanki* with Mushrooms and Onions (p. 101). For 6 people, increase the quantities and use 2 pans.

1 pound (450 grams) veal tenderloin
1½ teaspoons salt
4 grinds pepper
3 tablespoons flour
2 tablespoons vegetable oil
2 tablespoons butter
1 teaspoon lemon juice

Trim the meat of fat and cut it across the grain into slices ⅓ inch thick. Pummel the slices, not hard, with your fist, to make them very flat and even. Season them with salt and pepper and pat them with flour on both sides. In a frying pan heat the vegetable oil and sauté the slices 1 minute on each side. Then add the butter and cook another minute (being careful not to brown the meat). Serve immediately, sprinkled with a little lemon juice.

*Variation:* Sometimes I sprinkle the meat, just before it is done, with Parmesan cheese, a little Maggi extract, and ½ cup (1 deciliter) heavy cream.

# BREADED VEAL ESCALOPES

*Serves 4*

Even if you can obtain perfect pale veal, you will want to fuss with it a little for well-cooked scallops. Each piece should be of exactly the same thickness for even cooking, and preferably of the same length and width. Therefore I buy veal from the leg, cut across the grain and without membrane divisions. For 6 people, increase the quantities and use 2 pans.

1½ pounds (675 grams) veal slices from the leg
   (the butcher may call them cutlets)
1½ teaspoons salt
4 grinds pepper
2 eggs, beaten
About 4 tablespoons unseasoned bread crumbs
3 tablespoons or more vegetable shortening

With a mallet, or the edge of a can, pound the meat rather lightly, which will spread and flatten it, and will produce an even, quite dense texture. Very carefully cut off any gristle or membrane. Nick the edges of the slices all round so that they don't shrink or curl in the pan.

Dry the meat between paper towels. Pat salt and pepper into both sides of the pieces. Dip the pieces into the beaten egg, shaking off the excess drops, and coat them lightly with bread crumbs, patting off any excess.

In a large skillet over medium-high heat, brown the slices on both sides in the vegetable shortening. (If the pan gets dry, add a little more shortening.) Reduce the heat to medium-low to finish the cooking. When done, the escalopes are ivory-colored all through.

Since I prefer tenderness to crispness, I put the finished escalopes into an ovenproof dish, well covered with foil, and let them sit for 10 minutes in a warmer or slow oven before serving.

# VEAL ÉMINCÉ

*Serves 6*

For this dish you need veal tenderloin. I usually buy the whole fillet and trim the meat myself, saving some for Veal Piccata (p. 192) the next day or the day after. This dish is luscious and full-flavored, and very quick to make once the meat is nicely prepared. Serve it with rice or any kind of noodles or spätzle.

2 pounds (900 grams) veal tenderloin
4 tablespoons flour
1 teaspoon salt
3 grinds white pepper
2 tablespoons vegetable shortening
Salt and pepper to taste
Paprika to taste
1 cup (¼ liter) sour cream, at room temperature

Cut the meat across the grain into thin slices: it is easier to do when the meat is very cold. Lay the slices on waxed paper, cover them with waxed paper, and gently pound them as thin as you can, with a rubber mallet, bottle, or rolling pin, until they have spread out on the paper and are evenly thin. Cut these slices into finger-size strips. Pat them dry between towels and lightly coat them with the flour mixed with the salt and pepper. This is best done in a brown paper bag; shake off excess flour as you remove meat strips from the bag.

Sauté the veal strips in vegetable shortening until done, about 2 minutes. Taste one, and sauté them a little longer if necessary. Season very lightly with salt, pepper, and paprika, stir in the sour cream, and taste. Correct the seasoning if necessary. Some people like enough paprika to color the sauce; I prefer just a faint whiff of its flavor.

## VEAL CUTLETS
### (Ground meat)

*Serves 6*

These make a delicious and not too extravagant dish for parties. As with all dishes of ground meat, texture and juiciness are paramount. Veal is rather a dry meat, so I prefer, rather than buying it ground, to do all the preparations myself. Veal cutlets are delicious with lingonberries and with *Lazanki* with Mushrooms and Onions (p. 101).

2 pounds (900 grams) veal (use any cut)
4 tablespoons butter
¾ cup (1¾ deciliters) Chicken Broth (p. 8),
    or use ½ Knorr chicken bouillon cube
    dissolved in ¾ cup water
2 slices crustless white bread
2 eggs, beaten
2 tablespoons finely cut dill or parsley
1½ teaspoons salt, or to taste
½ teaspoon pepper, or to taste
4 dashes of Maggi extract
4–6 tablespoons flour
3 tablespoons vegetable shortening

Trim the meat of as many membranes as possible, especially if using stew veal. If you use a grinder, grind the veal with the medium blade. For the processor, cut the meat into 1-inch cubes, be particularly careful to trim off any bits of membrane or tendon, and process it with the steel blade in 1-second bursts. It should not be too finely chopped.

Melt the butter in the chicken broth, crumble the bread into it, add the eggs and the seasonings, and mix well with the ground veal. Taste for seasoning. Refrigerate the mixture for at least 1 hour. (*Note:* Up to this point, you can prepare ahead, even the night before, if you are planning a party.)

Form the cutlets into ovals about 3 inches by 2 inches across by ¾ inch thick. Roll them in flour, patting off the excess, and sauté them in the vegetable shortening over medium-high heat until they are lightly browned on all sides. Then lower the heat to finish them. Cut into one of them to test for doneness; you should see just a drop of very pale pink juice at the center. If they are not to be served immediately, you can cover the cutlets and keep them warm for 10 minutes.

## ℒamb

### ROAST LEG OF LAMB

*Serves 6–8*

Roast lamb has always been a great family favorite, so much so that it often appeared as the meat course for our Christmas Eve dinner when the children were young. I seldom order it in restaurants as they are a bit overprudent with garlic, and also because I like the meat fairly rare. Judging from the called-for interior temperature, 170°F (77°C), on meat thermometers in the U.S., the preference of the majority is for well-done lamb. If you are among these, may I urge you to try it "my" way? Delicate pink slices of lamb edged with a bit of crusty fat, with their own "jus," accompanied by a Polish-style Purée of Beets (p. 263) or white navy beans, are a veritable feast.

Shank half of 1 lamb leg (about 4 pounds or 1800 grams)
2 cloves garlic, slivered
Vegetable shortening or oil
Salt to taste
Pepper to taste
1 tablespoon flour (optional)
⅓ cup (¾ deciliter) heavy cream (optional)

Trim all but a thin layer of fat from the lamb leg and insert slivers of garlic in several places in the meat; to do this, make deep slits with the thinnest knife available and push the garlic slivers in with one finger. Rub the surface with shortening or oil and with salt and pepper all over. Preheat oven to 425°F (220°C). Let the lamb stand at room temperature while the oven heats, to absorb the perfume of the garlic. (It will not taste strongly of garlic, but the meat flavor will be much enhanced.)

Put the lamb leg in the middle of the oven in a roasting pan. After 10 minutes' roasting, the high temperature will brown and seal the meat; lower the oven heat to 350°F (180°C); continue roasting for about 50 minutes, basting the meat 2 or 3 times.

When the lamb is ready to remove, the interior temperature should be 125°F (52°C). Transfer the lamb to another pan or platter, and let it sit for 10–15 minutes in the *turned-off* oven, with the door open. The lamb's interior temperature will rise about 10°. Deglaze the roasting pan, adding a very small amount of water if necessary; remove as much fat as possible, using a fat-separating cup if you have one, or paper toweling to absorb it. Put the pan juices into a small saucepan. Carve the roast, preferably on a board or platter with hollows to collect the juices. Keep the slices warm and add the juices to the saucepan. Heat all the juices together for a moment, tasting for salt if you like. Pass the "jus" separately in a sauceboat.

If you prefer a slightly thickened sauce, after removing the juice stir about 1 tablespoon flour into the roasting pan, cook briefly, scraping up the dredgings, then gradually return meat juices plus about ½ cup water. Bring to the simmer and cook for a minute or so, stirring or whisking continuously, until the flour does not taste raw.

*Leftovers:* You will have some chunky rare bits clinging to the bone. They can be diced and warmed in Curry Sauce (p. 53) or ground for crêpe filling (p. 80) or for stuffing tomatoes or peppers.

# SHASHLIK

*Serves 6*

Shashlik—otherwise known as shish kebab, skewered lamb—is delicious with Kasha (p. 120) or couscous. Serve with it a crisp green salad. (And please cook the lamb rare.)

2 pounds (900 grams), after trimming, boneless lamb
  from the leg

THE MARINADE

2 medium onions, chopped
1 medium carrot, chopped
8 grinds pepper
1 bay leaf
½ cup (1 deciliter) water
3 tablespoons vinegar
1 teaspoon salt

THE SKEWERS

3 medium onions
8 strips bacon
24 large mushroom caps

Trim the meat of its fell (the outer membrane), if any, and of any surface fat. Cut the meat into 1½-inch cubes.

In a small pot, simmer, covered, the chopped onions and carrot, with pepper, bay leaf, water, vinegar, and salt, until the vegetables are soft but not mushy. Cool slightly. Place the lamb meat in a small bowl, so that the marinade will cover it, and pour the cooked marinade over it. Leave at room temperature for about 2–3 hours, turning the meat occasionally.

Assemble the skewers for baking, and choose a pan of the right size: deep enough so that none of the food touches the bottom. If you don't have the hairpin-shaped double skewers, use 2 skewers for each shashlik, so that the food cannot roll around on them.

For ease in skewering, slice the onions crosswise. Then, even if the skewer punches out the center, the slices will simply hang on it like curtain rings. (Vertically cut slices sometimes split and fall off.) Cut the bacon strips into twice as many squares, minus 1 for each skewer, as you have cubes of lamb. Assemble the shashliks: 1 mushroom cap (pierce it very gently to avoid splitting), 1 onion slice, 1 bacon square, 1 lamb cube, another bacon square, and repeat. If your first mushroom cap splits, as very crisp fresh ones sometimes do, stop. Bring the drained-off marinade to a boil and simmer the rest of the mushrooms for 2 minutes to make them more supple.

Preheat the oven to 450°F (230°C). Roasting works better than broiling for shashlik. All surfaces are equally exposed to the heat, making it unnecessary to turn the skewers often, and the meat is more quickly seared without being charred.

Arrange the shashliks so that the skewers rest on the edges of the baking pan. The cooking time will be about 15 minutes. After a few minutes, look to be sure that all the surfaces are browning evenly. If the skewers had to be crowded along the pan edges, you may have to turn them 90° to expose the inner sides to the heat. About halfway through, baste the shashliks with their juices, which have exuded into the baking pan. Do it with a siphon (bulb baster), or remove the skewers and roll them one at a time in the pan juices, then replace them and continue baking.

To serve, hold the skewers above the platter or plates, and push everything off with a long-tined cooking fork.

## LAMB CUTLETS
(Ground meat)

*Serves 6*

These I find even more delicious than hamburger, for they can be so much juicier. At cocktail parties they are very popular: in tiny meatball shapes, served on toothpicks, accompanied by a light mustard sauce.

2½ pounds (1125 grams) lamb, shoulder preferred
   (about 25 percent fat is just right)
3 eggs, beaten
2 medium cloves garlic, minced fine
Salt and pepper to taste
Flour for coating
2 tablespoons oil, or additional vegetable shortening

If you use a meat grinder, choose the fine blade to grind the meat; then mix the eggs, garlic, and salt and pepper in with the ground meat, and refrigerate the mixture for an hour before forming the cutlets. To prepare the lamb for grinding in the processor, cut it into ½-inch cubes. I would do the amount of meat for this recipe in 2 batches, as that makes it easier to get an even texture. Use the steel blade and process the meat in 1-second bursts. When the texture is as you like it (for me, quite fine), process the full amount of meat with the eggs, garlic, and salt and pepper: just long enough to blend the mixture well. Refrigerate it.

Form the meat into round patties, about ¾ inch thick and about 3 inches across. Dredge them in a little flour on both sides, shaking off excess. In a nonstick pan if possible, melt the oil or shortening, sauté the cutlets over high heat to brown them well and medium-high heat to finish. (For well-done meat, make the cutlets thinner, and use medium heat.) Let the cutlets sit, covered, for 5 minutes before serving. I consider them perfect when they are evenly pink inside and spurt a little juice when you cut into them.

## NAVARIN OF LAMB

*Serves 6*

When I make this classic French stew, I am aiming at a delicately flavored, light-colored sauce, with each of the vegetables cooked just until done and their individual flavors quite distinct. (The old-style Navarin usually had all the vegetables I use, with tomatoes, garlic, and string beans in addition: everything was cooked with the meat.) To get the vegetables just right, it is necessary to adjust their size to their density, and I always taste the carrots especially before trimming them. If they seem old and dry, I cut them smaller.

If you are in a hurry, you can make this dish beautifully in a pressure cooker.

3 pounds (1350 grams) lamb (shoulder preferred)
4 medium purple-topped turnips
4 medium carrots
2 medium baking potatoes
24–30 (depending on size) pearl onions, or use
    small "silverskins"
3 tablespoons oil or vegetable shortening
3 tablespoons flour
2 teaspoons Herbes de Provence
1 teaspoon salt, or more to taste
2 tablespoons butter
One 10-ounce (285-gram) package frozen peas, thawed
    in the box; or ½ pound (225 grams) very young
    fresh shelled peas (never use canned peas)

Cut the meat into sizable chunks, about 1 by 1 by 2 inches. Peel the turnips and cut in 1-inch dice. Peel the carrots, split them lengthwise, and cut them into 1½-inch lengths. Cut the peeled potatoes into ½-inch dice. Peel the onions by plunging them in boiling water for 1 minute, then slip off the skins; with scissors, cut off the little tails on the stem ends.

Brown the meat on all sides, over medium-high heat, in the oil or shortening. Sprinkle it with the flour, mixing well. Add water just to cover, about 2 cups. Cover the pot and cook slowly until the meat is tender, about 40 minutes for lamb shoulder, less if you used meat from the leg.

Now add the Herbes de Provence, taste the sauce, and add 1 teaspoon salt; add the cut turnips, carrots, and potatoes. In a separate, small, covered pot, stew the onions in the butter. The stew and the onions should be done in about 15 minutes. Meanwhile, boil the thawed or fresh peas until just done, and drain them: about a minute for the thawed peas, 5 minutes or more for fresh ones. Combine the onions and peas with the stew, taste it, and add salt if necessary.

*For the pressure cooker:* Trim the meat and the vegetables as above. Brown the meat in 3 tablespoons oil or shortening in the open pot, add 2 cups water, cover, and cook for 12 minutes after pressure is reached. During this time, the onions should be stewing in their separate pot. Cool and uncover the pressure cooker. Add the Herbes de Provence, salt to taste, and the cut turnips, carrots, and potatoes. Cook the peas in a separate pot, while you cover the pressure cooker and cook for 3 minutes after pressure is reached. Cool and uncover the pressure cooker. To thicken the sauce a little, blend ½ cup of the liquid with 1 tablespoon (or more) flour, and stir the mixture until it is smooth; then return it to the pot and simmer the stew until the sauce has thickened and the flour no longer tastes raw. Add the onions and the peas. Correct the seasoning.

# *Pork*

## ROAST PORK LOIN WITH BAKED APPLES (OR APPLESAUCE)

*Serves 6*

Pork must be very well done, to an internal temperature of 175°F (79°C), and cooked slowly to preserve its tenderness. With the pork, apple and onion flavors are the best—a way to roast pork with onions is suggested in Roast Pork Shoulder (following recipe).

Properly trimmed pork should have about ¼ inch of fat to keep it moist during its long cooking. Serve with mashed potatoes.

THE PORK

    1 pork loin center rib roast of 6 ribs, about 5 pounds
       (2¼ kilograms)
    2 tablespoons salt
    6 grinds black pepper
    ½ teaspoon fragrant dried thyme
    2 large onions, quartered

This cut of pork allows 1 chop per person and does not include the tenderloin. Ask the butcher to crack the chine (spine) between each rib and have him trim off the surface fat to leave a layer less than ¼ inch thick.

Mix the salt, pepper, and thyme, and rub them well into the top of the roast.

THE APPLES

    2 tablespoons butter
    6 tart apples (Rome Beauties are ideal)
    6 teaspoons sugar

Choose a pan in which the apples will fit closely and butter it heavily. Core the apples, set them in the pan, and fill the holes with sugar. Pour ½ cup water into the pan.

Preheat the oven to 300°F (150°C). Set the meat in a baking pan. You need no rack, since the ends of the ribs and the chine bone form a support. Place the apple pan in the same oven. Roast the pork for about 2 hours; low heat preserves the tenderness of pork. Remove the apples from the oven, as they should be done, raise the oven temperature to 350°F (180°C), and roast the pork for another 30 minutes. Halfway through the cooking, put the quartered onions around the meat, and baste them with the pan juices. When the interior temperature of the pork reaches 175°F (80°C), turn off the oven and let the roast sit for 15 minutes. The interior temperature will be 180°F (82°C) and the meat will be cream-colored with a dense but tender texture. To carve, simply divide the roast with 5 cuts, aimed straight down through the cracks in the chine, and serve with the onions.

Jelly will have formed on the bottom of the apple pan. Serve the apples with the pork either as they are, with a little jelly on top of each, or make applesauce by processing them, jelly, skins, and all. (This happens to be my favorite way of making applesauce in any case.)

## ROAST PORK SHOULDER

*Serves 6*

Often when preparing Pâté Barbarka (p. 217), I used to pause halfway along to smell the wonderful fragrance of this rich cut of pork combined with roast onions, and finally it occurred to me to stop right there and serve up the pork. What a good idea! Because this cut has more fat than the loin, you may think it less elegant. But the flavor and scent are incomparable, and if you choose a piece of meat without bone, it will be easy to carve.

3 pounds (1350 grams) boned or boneless pork shoulder
2 tablespoons salt
8 grinds black pepper
1 teaspoon crushed juniper berries (optional)
4 onions, quartered

Preheat the oven to 300°F (150°C). Immerse the pork shoulder in boiling water for 1 minute to seal the juices, and remove it immediately. Season the roast with salt and pepper, and the optional crushed juniper berries, if you like.

Roast the meat in the oven for 1½ hours, then put the onions around the meat. Roast for another hour, then raise the oven temperature to 350°F (180°C). Roast 30 minutes longer, or until the interior temperature is 175°F (79°C).

When the meat is done, remove it from the oven and let it sit for 15 minutes, or until the interior temperature has risen to 180°F (82°C). The roast meat may be sliced either with or against the grain. Serve it surrounded with the browned onions.

## HAM STEAKS

*Serves 6*

When we first came to America to live, in 1939, Arthur and I were delighted with the mildly cured, nicely trimmed ham to be found at any butcher's. From Kate, who was with us almost twenty years, I learned several new ways of cooking ham, and served it often.

Nowadays it is hard to find the tasty, close-textured ham I remember. Nevertheless, the packaged ½-inch-thick ham steaks in the supermarkets are too convenient to be overlooked. Their bland flavor and slightly too moist texture just need enlivening. Sometimes I heat them in an Onion or a Horseradish Sauce (pp. 58 and 60). More often, my choice is something sweet-and-sour: a Mustard Sauce (p. 51) with a little sugar, or Caramel Sauce with Raisins and Almonds (p. 62). Or I borrow from Kate's way with pineapple, and serve the following dish with mashed potatoes.

One small, ripe, fragrant fresh pineapple
4 tablespoons butter
3 tablespoons light brown sugar
1½ tablespoons cornstarch
2 pounds (900 grams) precooked packaged ham steaks
½ Knorr beef bouillon cube (optional)
Vinegar to taste (optional)

Trim the fresh pineapple, saving the juice that trickles out, and cut it in small wedges. Sauté these in the butter until they are lightly browned. In a small, heavy pan, melt the sugar, stirring constantly, until it is lightly caramelized; let it cool 2 minutes, then pour in 1 tablespoon hot water and mix well. (For full details on caramelized sugar, see page 66.) Strain the reserved pineapple juice and mix into it the cornstarch, whisking it carefully, and straining it if there are any lumps. Add it to the caramel.

Heat this mixture, stirring constantly, until it is thickened and glossy. If it is too thick, add a little water. In the pan in which you sautéed the pineapple, heat the ham. Deglaze the pan with a little hot water, and stir in the caramel/pineapple juice mixture. Taste it: if it seems too sweet, add ½ bouillon cube and a few drops of vinegar, tasting until the balance of flavors pleases you. Add the sautéed pineapple wedges and serve.

## ANIELA'S PORK FILLET MEDALLIONS

*Serves 6*

This is a nice dish for parties, because it is if anything improved by a wait in a warming oven (or at about 140°F/60°C); all the delicious flavors merge harmoniously. But don't let the word "medallions" make you think of this as a last-minute dish, like chicken medallions. Pork has to be slowly cooked, and I would allow a good 30 minutes for sautéing the thick slices of meat, then the mushrooms, and then for letting them sit together a little while.

2 pounds (900 grams) pork tenderloin
2 tablespoons butter
½ pound (225 grams) mushrooms, sliced thin
½ teaspoon salt
3 grinds white pepper
½ cup (1 deciliter) medium-dry sherry
   (for instance, Amontillado)
½ cup (1 deciliter) heavy cream

Cut the meat crosswise into slices 1 inch thick. Lay them between sheets of waxed paper and pound them with a mallet, not too hard, until they have spread out and are an even ½ inch thick. Pat them dry and sauté them very slowly in the butter, on both sides.

Remove the meat and keep it warm, covered, while you fry the sliced mushrooms in the same butter. Season the mushrooms with salt and pepper and combine them with the pork slices. Deglaze the pan with the sherry, over medium-high heat, mix in the cream, and pour this sauce over the pork and mushrooms. Taste it now, since the mushrooms will have lent it their salt and it may not need more. If you plan to keep the dish warm for much time, taste it again before serving, as there may have been some evaporation. If it has become too salty, stir in a little more cream.

# Offal

## CALVES' LIVER VENEZIANA

*Serves 6*

Unless you have a butcher who will remove the toughest membranes and veins from sliced liver, prepare liver this way and you make the chore easier. Cutting the liver into thin strips makes it quite easy to snip out anything unwelcome.

3 medium onions, sliced thin
3 tablespoons olive oil
1½ pounds (675 grams) calves' liver, in strips
   3 by ½ by ½ inch and trimmed of veins
About 4 tablespoons flour for coating
3 tablespoons butter
½ cup (1 deciliter) or more water
½ cup (1 deciliter) heavy cream
3 tablespoons dry sherry
5–7 dashes of Maggi extract
Salt and pepper to taste

Sauté the sliced onions in the olive oil, stirring often and covering the pan occasionally, until they are soft and lightly browned. If possible use a nonstick pan. Coat the liver strips with flour, shaking off the excess. Add the butter to the onion pan, add the liver, and stir well as you cook it over medium-high heat for about 2 minutes, tasting the meat for doneness. The liver should still be very rare. Add the water, stirring, then the cream, sherry, and Maggi extract. If the sauce seems too thick, add a little more water. By the time all is heated through, the liver strips will be a nice bright pink in the center. Taste the sauce, correct the seasoning, and serve immediately.

## CALVES' BRAINS EN COQUILLE

*Serves 6*

Baked and served in real scallop shells (hence its name), this makes an attractive and unusual first course or a light entrée. (Of course you can do it in a small gratin dish too.) This is similar to the mixture I use for stuffed and sautéed pancakes (p. 81), but richer, moister, and more highly seasoned.

2 pounds (900 grams) calves' brains (or 3 pairs)
4 bay leaves
10 peppercorns
2 tablespoons lemon juice or vinegar
6 tablespoons finely chopped onions or shallots
1 tablespoon butter
2 egg yolks, beaten
1 cup (¼ liter) sour cream
Salt and pepper to taste
½ cup (1 deciliter) freshly grated Parmesan
   or Swiss cheese

Soak the brains in cold water for 30 minutes, then place under cold running water then remove the outer membrane and/or any traces of blood. Poach the brains in salted water to cover with the bay leaves, peppercorns, and lemon juice or vinegar for 5 minutes. Drain the brains and keep them warm.

Preheat the oven to 350°F (180°C). Sauté the chopped onions or shallots in the butter and mix them well with the beaten egg yolks, sour cream, and salt and pepper; add this mixture to the warm brains and stir it in without mashing the brains or breaking them up too much. Turn the mixture into scallop shells or a gratin dish, not more than three-quarters full, since cooking will expand the mixture a little. Sprinkle the top with the grated cheese and set the shells or the dish in the oven for 5 minutes, then briefly under the broiler to brown lightly.

# VEAL KIDNEYS

*Serves 4–6*

Kidneys must be cooked at the last moment, but they are very quickly done, and the trimming, soaking, and cutting up can be all done ahead of time.

2 mature veal kidneys, about 1¼–1½ pounds
  (560–675 grams) in all
3 tablespoons vinegar
1 tablespoon plus 1 teaspoon salt
½ cup (70 grams) flour
4 grinds pepper
1 tablespoon oil
2 tablespoons butter
½ teaspoon Herbes de Provence
1 teaspoon marjoram
1 teaspoon Worcestershire Sauce or A-1 Steak Sauce
¾–1 cup (1¾ deciliters–¼ liter) Basic Beef Broth
  (p. 5), or use ½ Knorr beef bouillon cube
  dissolved in ¾–1 cup water
1 ounce (2 tablespoons) brandy

Trim the kidneys carefully of their central core of fat. You may find it easier to slice the kidneys (crosswise, ¼ inch thick) and then trim the slices of as much fat as possible. Soak the kidney slices for 30 minutes in a large bowl of cold water with the vinegar and 1 tablespoon of the salt.

Drain the kidneys well and pat them dry carefully. Mix the flour in a bag with the remaining teaspoon of salt and the pepper, shake the kidneys in it so that they are well coated, and shake off the excess flour.

Heat a large skillet. First put in the oil and, when this is hot, add the butter. It must not be heated to smoking point. If it gets too hot, pour it out and start again. Sauté the kidney slices for 1 minute on each side, then add the Herbes de Provence, the marjoram, and the Worcestershire or A-1 sauce. Add ¾ cup broth, mixing well, and stir the sauce until it thickens.

If it gets too thick, add ¼ cup more broth. Warm the brandy, add it to the sauce, ignite it, and serve the kidneys immediately, flaming.

## FRESH BEEF TONGUE

*Serves 8*

Fresh beef tongue has a very special delicate flavor, far superior to that of smoked or pickled tongue. Cooking it creates a wonderful broth that can be used as a base for other soups, and can provide the stock for an Onion Sauce (p. 58) or a Caramel Sauce with Raisins and Almonds (p. 62), either of which makes a delicious accompaniment along with mashed potatoes.

1 whole fresh beef tongue, about 3–4 pounds
   (1350–1800 grams)
2 teaspoons salt
2 leeks, including some of the green part
2 carrots
1 parsnip
3 stalks celery
3 onions
3 bay leaves
5 sprigs parsley
10 peppercorns
1 Knorr beef bouillon cube (optional)

Boil the tongue in water to cover (at least 3 quarts) with the salt for 1½ hours. Cut the leeks lengthwise, rinse, and cut crosswise into 2–3 pieces. Cut the carrots, parsnip, and celery into pieces and halve the onions for the pot. Remove the tongue from the pot, peel and trim it, and return it to the pot. Add the leek, carrot, parsnip, celery, onion, bay leaves, parsley, and peppercorns, and boil for 1½ hours longer; this way the peeled tongue will absorb the aromatic flavors of the broth. Discard the vegetables. Taste the broth, adding a beef bouillon cube if necessary. Use the broth to make the Onion Sauce or Caramel Sauce with Raisins and Almonds.

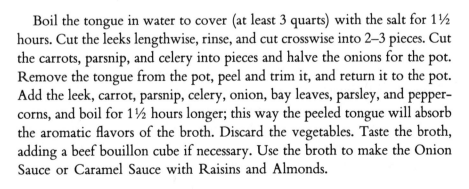

*For the pressure cooker:* Cook the tongue for 1 hour after pressure is reached, in enough water to cover it, with the salt. Remove the tongue, peel and trim it, and return it to the pot. Add the leek, carrot, parsnip, celery, onion, bay leaves, parsley, and peppercorns, and cook for 15 minutes after pressure is reached. Correct seasoning.

## TRIPES À LA VARSOVIENNE

*Serves 6*

This is one of my favorite dishes for really good eaters: richly seasoned, gelatinous, and cooked until the tripe is only slightly chewy (I like it quite soft). I find that most tripe bought in supermarkets in America has been precooked and requires only about 1½ hours' cooking. However, if you buy it directly from a butcher, be sure to ask whether it has been precooked; if it has not, the cooking time may be three times as long. I'd call this a ragout—wetter than a stew, more solid than most soups—and accordingly,

I serve it in soup plates. Marrow and Matzo Dumplings (p. 96) are a traditional Polish accompaniment, but one can substitute boiled waxy potatoes. In France, they add more garlic and a calf's foot, and in Spain a sliced chorizo sausage as well.

One hears often that tripe must be cooked slowly, but I do this dish in the pressure cooker with complete success. The method for an ordinary casserole is at the end of the recipe.

This is a good dish for parties, since you can hold it on a warmer for a long time without doing it any harm at all. It also freezes perfectly, so I often make double quantities. The servings may seem large to you, in comparison to what is allotted in my other recipes, but they are based on long experience. People love this dish, and they eat a lot of it.

4 pounds (1800 grams) fresh honeycomb tripe
Baking soda
2 medium carrots, cut in julienne to make 1 cup
1 large onion, sliced thin
1 small celery heart, with a few leaves, cut in
    julienne to make 1 cup
4 small cloves garlic, minced (optional)
1½ cups (3½ deciliters) unsalted beef broth*
4 teaspoons fragrant dried leaf marjoram
1 teaspoon thyme
1 teaspoon cracked black pepper
3 tablespoons chopped parsley
Grated nutmeg
3 tablespoons flour
3 tablespoons butter
Salt to taste

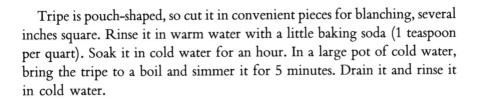

Tripe is pouch-shaped, so cut it in convenient pieces for blanching, several inches square. Rinse it in warm water with a little baking soda (1 teaspoon per quart). Soak it in cold water for an hour. In a large pot of cold water, bring the tripe to a boil and simmer it for 5 minutes. Drain it and rinse it in cold water.

*If you don't have unsalted beef broth, use 1–2 Knorr beef bouillon cubes, but don't add them until after the tripe has cooked.

Cut the blanched tripe into fine strips
2 by ½ inch. In the open pressure
cooker, put the tripe, carrots, onion,
celery, optional garlic, and the cold
broth or water (if you will be using
bouillon cubes). Bring it to pressure
over moderate heat, which may take
15 minutes, and cook it for 15 minutes
after pressure is reached. Cool and un-
cover the cooker, and taste the tripe. It should not be actually chewy, yet
it should have a little bite to it. Add the marjoram, thyme, pepper, parsley,
nutmeg, and bouillon cubes to taste, if you are using them, and cover the
cooker but do not weight it. Cook the tripe over low-medium heat for 15
minutes more. Measure the soup liquid if you had to add broth; if not, you
should have about 2½ cups. For this amount, cook 3 tablespoons flour in
3 tablespoons butter until thickened and smooth, add a little soup liquid,
stirring to keep it smooth, and return it to the pot. Salt to taste. Cook a
little longer, until the broth is lightly thickened.

*For an ordinary casserole:* Follow the recipe exactly as given, but simmer the
tripe for 1¾ hours, then add the marjoram, thyme, pepper, parsley, and
nutmeg, and simmer for 15 minutes more.

## CABBAGE ROLLS

*Makes 18 rolls*

Cabbage rolls done this way are not only good, but also extremely practical
for several reasons—they can be made ahead, in large quantities, for parties;
once cooked, they can be frozen, and, refrigerated, they keep for days, even
improving from being reheated. Accompanied by potatoes or Kasha (p. 120),
they make a complete meal.

An important step in the recipe is first to sauté the cabbage-wrapped parcels in order to brown them; this adds flavor as well as color.

1 pound (450 grams) ground beef
1 pound (450 grams) ground pork shoulder
1 cup (¼ liter) cooked Rice (p. 122)
1 teaspoon dried leaf marjoram
1 teaspoon Italian seasoning or Herbes de Provence
1 teaspoon salt
Several grinds pepper
1 medium-to-large head cabbage, winter or white
3 tablespoons oil or vegetable shortening
12 ounces (340 grams) fresh mushrooms, caps only,
   sliced (optional)
Maggi extract (optional)
1½ cups (3½ deciliters) strong Basic Beef Broth
   (p. 5), or use 1 Knorr beef bouillon cube
   dissolved in 1½ cups water
½ cup (1 deciliter) sour cream
4 teaspoons flour

Mix the ground meat with the rice, marjoram, Italian seasoning, salt, and pepper, and set the mixture aside.

In a large pot of boiling water, immerse the cabbage head until the outer leaves are barely tender (5 minutes). Remove these outer leaves, and repeat, until 18 leaves have been removed.

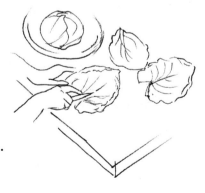

Cut out the thick center vein running partway up each leaf. The remaining cabbage leaves should be roughly chopped, blanched, drained, and reserved.

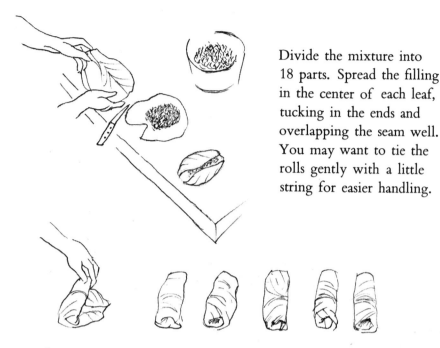

Divide the mixture into 18 parts. Spread the filling in the center of each leaf, tucking in the ends and overlapping the seam well. You may want to tie the rolls gently with a little string for easier handling.

In a frying pan, brown the rolls on all sides in the oil or shortening. Make a bed of the reserved chopped cabbage leaves in a Dutch oven or heavy casserole, the widest and shallowest you have, then put a layer of rolls, then more cabbage until all the rolls and cabbage are used up, finishing with cabbage and optional mushrooms. Sprinkle a little Maggi extract on top, if you like.

Pour the beef broth over rolls, adding more if the liquid does not reach halfway up the rolls. Cover the pot tightly and cook over a medium flame for about 1 hour, or until the cabbage is soft. Occasionally spoon the liquid over the rolls, making sure it does not evaporate; add a little more if necessary.

Pour or draw off ½ cup of the liquid in the pot, mix it with the sour cream and flour, blending well, and heat it slowly, stirring, in a small saucepan until thickened. Pour this over the cabbage rolls, shaking the pot or dish gently to blend in the thickened liquid with the pot juices, and return the pot or dish to the stove for a few minutes.

*For the pressure cooker:* Mix the meat, rice, and seasonings. Blanch the cabbage in the open pot. Sauté the rolls in a skillet. Layer rolls and cabbage as above. Pour over them only 1 cup strong broth. (In spite of the preliminary sautéing, pressure cooking extracts more juice from the cabbage than regular cooking would.) Cook for 15 minutes after pressure is reached, then cool and uncover the pot, drain off some of the cooking liquid, and thicken it as above.

# Mixed Meats

## PÂTÉ BARBARKA

*Makes 1 loaf 9 by 5 by 3 inches*

Since this very old recipe, from my mother's cook Barbarka, was published in the *New York Times* twenty years ago, I have seen it crop up in lots of places—most recently, an excellent cookbook published to benefit a children's school. But one error persists in these versions: the use of salt pork to line the roasting pan. Please use *fat* bacon—not lean.

The pâté is dark brown and very densely textured, making it good for small open-faced sandwiches. Unlike most French pâtés, the meats are first cooked separately so each is done just the right amount of time before they are combined and baked, and though lightly seasoned, the pâté has a hearty taste. It keeps for at least a week in the refrigerator, but like most pâtés is better not frozen. (You can freeze it, but its characteristically fresh flavor gets somewhat lost.)

¼ pound (115 grams) fresh pork fat,
  in small pieces (it need not be sliced),
  or lard or vegetable shortening
1½ pounds (675 grams) fresh pork shoulder
4 medium onions, quartered
1 pound (450 grams) fresh pork liver*
2 eggs
1 teaspoon marjoram
½ teaspoon nutmeg
½ teaspoon allspice
1 tablespoon Maggi extract
Salt and pepper to taste
½ pound (225 grams) sliced fat bacon

Preheat the oven to 300°F (150°C). Distribute the fresh pork fat or lard or shortening in an open roasting pan, add the pork shoulder, and roast for about 1 hour. At this point, strew the quartered onions around the pork, then continue roasting until it is well done, about another hour. The interior temperature should be 170°F (77°C). Remove the pork. Do not drain the roasting pan.

Cut the pork liver into several pieces. Raise the oven temperature to 350°F (180°C) and roast the liver with the onions for 15–20 minutes. Lower the oven temperature again to 300°F (150°C).

If there are any burned edges or other burned spots on the pork shoulder or liver, trim them off. Remove the pork bones and cut the shoulder meat into 1-inch dice. Cut the liver into strips and trim out any tubes. For the grinding, you can use the processor, which produces a fluffier texture than I quite like, or an old-fashioned meat grinder, which does it perfectly. Grind the meats together through the small-holed disk with the onions and pan juices and mix them together. Or else process the onions and pan juices with the meats (it will have to be done in 2 batches). Add the eggs, marjoram,

*Do *not* substitute calves' or beef liver.

nutmeg, allspice, and Maggi extract, mix thoroughly, and taste. Add salt and pepper to taste.

The pâté can be baked in a bread pan 9 by 5 by 3 inches or in 2 small pans. Line your pan or pans with the bacon, allowing 2–3 inches overhang, fill with the pâté mixture, smooth the top, and fold the bacon over. Bake for about 30 minutes. The internal temperature of the pâté should be about 155°F (68°C). Cool and chill it in the baking pan or pans.

## MEAT LOAF

*Serves 6–8*

This fine-grained meat loaf slices well and makes good sandwiches if you have leftovers. I particularly like in it the fresh—yet not too "green"— flavor of marjoram, one of my favorite herbs. The meat loaf is nice accompanied with a sauce (perhaps Dill, p. 49; Mushroom, p. 51; or Onion, p. 58).

2 slices bread
½ cup (1 deciliter) Basic Beef Broth (p. 5)
1 pound (450 grams) ground round beef,
   or hamburger
1 pound (450 grams) ground pork shoulder
2 eggs
1 medium onion, minced
1 tablespoon finely cut fresh dill
½ teaspoon Italian seasoning
1 teaspoon fragrant dried marjoram
6 grinds black pepper
1 teaspoon salt, or to taste
Maggi extract (optional)
2 hard-boiled eggs, peeled
2 tablespoons flour
2 tablespoons butter

Crumble the bread into the beef broth and let it soak while you mix the meats, eggs, onion, dill, Italian seasoning, marjoram, pepper, salt, and Maggi extract, if you like. Preheat the oven to 375°F (190°C). Lightly butter a large roasting pan. Now with floured hands shape the meat into a free-form loaf and place in the center of the roasting pan. Make a trench down the center and embed the hard-boiled eggs end to end lengthwise. Close the meat over the eggs, sprinkle the loaf with flour, and dot it with a little butter. Bake for about 45 minutes.

## Bigos

Traditional in Poland for centuries, *bigos* is a fragrant stew of fresh meat, smoked bacon and sausage, sauerkraut, onions, apples, herbs, spices, and juniper berries. Of all the dishes in this book, *bigos* is the one I commend to you most enthusiastically.

Although I don't get sentimental about food, *bigos* is a friend and standby to cook and hostess, and I have counted on it on many occasions. People always seem to love this delicious dish, and it is easy to make, even in enormous quantities (just allow time for all the chopping and slicing). The dish can be kept hot for hours; it can be reheated; it can be refrigerated for days; it can be frozen; pressure cooking does it fast and well; and the ingredients are usually easy to find.

*Bigos* began as a hunters' stew. The forests of Poland have always teemed with game, and hunters, setting out on week-long winter expeditions, would bring with them the sauerkraut, smoked meats, and spices to heat over log fires after a day's stalking, when they would find fresh meat for the pot: rabbit, hare, venison, boar, and feathered game like grouse and pheasant. With them they had potatoes to roast in the embers and plenty of vodka to wash the whole thing down—and I still serve vodka and potatoes with *bigos*. But by the time I "inherited" this dish, it was no longer a primitive thing. Generations of good cooks at Ilgovo, my mother's family place on the Niemen, had refined it to create a subtle basic recipe, which of course varied a little with the seasons.

It is typical of the cooking I first knew, for it speaks so plainly of its origins. Except for the salt and spices, which were brought by the weekly

peddler, all the ingredients came from home. In those days of no refrigeration, the arts of preserving food were much prized. From the cool, half-underground larder, where dried mushrooms hung on strings above shelves of ranked crocks and barrels, came the tomatoes (dried or cooked down in their summer prime for use in winter), the sauerkraut that was brined in early fall, and smoked sausage and lean bacon from the pigs killed after the first frost. Apples could be taken all through the winter from the special fruit cellar where they lay in straw, on shelves built with slats so that air could circulate. As for the fresh meat, one of my earliest memories is of my slim, straight grandmother in our big kitchen, demonstrating to Chef Antony how to cut up a carcass: which cuts to hang before cooking, which to smoke, which to be rendered, which to be ground for sausages and pâtés.

In 1932 I cooked a *bigos* for our first party in Paris in our little place in Montmartre, and it was such a success among Arthur's sophisticated friends that it became my *plat de résistance.* For our first Hollywood party in 1941 we invited the whole Ballets Russes as well as the movie stars, and of course we had *bigos.* Then, naturally, it was our first choice to serve to compatriots; *bigos* was my contribution to the dinner at the first *Bal Polonais* given in New York after the war—a charity party to raise money for Polish refugees, so we kept down expenses by doing all the cooking ourselves. (Later I taught *bigos* to professional chefs when the ball outgrew private quarters and moved to a hotel.) I cooked *bigos,* too, at a party for the Warsaw Philharmonic, which my father had founded and directed, when the orchestra came to New York. Once, for a midnight supper in honor of Stravinsky, I cooked *bigos* in Venice, though in that city sauerkraut was hard to find. And I remember cooking it for a wartime party that Ouida and Basil Rathbone gave for a great crowd of American servicemen who happened to be stationed near Los Angeles: none of them had ever tasted it before, but they gobbled it up and all demanded second helpings. So perhaps you will agree with me that this very Polish dish deserves to become international.

Not only can you serve it anywhere, to anyone, but you can cook it anywhere. A knife, a big pot, a wooden spoon, heat of some kind, and there you are. Just lately when the play *Children of a Lesser God,* which my son John starred in, had such a success on Broadway, I was staying in a small hotel apartment with a two-burner kitchenette, but I wanted to give the cast and crew a party. My photographer daughter Eva lent her loft in Chelsea and I shopped for forty-five guests, cooked up *bigos* in that little closet kitchen, and carried the whole feast down to Eva's studio in plastic pails. It was a lovely party.

On that particular night, all the guests were good friends, happy about working together, happy to celebrate. And of course good feeling counts as much as good food—but they come together in the word "hospitality." And to express this, I know nothing better than a big pot of savory *bigos.*

Once the meat is roasted and the cèpes have been soaked, which can be done the night before, this recipe takes only 30 minutes of actual cooking in the pressure cooker. In an ordinary pot, it takes about 45 minutes. Either way, one can do what little cutting and trimming are needed during the 2½ hours' preparatory time of cooking and cooling the meat.

Serve with boiled potatoes or rye bread. Good drinks with *bigos* are iced vodka, beer, or red wine.

# BIGOS

*Serves 10 as a main course, 15 as a first course*

4 ounces (115 grams) dried cèpes
3 cups (¾ liter) strong Basic Beef Broth (p. 5),
   or use 2 Knorr beef bouillon cubes dissolved
   in 3 cups water
2 pounds (900 grams) fresh pork shoulder
   (or beef, or venison)*
Salt and pepper
3 tablespoons solid vegetable shortening
4 pounds (1800 grams) sauerkraut, canned or fresh
1 pound (450 grams) slab bacon, smoked or salted
4 apples
2 pounds (900 grams) canned whole peeled tomatoes,
   drained
12 crushed juniper berries, or 1 tablespoon caraway seeds
12 peppercorns
2 bay leaves
4 medium onions
1 pound (450 grams) Polish sausage, precooked or not
½ pound (225 grams) cooked ham (in a chunk)
2 tablespoons sugar (optional)
½ cup (1 deciliter) dry wine, red or white (optional)
1 Knorr beef bouillon cube (optional)

Preheat the oven to 300°F (150°C). While the oven is heating, put the cèpes to soak in the beef broth. Season the pork shoulder with salt and pepper and spread the shortening all over it. Add ½ cup (1 deciliter) water to the roasting pan and set the meat in the oven. During the first hour of its roasting, you need not baste pork or beef. But if you use venison, which can be very lean, baste it twice with melted butter.

*You may also use leftover roast lamb, beef, or venison.

During this first hour's roasting time, you can do the following:

- Rinse the sauerkraut in cold water until it no longer tastes too sour. Drain it well, pressing down, and reserve it.
- Dice the slab bacon and cook it until it is slightly brown.
- Peel, core, and grate the apples.
- After they have soaked an hour, drain the cèpes, reserving their broth, and slice them thinly.
- With the above ingredients, prepare the first-stage casserole. In a heavy, covered casserole, layer the diced browned bacon, the rinsed sauerkraut, the soaked sliced cèpes, the tomatoes, and the grated apples, interspersing them with the juniper berries or caraway seeds, the peppercorns, and the bay leaves. Cover the casserole and simmer it over low heat for 1½ hours.

When the fresh meat has roasted for an hour, quarter the onions and strew them around the meat, then sprinkle with salt. If the pan has become dry, add a little water. Raise the oven heat to 350°F (180°C) and cook the meat an hour longer, or until tender.

While the casserole continues to simmer and the meat to roast, skin the Polish sausage, if necessary, and dice it. If it is not the precooked kind, sauté it slowly until it is half done, about 10 minutes. Reserve it.

Dice the cooked ham and reserve it.

At this stage sugar is caramelized by melting it in a small, heavy pan over medium-high heat until it begins to color, to add richness; this step is optional. (For full details about caramel, see page 66.) Let it cool off heat for 2 minutes, then combine it with the reserved broth from the cèpes.

When the roast meat is done, set it aside to cool, then dice it.

When the casserole has simmered for 1½ hours, remove it from the heat and add to it the caramel-broth mixture. When the roast meat is ready and diced, add it to the casserole. Add also the diced precooked or half-cooked sausage, the diced cooked ham, and the wine, if you like. Mix all these ingredients well with the contents of the casserole, then simmer it for 30 minutes over low heat, being careful that the *bigos* does not burn. Taste it carefully: it may need a bouillon cube dissolved in it; it may need salt.

*For the pressure cooker:* Begin as above by soaking the cèpes (but use only 1 cup broth) and roasting the pork. After the pork has been roasted 1 hour and strewn with onions, and the oven heat raised, start dicing the bacon, and then lightly brown it in the open pressure cooker. Rinse the sauerkraut and skin and dice the Polish sausage; if necessary, cook the sausage 10 minutes or until half done.

Before the pork is done, slice the cèpes (reserving their broth), and arrange the "first-stage casserole" in the pressure cooker. Combine the bacon, sauerkraut, tomatoes, cèpes, juniper (or caraway), and apples with the peppercorns and bay leaves. Cook for 12 minutes after pressure is reached; then cool the pot under running water and open it.

When the roast pork is cooked and diced, do the second stage of cooking in the pot. Caramelize the sugar and add to it the reserved cèpes broth. Combine the caramel-broth mixture with the ingredients already in the pressure cooker, and add, mixing well, the diced meats: sausage, ham, and pork. Taste: you may wish to add a bouillon cube. Add the optional wine. Cook the assembled dish in the open pot for about 10 minutes, until all the flavors have blended. Taste, season if necessary, and serve.

*Note:* As mentioned earlier, *bigos* may be kept warm for hours, may be refrigerated and reheated, and may be frozen.

# Chicken

## CHICKEN WITH PRUNES

*Serves 6*

To make this easy, fragrant dish, you just put together three simple things
—chicken, prunes, and butter—and let them improve each other. The juices
in the roasting pan reduce, blend, and thicken into the consistency of a light
syrup, which beautifully flavors the bird as you baste it.

1 roasting chicken, about 4 pounds (1800 grams)
Salt and pepper to taste
8 tablespoons butter
1 tablespoon oil
1 cup (¼ liter) Chicken Broth (p. 8), or use
   ½ Knorr chicken bouillon cube dissolved
   in 1 cup water; plus enough additional
   broth to cover prunes and raisins
24 dried prunes
½ cup (1 deciliter) raisins
Rice (p. 122)

Wash and dry the chicken, and salt and pepper it inside and out. Put a 2-tablespoon lump of butter in the cavity and truss the bird. Place it in a low-sided roasting pan greased with the oil. Add the cup of chicken broth to the roasting pan.

Preheat the oven to 350°F (180°C). Into a medium bowl pour enough boiling chicken broth to cover over the prunes and raisins and let them soak. Roast the chicken for about 45 minutes or until half done, basting it often by rubbing it with the remaining 6 tablespoons of butter, and later spooning pan juices over it. Turn the chicken when basting it, so that it will color evenly.

When the chicken is half done, add the soaked prunes and raisins to the pan with their soaking liquid, basting the bird well and often then and thereafter. When the chicken is done, in about 1½ hours, the pan juices should have the consistency of a light syrup. If they don't, siphon off the juices and boil them down rapidly.

Carve the chicken and serve it over plain boiled rice surrounded by the prunes and raisins, with the pan juice poured over.

## ROAST CORNISH HENS POLONAISE

*Serves 3–6*

In Poland in the spring, we used to have little chickens, about a pound each (like a Cornish hen), which we stuffed with buttery bread crumbs and fresh dill. To do this in Paris I use the *"coquelets"* or even the tiny *"poussins."* As it is difficult to find birds this small on the market, I suggest you use Cornish hens or small broilers.

Serve with them a salad of Boston lettuce with Sour Cream Dressing (p. 294), or Cucumber Salad (p. 300), or both.

3 small chickens (2–2½ pounds or 900–1125 grams each)
Salt to taste

THE FILLING

2 cups (½ liter) unseasoned bread crumbs
¼ cup (1 deciliter) finely cut fresh dill
1 stick plus 2 tablespoons (145 grams) butter,
    at room temperature
½ teaspoon or more salt
Livers from the chickens
4 or more dashes of Maggi extract
Soft butter

Wash and dry the insides of the chickens and salt to taste. In a wooden bowl place the bread crumbs, dill, and butter. Add the ½ teaspoon salt. Chop the raw chicken livers into a paste, removing any bits of membrane, and mix with the bread-crumb mixture. Pour ½ cup boiling water over, and mix quickly. Add the Maggi extract and mix well.

Preheat the oven to 350°F (180°C). Divide the filling in 3 portions and put into the cavities of the chickens. Skewer or sew up the cavities, truss the birds, rub butter over them, and salt and pepper lightly. Cover the breast areas with aluminum foil. Roast for 25 minutes per pound of *one unstuffed bird,* removing the foil and basting with the pan drippings after 15 minutes, and once or twice more during the roasting. Test for doneness by pricking the leg joint; the juice should not be at all pink. Remove the birds to a platter, deglaze the pan with ½ cup boiling water, and pass this "sauce" separately. Serve either a whole bird or half a bird, split down the middle, to each person, depending on appetites.

## CHICKEN WITH ORANGE

*Serves 4*

This dish was served to me by my daughter Alina on my birthday a few years ago. It is divine.

3 pounds (1350 grams) chicken, cut in 8 serving pieces
Salt and pepper to taste
About 4 tablespoons flour
3 tablespoons oil
1 tart apple, cored, peeled, and chopped
1 rib celery, chopped
1 carrot, chopped
1 onion, chopped
2 tablespoons curry powder
½ cup (1 deciliter) orange juice
¾ cup (1¾ deciliters) Chicken Broth (p. 8),
    or use ½ Knorr chicken bouillon cube
    dissolved in ¾ cup water
2 teaspoons grated orange rind
⅓ cup (¾ deciliter) chopped mango chutney
1 bay leaf, crumpled
GARNISH: 1 small navel orange, peeled and sectioned

Pat the chicken pieces with salt, pepper, and flour, shaking off the excess. Brown the chicken in the oil in a heavy skillet. Remove the chicken and keep it warm. Discard all but 1 tablespoon of oil.

Add the apple, celery, carrot, and onion to the oil and cook, stirring, for 4 minutes. Sprinkle the mixture with curry powder and cook, stirring, for 1 minute more.

Stir in the orange juice and chicken broth, the orange rind, the chopped chutney, and the bay leaf, and bring to a boil. Add the chicken pieces, cover the pan, and simmer for 30 minutes. Serve garnished with orange sections.

# CHICKEN FRICASSEE, ANDALUSIAN STYLE

*Serves 6*

I learned this recipe from Pepa, our caretaker in Spain for many years. She was not really a cook, but once offered to make this dish as she did it for her family at home. Having tasted it, I found it so good that I "adopted" it.

In Spain this dish is eaten with fried potatoes, but my preferred accompaniment is rice flavored with saffron.

2 chickens, each under 2 pounds (900 grams),
   if possible
2 teaspoons salt
½ teaspoon pepper
About 4 tablespoons flour
4 tablespoons olive oil for frying
6, or even 8, large whole cloves garlic, peeled
2 cups (½ liter) dry white wine
1 cup (¼ liter) strong Chicken Broth (p. 8),
   or use 1 Knorr chicken bouillon cube
   dissolved in 1 cup water

Cut the chickens into 8 pieces each, wipe them dry, salt and pepper them, and flour them lightly all over. Fry the pieces in olive oil in a small, heavy casserole over medium-high heat until golden-brown. Add the garlic cloves, the wine, and the chicken broth, cover the pot, and simmer for 15 minutes, or until the chicken pieces are tender. Uncover the pot, raise the heat, and cook for 15 minutes more, or until the winy sauce is reduced by at least one-third. Taste it and add salt if necessary.

## LEMON CHICKEN AND
## LEMON CHICKEN EN CHAUD-FROID

*Serves 4 (hot) today and 4 (cold) later*

For many years it was difficult for me to plan more than one day's meals at a time. My cooking had to be quick and resourceful, to accommodate all the surprises—and surprise guests—of an exciting and changeable life.

But quite often now I can plan for one dish from which another will evolve. Though of course this sequence is possible with many recipes, I chose this one as an example because it offers an ideal, not just a convenient, way to arrive at a good chaud-froid and a pleasantly simple way to present it. A chaud-froid is an ivory-colored jellied sauce, and usually, when one is served a *poulet en chaud-froid,* it is a whole bird, elegantly clothed in a thick, opaque, gleaming aspic: pretty, but not so pretty after carving, and one rarely gets enough sauce for each portion. Moreover, the sauce has to be made thick and rubbery to keep it from sliding off the bird. My method is to cook two whole birds and serve the first hot, with a good ivory sauce flavored with lemon peel, then let the second bird cool before carving it, skinning it, and arranging it on a platter. Then it is blanketed with a creamy, just lightly jelled version of the original sauce.

Even if you want to cook only one bird, don't ignore this recipe; the lemon peel flavor is very subtle and fine. For one bird, do not divide the quantities, except for omitting extra broth, as noted in the recipe.

Two 3-pound (1350-gram) frying chickens
6 ribs celery, cut coarse
3 carrots, cut coarse
2 medium onions, cut coarse
4 cups (1 liter) strong Chicken Broth (p. 8),
   or use 3 Knorr chicken bouillon cubes
   dissolved in 4 cups water
3 tablespoons flour
3 tablespoons butter
Grated zest of 1 lemon (about 1 tablespoon)
   or more, to taste
½ cup (1 deciliter) heavy cream
Rice (p. 122)


THE CHAUD-FROID

½ envelope gelatin, if needed
1½ cups (3½ deciliters) heavy cream
2 tablespoons cornstarch or rice flour
White pepper to taste

Put the chickens, whole and trussed, with the celery, carrots, and onions, into a pot close fitting enough so that 4 cups broth will cover the birds. If you are cooking only 1 bird, you will need only 2 cups of broth for the sauce, but you are likely to need 4 cups for the pot, to cover the bird. The extra broth will be good in a soup anyway. If you need more than 4 cups of broth to cover 2 birds, add ½ bouillon cube per cup of extra water.

Cover the pot and simmer until the bird or birds are done: about 1¼ hours for 1 bird, a little longer for 2. Remove the birds and strain the broth, discarding the vegetables.

In a saucepan, cook the flour in the butter, stirring, until thick and smooth. (For a single bird, use 2 tablespoons each of butter and flour.) Add 2 cups of the strained broth for 1 bird, 4 for 2 birds, stirring constantly, until the sauce is smooth and lightly thickened. Add the lemon zest. Reserve 2 cups of sauce.

For the Lemon Chicken, add the ½ cup heavy cream to 2 cups of the sauce, and heat thoroughly. Carve the chicken and arrange the pieces in a deep serving dish and pour the hot sauce over it. Serve with boiled rice.

For the Lemon Chicken en Chaud-froid, let the second bird cool, then refrigerate it. Test a spoonful of the Lemon Chicken sauce for jelling power, as chicken bones have a good deal of gelatin. Put a spoonful of thickened sauce in the refrigerator for 10 minutes. If after that time it has stiffened only a little, you will need ½ envelope powdered gelatin for the whole amount. Soften the gelatin in ½ cup of the heavy cream.

Mix the cornstarch or rice flour with the remaining cup of heavy cream, add it to the reserved thickened sauce, and heat, stirring constantly, until it is smooth and further thickened. Taste it, add white pepper, and more lemon zest, if you like. Add the gelatin-cream mixture and stir until it is well dissolved in the sauce. Chill a spoonful of the sauce for 10 minutes again, and taste it. It should feel smooth and just firm enough to cling to a spoon turned upside down. Correct the seasoning and leave the saucepan at room temperature while you carve the chilled reserved bird into serving pieces, skin the pieces, and arrange them on a serving platter. Spoon the sauce over the chicken, making sure all the pieces are well covered, and shake the dish so that the sauce will penetrate among the pieces. Chill it for a minimum of 3 hours before serving.

## DEVILED CHICKEN LEGS

*Serves 6*

This is the simplest possible chicken dish, inexpensive, savory, and appetizing. Children love it hot or cold, and the skin (not always nice on cold chicken) is crisp and good.

To brush over the legs, I use Escoffier Sauce Diable, available bottled in most markets. You may prefer some other bottled sauce, or you may like to make your own deviling sauce by mixing ketchup, mustard, and A-1 Steak Sauce in whatever proportions please you.

> 6 whole chicken legs, about 2½ pounds (1125 grams)
> 4 tablespoons butter
> 1 teaspoon salt
> ½ teaspoon pepper
> ½ cup (1 deciliter) Escoffier Sauce Diable,
>    or your own choice

Preheat the broiler. Wash and carefully dry the chicken legs. Sauté them briefly in the butter, about 5 minutes on each side. Salt and pepper the browned side of the chicken as it sautés. Set them skin side down in a greased shallow pan, about 8 inches from the broiler unit. Brush them with about one-third of the Sauce Diable, and broil them for 8 minutes, or until the drumstick skin is pale golden-brown, with blistered spots. Turn the chicken legs over, brush them with another third of the sauce, and broil them 8 minutes more. Raise the rack closer to the broiler if you want more color. The legs are done when you prick the thigh and the juices are colorless.

## CHICKEN MEDALLIONS

*Serves 4 to 6*

These are sautéed slices of chicken meat, with the fibers shortened and evened by pounding, so that a bite has the velvet consistency of fine veal. With each serving you get just a small spoonful of creamy golden-beige sauce. I like these medallions with noodles and a green vegetable or a purée of carrots (p. 268).

For simplicity, the dish can be quickly completed in the sauté pan. But if you don't want to leave your guests after the first course, you can sauté the chicken before dinner and leave it to finish in a moderate oven for 20 minutes, while you enjoy your first course.

One 3½–4-pound (1500–1800 grams) chicken, or
    approximately 3 pounds (1350 grams) chicken
    breasts and thighs
2 teaspoons salt
½ teaspoon pepper
½ cup (70 grams) flour
2 eggs, beaten
3 tablespoons butter or vegetable shortening
½ cup (1 deciliter) heavy cream
Maggi extract to taste
1 tablespoon finely cut dill or parsley
Freshly grated Parmesan cheese (optional)

Skin the chicken or the chicken breasts and thighs, if you are using them. Remove the meat from the bones in large pieces: 2 from each breast half (cut across diagonally), 1 from each thigh, and 1 from each drumstick. (If the thigh meat breaks apart, don't worry. Pounding will weave the meat fibers back together again.) Extract the 2 long breast and leg tendons if they come easily. If not, don't worry, because they will come to the surface during the pounding and can easily be tweaked out then. You will have 8 serving portions. Cut them smaller if you want to offer more choices of light and dark meat.

Flatten the portions with a mallet. This is done with short, light whacks, twisting the mallet a quarter-turn as it hits, which gives you nice firm pieces. Don't worry if the meat breaks apart a little—it will come together again. Combine salt and pepper with flour. Dip each prepared chicken piece into beaten egg, shake off excess drops, and coat it with the seasoned flour, patting off the excess. Over medium-high heat, brown the pieces quickly on each side in the butter or vegetable shortening.

Here you have a choice.

You can reduce the heat to low-medium (about egg-frying temperature) and continue sautéing for about 8–10 minutes, or until the pieces are cooked through. (Cut into one; no pink will be left.) Then set the pieces on a hot serving dish and pour the cream into the sauté pan to deglaze it, loosening and incorporating all the delicious brown specks. Taste the sauce and add dashes of Maggi extract. Drizzle it over the chicken pieces and sprinkle the dish with the dill or parsley.

Or, having browned the chicken pieces on each side so that the meat has stiffened but is not cooked through, you can place the pieces in a buttered ovenproof dish. Preheat the oven to 300°F (150°C). Deglaze the sauté pan with cream, add Maggi extract to taste, and drizzle the flavored cream over the chicken pieces. Sprinkle with a little grated Parmesan, if you like. Cover the dish and set it in the oven for 20 minutes to finish cooking.

# CHICKEN CUTLETS
## (Ground meat)

*Serves 6*

Plump, succulent, and juicy, these golden-brown cutlets are my most practical party dish—these and *Bigos* (p. 223). You can make the mixture ahead of time and cook the cutlets up to 30 minutes or so before the party, keeping them in a very low oven and basting them now and then with cream, which thickens and takes on color and flavor to make a rich little sauce. The dish is at its best served with *Lazanki* with Mushrooms and Onions (p. 101).

If you don't want to bother with whole chickens and prefer to buy chicken parts, buy a greater proportion of thighs than breasts and don't buy drumsticks (too hard to get the meat off). The dish should have a rather rich taste, which means using plenty of dark meat. You will get about 1½ pounds (675 grams) of meat from a 3-pound (1350-gram) chicken, and a larger proportion from a capon.

2 pounds (900 grams) chicken meat, light and dark
1 stick (4 ounces or 115 grams) butter
½ cup (1 deciliter) strong Chicken Broth (p. 8),
    or use 1 Knorr chicken bouillon cube
    dissolved in ½ cup water
2 slices crustless white bread
2 eggs, beaten
2 tablespoons finely cut dill or parsley
1½ teaspoons salt
10 grinds pepper
4 dashes of Maggi extract
About 6 tablespoons flour for coating
2–3 tablespoons butter or vegetable shortening
    for sautéing
¾ cup (1¾ deciliters) heavy cream
    (if preparing dish in advance)

Remove all the meat from the chicken bones, and skin it. Trim it carefully and cut it into cubes. I have always used a meat grinder, fitted with the medium disk, but have found that the processor will grind chicken nicely if you cut carefully across the tendons in advance, and process the meat, using the steel blade, in 1-second bursts. The texture should not be too fine, a little coarser than hamburger.

Melt the butter in the chicken broth; crumble the bread into this liquid, add the beaten eggs, dill or parsley, salt, pepper, and Maggi extract, and mix thoroughly. When the mixture has cooled, blend in the ground chicken meat and refrigerate it for at least 1 hour.

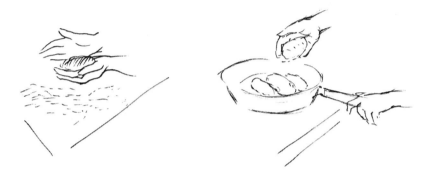

Form the mixture into cutlets 3 by 2 inches, and ¾ inch thick. Then roll them in flour, patting off the excess. Sauté the cutlets in the butter or vegetable shortening over medium-high heat until they are golden-brown all over, then lower the heat and cook them until they are done—approximately 5–7 minutes: they should be springy to the touch and not pink inside.

*Note:* To prepare the cutlets in advance for a party, proceed through forming the cutlets and rolling them in flour. You can then put them in the refrigerator on a platter or cookie sheet, lightly covered, until you are ready to cook them. For a wait of not more than 30 minutes or so, you can sauté them and remove them when they are not quite done (the centers are still pinkish). Arrange them in a buttered baking dish, pour the heavy cream over them, and leave them, covered with foil, in a very slow oven, basting occasionally, until you are ready to serve. The cream will reduce a bit, and the basting will color it a pale caramel.

## CHICKEN LIVER AND EGG PÂTÉ

*Makes about 2 cups*

For a rich, dense meat pâté you can slice for a first course, see page 217. This light pâté is simple and fresh tasting, nice with thin toast, or as canapés. It is best eaten one day after you make it (so that it has had time to mellow in the refrigerator) or up to four days. After that, though it keeps a week, it loses its fresh flavor.

About chicken fat, which you will need: Keep the pieces of yellow fat you take off chickens, and collect them in the freezer. A large (6-pound or 2¾-kilogram) bird will give you nearly ⅔ cup fat, melted. Chicken fat— "schmaltz"—can also be bought separately (Jewish butchers always have it —and supermarkets in large cities as well). It keeps a long time chilled and can be frozen indefinitely.

3 medium onions, chopped coarse
9 tablespoons melted, strained chicken fat
12 ounces (340 grams) very fresh chicken livers
2 hard-boiled eggs
1 tablespoon salt
8 grinds black pepper

Sauté the chopped onions slowly in 2 tablespoons of the chicken fat, until the onions are very soft and barely colored. Add the chicken livers, whole, and cook them over medium heat until lightly browned. Cut one open to inspect the center. It should be pale pink, and no longer exuding juice.

Now grind or process the onions and chicken livers with the pan juices and the hard-boiled eggs. The texture should not be smooth or pasty, but should have a little grain the size of a seed pearl. With the grinder, pass the mixture twice through the medium disk. With the processor, taste it after three 1-second bursts.

Add the salt and pepper and the remaining 7 tablespoons melted chicken fat. Taste the mixture, let it cool to room temperature, and taste it again for seasoning. Pack it closely in a crock or bowl, slashing through it with a knife blade and pressing down to eliminate all air pockets, and cover it closely with plastic wrap (exposure to air will darken the surface).

## CHICKEN LIVER PÂTÉ IN ASPIC

*Makes about 3 cups*

Years ago a friend in California gave me this recipe for a delicious and elegant way to make chicken livers taste (and feel) almost like real "foie gras." The pâté, in a ring mold glazed with aspic, looks very attractive on a buffet table.

Make this pâté a day ahead—it "mellows" and tastes even better. Be sure to allow time for "glazing" the mold.

One 10-ounce (285-gram) can beef consommé with gelatin,
    or 1 can beef broth and 1 envelope gelatin*
1 pound (450 grams) chicken livers
1 small onion, minced fine
1 stick (4 ounces or 115 grams) plus 1 tablespoon butter
8 ounces (225 grams) cream cheese
1 ounce (30 grams) Roquefort cheese
1 clove garlic, mashed (about ¼ teaspoon)
¼ teaspoon salt, or to taste
1 shot glass brandy
2 teaspoons pitted and minced black olives (*or,* if possible,
    2 teaspoons drained chopped black truffles)
GARNISH: watercress or parsley

Chill a 1-quart ring mold (preferably aluminum) for at least 1 hour. Prepare a large bowl of ice water with ice cubes, about two-thirds full. Pour the chilled consommé or broth with gelatin into the cold mold, and, holding

*If you use a canned beef broth that has no gelatin in it, soften 1 envelope gelatin in ¼ cup of the broth, heat the remaining broth, and dissolve the gelatin mixture in it. Cool, and chill for at least 15 minutes but no longer than 30 minutes, before proceeding. Canned consommé with gelatin should also be prechilled.

the mold carefully, turn and tip it, allowing the outside to dip into the ice cubes and water in the bowl. Keep turning the mold slowly enough to let the gelatin mixture adhere to all the inner surfaces as evenly as possible, until all of it has "glazed" the interior of the mold. Then chill it again, so that the "glaze" becomes as firm as possible.

Clean the livers of membranes and fatty tissue. Sauté the onion gently, over a low fire, in the 1 tablespoon of butter until it is translucent but not colored. (Remove any bits that may have browned.) Add the stick of butter, raise the heat to medium; when the butter foams, add the chicken livers. Sauté gently, turning them occasionally, until they are cooked through but still slightly pink inside. (Cut one and peek.)

Put into a blender or processor (with the steel blade) the livers, onion, and their butter, the cream cheese, Roquefort, garlic, salt, and brandy. Blend or process until the mixture is very smooth and creamy, then taste for salt, adding a bit more to taste. Mix in, by hand, the olives (or truffle pieces!). Gently spoon the mixture into the prepared mold so that you don't make air pockets. Smooth the top, cover with plastic wrap, and refrigerate overnight or a little longer.

To serve, unmold onto a platter, and garnish with sprigs of watercress or parsley.

# ROAST TURKEY

*Serves 10–12*

I don't believe in big turkeys. For me the ideal, for roasting, is a hen weighing from 10 to 12 pounds. Tom turkeys are not so plump and compact as hens, and too much of their weight is in the legs.

The stuffing must be very buttery, since this helps to prevent the lean breast meat from drying out. I like it flavored simply with onions, celery, herbs, and the raw turkey liver, very finely chopped. Without stuffing the bird must be basted much more often. In order that the butter, and the juices of the meat, be concentrated in the breast, I roast the bird upside down for part of the time, on one of those jointed racks whose sides make a V. Though you do get grill marks on the breast, these are, for me, a promise of succulence.

It is difficult to predict turkey roasting time to the minute. Turkeys of this general size average 15 minutes to the pound. At any rate, the turkey, once cooked, only improves by sitting; and it gets cool slowly, especially when stuffed. So I allow about 3½ hours in all, with the turkey at room temperature when it goes into the oven; then I keep a close eye on it and take it out when it seems done.

For a festive occasion, I might serve the turkey with boiled peas, Onions with Raisins and Port (p. 277), Cucumber Salad with dill (p. 300), Carrot and Apple Salad (with or without the raisins) (p. 299), or a green salad. No potatoes, as the stuffing is very rich and starchy, but certainly bowls of Spiced Fruit compote (p. 70), lingonberries, and cranberry jelly.

A hen turkey of 10–12 pounds (4½–5½ kilograms)
Salt

THE SAUCE

Neck, heart, and gizzard of the turkey
1 large carrot
1 onion, chopped coarse
2 ribs celery, chopped coarse

THE STUFFING

Liver of the turkey
2–3 chicken livers
4 sticks (1 pound or 450 grams) butter
4 large onions, chopped fine
4 small celery hearts, without leaves, chopped fine
1 pound (450 grams), or about 1 loaf, good stale
   white bread
2 teaspoons each: dried tarragon, thyme,
   rosemary, marjoram
2 tablespoons Herbes de Provence
4 tablespoons finely cut fresh dill, if available
2 teaspoons salt, or to taste
10 grinds black pepper, or to taste
3 tablespoons butter

1 Knorr chicken bouillon cube (optional)
3 tablespoons flour
4–8 tablespoons heavy cream (optional)

Pat the turkey dry inside and out. Rub a little salt around the cavity. Remove and reserve any excess fat from just inside the vent.

To make the sauce: In a pot or pressure cooker, place the turkey neck, heart, and gizzard with the carrot, split lengthwise and cut in 1-inch pieces, and the chopped onion and celery. Add 2 cups water. Simmer for 20 minutes after pressure is reached, or for 1 hour in an ordinary pot, and set aside.

To make the stuffing: Chop very finely the *raw* turkey and chicken livers and remove the veins; melt 1 stick of the butter in a large skillet and sauté in it the chopped onions and celery hearts until they are golden. Melt the remaining 3 sticks of butter in a pot.

Tear the bread, with the crusts left on, into roughly 1-inch pieces and toss in a large bowl with the sautéed vegetables and the raw livers; add the dried tarragon, thyme, rosemary, and marjoram, the Herbes de Provence, the dill, if available, and salt and pepper. Pour over the mixture the melted butter, and mix well again. Let it cool to room temperature.

Bend the turkey wings backward, so that the wingtips are pointing at each other and the turkey looks square-shouldered. Stuff both cavities loosely.

You can fasten the neck flap to the back, under the wingtips, with a large safety pin. The other cavity should be laced up with small skewers and string, or sewn up with kitchen thread. Cross the drumstick tips over the rear cavity and tie them to the tail stub. Tie together the triangles formed by the wings.

Preheat the oven to 325°F (165°C). Rub the turkey all over with the 3 tablespoons of butter, and set it breast up on the rack in a roasting pan. Place on the breast the reserved fat from inside the vent. Roast the turkey for 30 minutes. Now turn the bird breast side down on the rack and baste it with the reserved broth. Baste it again every 30 minutes, using the pan juices and additional broth as needed, since the pan juices will evaporate somewhat.

After 2½ hours, start testing the bird for doneness. When it is done, an "instant" or microwave-type thermometer, pushed into the center of the thigh, will register 175°F (80°C). Juices from the thigh will be only very faintly tinged with pink. The feel of the breast, when poked with a fingertip, will be dense and solid; the joint between thigh and drumstick will feel loose. Don't forget that the turkey will cook a little more as it rests outside the oven.

When you have removed the bird, combine any remaining broth with the pan juices, and quickly chill this liquid for ease in degreasing it. Reserve 3 tablespoons of the fat from the liquid. Taste the liquid for flavor, adding a bouillon cube if it seems weak, or water if it seems too strong.

Melt the reserved fat, and cook in it the flour, stirring until thickened and smooth; then add the liquid (you should have about 1½ cups), stirring constantly, and cook until the broth is thickened and the flour no longer tastes raw. At this point I like to add a few spoonfuls of heavy cream to the sauce. Taste it for seasoning, adding more cream if the flavor is still too intense.

When the roast turkey has sat for 15 minutes outside the oven, it is ready to untruss and carve, but it can safely wait at least 15 minutes longer.

*Note:* Turkey leftovers, mixed with sauce and mushrooms and pimientos, are very good served as a deep dish pie or in a curry, and of course the bird's carcass makes a wonderful soup.

# $\mathcal{D}uck$

French markets offer a choice of several kinds of duck. The one I use most frequently is called *Croisé,* which really serves only two. I also like the *Nantais,* which is known for its flavor. The *Barbarie,* which is the meatiest, is sometimes a bit dry.

Here I buy the standard Long Island duck, which most resembles the *Nantais,* fresh if possible, and allow one bird for three people. This duck is a fat fellow, but nicely flavored, and the skin can be delicious. The following recipes are intended for this kind of duck.

The only real secrets to roasting duck are to cook it very slowly and to pour off the fat during roasting.

*Note on frozen ducks:* They should be defrosted in the refrigerator; this takes at least 36 hours.

## ROAST DUCK À L'ORANGE

*Makes 4 small servings*

Using only the juice and the zest of the oranges and deepening the flavor with orange liqueur, you get a beautifully fragrant orange sauce, which tastes rich and meaty because it is made of the basting liquid.

This dish is particularly good with fresh boiled peas and a green salad.

1 duck, about 4½ pounds (2 kilograms)
Salt and pepper to taste

THE SAUCE

4 juice (not navel) oranges
½ cup (1 deciliter) sugar
3 tablespoons orange liqueur (for instance, Grand Marnier)

Preheat the oven to 325°F (165°C). Rub the duck inside and out with salt and pepper. Prick or lightly slash the skin all over, not piercing the meat. Roast for 45 minutes. Pour the fat from the pan, discard it, and raise the oven temperature to 350°F (180°C). Roast the duck 45 minutes more, occasionally pouring off the fat in the pan. Now, with a pointed knife, make a long slash on each side, between the legs and the body, and lightly prick or slash the skin in that area. Pour off the fat. Return the duck to the oven while you make the sauce for the last stage of roasting (about 30 minutes).

With a peeler, carefully remove the zests of the oranges. Cut them in very fine julienne. Squeeze the oranges and strain the juice. Cook together for 10 minutes the zests and juice with the sugar. Several times during the final roasting, baste the duck with this liquid. If you smell sugar beginning to burn in the hot roasting pan (unlikely but possible if the pan was very dry), remove the pan from the oven and cool it with a little cold water, scraping the bottom, then return it to the oven.

When the duck is done after 1 more hour (total roasting time is about 2½ hours), turn off the oven. Turn the bird over a frying pan, to pour out its cavity juices. Put the bird on a platter and place in the turned-off oven. Pour the juices from the roasting pan, with any brown bits into the frying pan. Quickly reduce the collected juices over high heat to half their volume.

When the duck, carved or not, is on its warm platter and ready to serve, flame the sauce: warm the orange liqueur (in a metal ladle, for instance, over a burner, or a metal cup set right in the frying pan with the hot liquid). Pour it into the sauce and ignite. When the flame dies down, serve this sauce in a separate bowl.

## PLAIN ROAST DUCK

*Makes 4 small servings*

Omitting the oranges, sugar, and liqueur, follow the method for Roast Duck à l'Orange (preceding recipe); but begin by cooking the duck giblets (not the liver) in 2 cups of water with 1 chopped carrot, 1 chopped celery rib, and salt and pepper. Use this liquid for basting, and reserve it to make Duck Soup with Barley (p. 13), which uses the carcass.

## ROAST DUCK WITH APPLES

*Serves 6–8*

Cooking apples with marjoram in the duck cavities gives you nice fragrant meat; then extra apples and marjoram are sautéed separately and served on the platter with the carved ducks. Or you can serve the apple-flavored ducks with baked apples, one per person, as noted in the Variation at the end of the recipe. These are superb, if slightly extravagant, with wild rice.

2 ducks, about 4½ pounds (2 kilograms) each
3 teaspoons salt
1 teaspoon pepper
4 teaspoons marjoram
6–8 good tart apples
1 teaspoon sugar
3–5 teaspoons lemon juice

Massage the ducks' breasts firmly with your fingertips—this helps to break up the fat so that it melts off better. Rub each duck inside and out with 1½ teaspoons salt, ½ teaspoon pepper, and 1 teaspoon marjoram, using more in the cavity than on the skin.

Preheat the oven to 325°F (165°C). Peel, core, and quarter 2 or 3 of the apples, then cut each quarter crosswise into ¼-inch slices. Mix 1 teaspoon marjoram with the slices, and divide them between the duck cavities. It is unnecessary to truss the ducks or to close the cavities.

Put the ducks in a large, lightly oiled roasting pan, and put it in the oven. After 30 minutes' roasting, when the ducks' skin has begun to color and stiffen, make tiny slashes in it with a pointed knife, taking care not to pierce the meat. At 30-minute intervals, pour off the fat accumulated in the bottom of the pan. Reserve 2 tablespoons of the fat. No basting is necessary, since the apple stuffing flavors the meat.

The total roasting time is about 2½ hours. After 2 hours, slash the skin between the leg and body of each duck on each side. Fat will pour out, and the inside of the leg will cook a bit faster. At this point, peel, core, quarter, and slice the remaining apples, as above. Sauté the apple slices with the remaining teaspoon of marjoram and the sugar in the reserved duck fat over very low heat, until the slices are soft but not mushy. Cover the pan and let it sit for 10 minutes off the heat. Taste the mixture and add lemon juice to taste. This apple sauté is to be served on the platter with the ducks.

For a sauce or gravy: Chop the duck giblets (not the liver) and cook them in a little chicken broth (7 minutes in the pressure cooker, 20 minutes in an ordinary pot). Strain the liquid. After all the fat has been poured out of the roasting pan, pour in this broth to collect any brown bits, which will flavor and color it. It may be served as is, or thickened with 1 tablespoon flour per cup of liquid, cooked until smooth in 1 tablespoon butter; add this roux to the broth and cook, stirring constantly, until it is lightly thickened and the flour no longer tastes raw.

*Variation: Duck with Baked Apples*

As above, put apple slices in the duck cavities. In addition, core but do not peel 1 baking apple per person; put 1 teaspoon sugar and 1 teaspoon butter in each hollow, and put water ¼ inch deep in the apple pan. Bake the apples in the oven with the duck, for about 1 hour. A little pink jelly will have formed in the bottom of the apple pan; scrape this up, to top each apple.

Instead of sugar, you may use 1 teaspoon red currant jelly or cherry jam per apple.

# Guinea Hens and Game Birds

Guinea hens, which shriek and strut with the commoner fowl in every French *basse-cour,* are not game, but they have a lovely little wild taste, and so do squab. I usually cook these savory birds by one general method that guarantees they will not be tough, as wild game can be. Of course there are other ways (and I give one for squab and two for pheasant), but this system of casserole roasting is reliable for ensuring the birds' tenderness and bringing out their haunting flavor.

Guinea hen, like game birds, is good with *Pommes Allumettes* (p. 281) or *Pommes Rissolées* (p. 280), and either a preserve of lingonberries or cranberry relish or the sweet and sour compote on page 70.

# GUINEA HEN

*Serves 3–4*

1 large guinea hen
Salt and pepper
About 1 pound (450 grams) barding fat
   (also called fatback)
1 cup (¼ liter) sour cream
½ cup (1 deciliter) heavy cream
4 dashes of Maggi extract
1 small truffle, in pieces (optional)
2 tablespoons flour

Rub the bird inside and out with salt and pepper. Prepare the barding fat. This consists of fresh pork fat; you want it in thin pieces, which you can wrap and tie around the bird to make it self-basting. It is usually available in markets in irregular, thick pieces. Slice these into *very* thin strips. If you cannot obtain barding fat, use slices of bacon that have been simmered in water for 10 minutes (to eliminate the salty taste).

Preheat the oven to 400°F (205°C). Truss the bird, twisting the wingtips backward under the back and tying the crossed drumsticks to the tail stub. Wrap it in the barding fat and wind a long piece of white string over and around it to keep the fat on. Place the bird in a Dutch oven or a heavy casserole with a lid. Roast it uncovered for 20 minutes. Turn the oven down to 350°F (180°C). Cut off the bard, leaving it in the casserole, and cook the bird, basting with the barding fat, for about 15–20 minutes, or until it is nicely browned on both sides. Remove the bird briefly, discard the bard and melted fat, and deglaze the casserole with ½ cup water. Return the bird, and pour over it ½ cup of the sour cream, mixed with the heavy cream, and the Maggi extract. At this point you may add the truffle pieces and their juice. Cover the casserole and cook for another 10 minutes, basting once.

Check the bird for doneness; the leg joints should move easily, the breast should feel dense and firm, and, if you prick the thigh (holding a bit of paper toweling to it), the juice should not be pink. On an "instant" or microwave thermometer, the interior temperature of the thigh should be 170°F (77°C). Put the bird on a warm platter. Thicken the sauce with 2 tablespoons flour mixed with the remaining ½ cup sour cream; bring it to the simmer on top of the stove and cook, stirring well, for a minute or so, or until the flour no longer tastes raw. Correct the seasoning and serve the sauce separately with the carved bird.

*Note on truffles:* Whole ones are priced beyond reason. You can buy tiny cans of truffle bits or peelings. Use the juice too.

## PHEASANT

*Serves 3*

Commercially raised pheasants are quite plump, but if you have a wild bird you think may be dry, cook it with 2 ounces (60 grams) cream cheese or Petit Suisse in the washed, dried, salted and peppered cavity.

Then follow exactly the preceding recipe for Guinea Hen; again, the truffle is optional.

When the bird is done (test as for guinea hen), usually in about an hour, pour all but 2 tablespoons fat out of the casserole; add ½ cup (1 deciliter) sour cream and a little Maggi extract, and blend it all into a little sauce.

# PHEASANT SMOTHERED IN CABBAGE

*Serves 6*

Here is another delicious way to cook pheasant—absolutely guaranteed to be moist and juicy—lovely with steamed potatoes.

2 medium heads Savoy or white cabbage
1 slice lemon
1 medium onion, chopped coarse
1 large carrot, chopped coarse
3 stalks celery, chopped coarse
¾-pound (340-gram) piece of slab bacon
1 bay leaf
6 peppercorns
½ teaspoon Maggi extract
2 pheasants, quartered
Flour for dredging
½ teaspoon salt
2 tablespoons vegetable oil
2 tablespoons butter
2 tablespoons flour
2 knackwurst sausages
    (or 4 frankfurters or ½ Polish kielbasa)

Chop the cabbage very coarsely, discarding the center core, and blanch in boiling salted water with a slice of lemon for 10 minutes. Drain thoroughly and reserve.

Put the onion, carrot, and celery pieces into a saucepan with the piece of slab bacon; add the bay leaf and peppercorns and 2 cups water. Bring to the boil, then simmer gently for 30 minutes. Remove the bacon, strain and reserve the liquid, discarding the vegetables. Add the Maggi extract to the broth.

Slice the bacon into strips. Dredge the pheasant pieces in flour mixed with the salt, and sauté in the oil and butter until a light golden-brown on both sides. (Reserve the oil and butter in the skillet.)

Preheat the oven to 350°F (180°C). Make a bed of half of the reserved drained cabbage in a Dutch oven or heavy, lidded casserole. Then add in layers the pieces of pheasant with the strips of bacon, and top off with the other half of the cabbage. Into the reserved oil and butter in the skillet stir the 2 tablespoons of flour, cooking and stirring to make a roux. Add the reserved broth, stirring, and simmer briefly.

Pour this sauce over the contents of the casserole, cover, and bake for 1 hour. For the last 20 minutes, put ¼-inch-thick slices of the knackwurst on top of the cabbage.

## SQUABS WITH GRAPES AND RAISINS

*Serves 6*

This is a most luxurious dish, but it reminds me of a very thin time indeed. When we lived in Moscow during the Russian Revolution of 1917, food was scarce, and our cook Barbarka found an ingenious way of supplementing our scanty diet. She would open the *vasistas,* a hinged pane in the outer window (most houses in northern Russia are double-glazed), and strew a few crumbs on the sill. When a pigeon spotted them and hopped in to peck, snap! And there was our dinner. There were always plenty of pigeons around, since in Russia they were considered holy. We Poles had no such superstitions.

A squab is simply a very young pigeon, and the frozen squab you find in many American markets has been commercially raised. It is lean but not tough (as some of those Moscow street pigeons were). This recipe gives you quite a lot of juice, with a lovely aroma. One can accompany the birds with Rice (p. 122), Kasha (p. 120), or the excellent American wild rice, to absorb some of the delicious sauce.

6 squabs, about ¾ pound (340 grams) each,
    defrosted overnight in the refrigerator
Salt and pepper
1 teaspoon Herbes de Provence
1¼ pounds (560 grams) Ribier grapes,
    slit and seeded
⅔ cup (1½ deciliters) raisins
1 pound (450 grams) barding fat
    (also called fatback)
½ cup (1 deciliter) Marsala wine

Wipe each bird's cavity dry, rub it with salt, pepper, and a small pinch of Herbes de Provence, and put inside it a small handful of the grapes with a few raisins (which intensify the flavor a little and also absorb some of the grapes' moisture). Reserve about ¼ pound of the grapes for the casserole.

Preheat the oven to 350°F (180°C). See the recipe for Guinea Hen (p. 250) for how to prepare the barding fat and how to truss the birds. Lay a thin piece of bard on the bottom of the casserole, put the birds on it, and lay thin pieces on top of the birds. Put the reserved grapes around them.

Cook the birds, uncovered, in the oven for 45 minutes, basting once or twice. Remove the barding for the last 10 minutes of roasting.

Lift the birds carefully from the pan, so that juice is not spilled from their cavities. Pour off and reserve all the pan juices (the grapes can stay), and replace the birds. Sprinkle them with the Marsala, cover the casserole, and return it to the oven. Turn off the oven and let the casserole sit for 10 minutes. During this time the fat will separate from the pan juices. Remove most of it. The birds will be moist and tender, served just as is, with the grapes and raisins inside each, and the pan juices and grapes poured over them.

## VEGETABLES

Artichokes
Boiled Asparagus
Purée of Beets
Old-fashioned Beets
Boiled Cabbage
Cabbage Timbale
Glazed Carrots
Carrot Purée
Cauliflower au Gratin
Cauliflower à la Polonaise
Cauliflower Purée
Boiled Sweet Corn
Green Beans
Creamed Mushrooms, Polish Style
Stuffed Sautéed Mushrooms
Pickled Mushrooms
Onions with Raisins and Port
Smothered Onions
Boiled Potatoes with Bacon and Onion
Lithuanian Potatoes
Pommes Rissolées
Pommes Allumettes
Potatoes à la Barbarka
Röstli
Potato Pancakes
Rutabaga with Diced Bacon Skwarki
Épinards en Branches (Leaf Spinach)
Creamed Spinach
Stuffed Zucchini, Hot and Cold
Deep-fried Zucchini
Vegetable Julienne

## SALADS

Vinaigrette
Sour Cream Dressing
Mayonnaise
Black Radish Relish
Celery Root (Celeriac) Relish
Green Salads
Combination Salads
Bean Sprouts Salad
Carrot and Apple Salad
Red Cabbage Salad
Cucumber Salad
Green Bean Salad
Red Pepper Salad
Hot Potato Salad
Zucchini, Watercress, and
    Red Onion Salad

# Vegetables and Salads

This is not a long chapter, although vegetables appear in several other places in the book: cauliflower and eggplant illustrate two ways of frying in batter (pp. 88 and 89); cabbage and mushrooms in a *Coulibiac* (p. 115) show how a moist and succulent filling can combine with a crisp pastry; and Adam's Vegetable Soup (p. 28) is an example of how careful proportions and attention to texture can transform the most ordinary ingredients into something quite special.

I assume everyone has tried and true recipes in the steam or boil-and-butter traditions. The only ones here are for asparagus and corn, since I add some personal touches. So for this chapter I have chosen mainly those recipes that may be somewhat less familiar, or even special to a Polish-Lithuanian kitchen. Surprisingly, perhaps, there are only two recipes for beets, although beets certainly reign among my soups. As for salads, they and vegetables so often take the place of one another that it seemed logical to include them in this chapter.

Potatoes, however, are another matter. They are without question my favorite vegetable, as they can be cooked in an almost infinite number of ways, can complement so many varied dishes, and can literally change their personalities to suit the meal and the occasion.

Sadly, many people stop at French fries and mashed potatoes, although this lowly tuber can offer the most painstaking as well as the laziest cook such variety as: Lithuanian Potatoes with sour cream and onions (p. 279), *Pommes Rissolées* (p. 280), potatoes with dill and butter, or boiled and served sprinkled with diced bacon and onions as a summer meal with Clabbered Milk (p. 64), or the wonderful baked Potatoes à la Barbarka (p. 282) filled with mushrooms and onions.

And I include our home version of thin potato pancakes *(bliny kartoflane),* which frequently became a meal in themselves and would send the children scurrying for sour cream and forks to be ready as each batch fell hot from the pan onto their plates.

These same "blinis" are not shy in more elegant company, however. Just before the war in 1938, the American Ambassador, William Bullitt, gave a cocktail party on the same day as we were having one in Montmartre. When the embassy party was over, Ambassador Bullitt, with the Polish

Ambassador Lukasiewicz, came to our house. Most of our guests had left and all the food was gone. Potatoes to the rescue! I made pan after pan of these "blinis," as they were devoured and I found myself running in and out the window entrance of the cubbyhole kitchen to serve them piping hot, to the delight of the guests. So much for the "lowly spud"!

# *Vegetables*

## ARTICHOKES

*Serves 6*

These uniquely formed and quite wonderful vegetables still occasionally put people off with their almost forbidding appearance and somewhat mysterious construction, but their prickly exteriors hide a soft heart well worth the pursuit. Artichokes are certainly among the most versatile of vegetables and can serve as "green," starch, or salad, or all three at once. They are delicious with such a variety of dressings and sauces that I will mention only a few here: have them hot with lemon-flavored melted Clarified Butter (p. 63), hot or cold with a Vinaigrette (p. 294), or warm with a luxurious Hollandaise or Mousseline (p. 55).

Children will eat just the leaves for the slightly messy fun of it, but don't complain—save the hearts and next day dechoke them, mound them with a savory mixture such as the chopped mushroom filling (p. 111), and eat them yourself!

Choose artichokes that are green and rounded, with leaves tightly closed and the fewest possible brown spots.

6 medium artichokes
Drops of oil (olive or vegetable)
½ lemon
1–2 bay leaves
8–10 peppercorns
1 medium clove garlic, peeled (optional)

Cut about one-quarter off the top of each artichoke—a bread knife does this easily—and cut the stems off so the artichoke sits level. Clip off the sharp points of the remaining leaves with scissors. Spread the leaves apart slightly and rinse well under cold running water. Dribble 2 or 3 drops of oil into each center, and rub all the cut surfaces with the ½ lemon.

In a pot or kettle large enough to hold the artichokes, bring to the boil enough lightly salted water to fill it halfway and add the bay leaf or leaves, peppercorns, the same ½ lemon, and the optional garlic, if you like. Add the artichokes, and after the water comes to the boil again turn the heat down a little, cover the pot, and cook the artichokes for 35–40 minutes. Test the bottom of one with a kitchen fork—it should be very tender. The time depends a little on the size and freshness of the artichokes; sometimes they need another 5 or 10 minutes. This is one vegetable that is better slightly *over-*cooked than *under-,* so don't worry.

When they are done, remove the artichokes with tongs, and let them drain well *upside down*—a dish-draining rack is perfect.

If you want to present them in an extra-elegant way, spread the center leaves as far apart as necessary to scoop out the "choke" with a grapefruit knife (or better yet, grapefruit spoon) and serve them on individual plates with the sauce or dressing in the hollowed-out bottom.

I often serve artichokes as a separate course, either before or after the entrée.

### BOILED ASPARAGUS

*Serves 6*

Asparagus is nice *à la polonaise* (scattered with bread crumbs that have been fried in butter), or with Garlic Butter (p. 50), Sauce aux Oeufs Durs (p. 61), or Hollandaise (p. 55), or served cold with a Vinaigrette (p. 294). I take great care in shopping for it, to get stalks of uniform thickness (for even cooking) and perfect freshness, and to find ones with young, tight (not old, seedy) tips. But then I cook it in the simplest possible manner. Peeling is optional; it does make thicker stalks more tender. But it is a chore.

3 pounds (1350 grams) fresh asparagus
Pinch of sugar
Pinch of salt

Buy or pick the asparagus as soon as possible before using it, and keep the base of the stalks immersed in an inch or so of water; don't refrigerate them. Break or cut off the tough lower part of the stalks (which can be peeled and cut up for soup). Lay the stalks in a large frying pan, and pour over them enough boiling water to cover. Add a pinch each of sugar and salt.

After the water has returned to a boil, the very young, pencil-thin stalks may be cooked in 2 minutes. Thick, older stalks may take up to 8 minutes. One must simply taste once or twice. Drain the asparagus very well when it seems tender, and serve it at once.

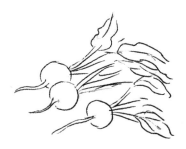

## Beets

Raw beets are hard to handle. Cook them whole, unpeeled, and leaving at least 1 inch of their tops, and the root end. In an open pot they can take 1½ hours or more, depending on their size. Cook them until they are tender. Start them in cold water to cover deeply, adding water if necessary as they cook. Do not salt. *Discard the water.* It is bitter. When cool enough to handle, slide the skins off, and trim them, then cut them according to the recipe you are making.

*For the pressure cooker:* Cook for 35–40 minutes after pressure is reached, using at least 2 cups water, and the pressure cooker's rack. Prepare the beets the same way as for an open pot, again discarding the water.

## PURÉE OF BEETS

*Serves 4*

This nice sweet-sour dish is delicious with a full-flavored plain meat dish —game, beef, or lamb. In fact I seldom serve lamb without it.

1 pound (450 grams) fresh beets
2 tablespoons butter
2 tablespoons flour
2 tablespoons vinegar
8 dashes of Maggi extract
Sugar, if necessary
½ cup (1 deciliter) sour cream (optional)
Salt, if necessary

Wash the beets, but do not peel them. Trim them, leaving the root end and about 1 inch of the tops intact. Cook them in water to cover for about 1½ hours, or until tender. If you have a pressure cooker, cook for 40–45 minutes, depending on the size of the beets. Discard the water; it will be bitterish. When the beets can be handled, peel them and cut off root and tops. Grate them or put them through the fine blade of a meat grinder. In a processor, use the serrated knife, and be careful to leave a little texture.

In a saucepan make a roux with the butter and flour, and cook for a few moments. Add 1 cup water, stirring constantly, and cook until the mixture is very smooth and thickened. Add the beets, stirring them well, then the vinegar and Maggi extract. Cook, stirring constantly, over a low fire for about 10 minutes. Taste; if you find the beets too much on the sour side, carefully add a little sugar, no more than ½ teaspoon at a time. Let the sugar melt and blend in well with the beet mixture before adding any more. Taste again.

When you have a pleasing balance of sweet and sour, add the optional sour cream, if you like, cook for a few moments, and taste again for seasonings. (The Maggi extract should have added enough salt.)

*Note:* Should you wish to make this dish with bottled or canned beets, make the following adjustments: Drain the beets well and reserve their juice. Use the juice in place of water in the roux, but use only half the volume, as the beets themselves have more liquid content than fresh-cooked ones. There is usually a little sugar already in the jar or can, so taste carefully before adding any more. Use the remaining beet juice (there will be quite a lot) to make *barszcz* (p. 18).

## OLD-FASHIONED BEETS

*Serves 4–5*

This is a very old Lithuanian recipe, a variation on the previous one, but with a quite different texture. Again, wonderful with simple roasts, especially lamb. It gains greatly in flavor by being allowed to sit a little after all the ingredients are combined.

1 pound (450 grams) cooked fresh beets, or canned beets*
2 tablespoons cider vinegar
2 tablespoons water
⅓ cup (¾ deciliter) seedless white raisins
1 medium onion, chopped fine
2 tablespoons vegetable oil
1 tablespoon flour
½ cup (1 deciliter) sour cream
5 dashes of Maggi extract, or more

Chop the cooked beets, or well-drained canned beets, with a chopper in a wooden bowl, to a medium-coarse but fairly even texture. (I don't recommend you use the processor for this, as it goes almost too fast to control—but if you do, do it in 3 or 4 rapid spurts.)

In a small pan, bring the vinegar, water, and raisins to a boil. Immediately

*I use canned beets interchangeably with fresh-cooked ones. What one loses in ruby red color, one gains in time! For full details on cooking beets, see Purée of Beets (preceding recipe).

take them off the heat, cover them, and let them stand for a few minutes to absorb the liquid.

Sauté the onion in the oil until it has colored slightly.

In a heavy-bottomed pan, combine the beets, raisins, and onion. Thoroughly blend the flour with the sour cream, and stir it in. Add a little Maggi extract, taste, and cautiously add more if you wish. Cook the mixture very slowly for 10 minutes, during which it will thicken, darken, and intensify in flavor. Taste it before serving; you will probably not want salt, but you may want more Maggi.

## *Cabbage*

This chapter has only two cabbage recipes, but there are several elsewhere in the book: a sauerkraut soup (p. 23), a filling for pastry, Cabbage Rolls, and so on. Two things are worth remembering when you cook cabbage: blanch it with a bit of lemon peel and then drain it, discarding the water, before proceeding further. Second, let it sit a little, covered, after cooking, as it develops more flavor.

### BOILED CABBAGE

*Serves 6–8*

A Savoy, or frilly, cabbage is nicest for this.

   1 medium head cabbage
   1 piece of lemon zest 1 by 2 inches, including the
      white pith, or 1 whole unshelled walnut
   2 tablespoons butter
   1 teaspoon sugar
   1 teaspoon salt
   6 grinds pepper

Quarter the cabbage, core it, and blanch it in a large, uncovered pot of furiously boiling water containing the lemon zest (which helps to cut down on the cabbagy smell). When the cabbage has softened a bit, usually in 5 minutes, drain it, and chop it coarsely. Wash the blanching pot, and return to it the blanched cabbage, discarding the lemon zest and adding the butter, sugar, salt, and pepper. Mix the ingredients well, cover the pot, and cook slowly until the cabbage is tender, about 15 minutes. Taste for seasoning, cover the pot, and let it sit off the heat for a few minutes before serving.

## CABBAGE TIMBALE

*Serves 6–8*

With an Onion or Mushroom Sauce (pp. 58 and 57), this makes a nice light entrée. Like most timbales, it can either be baked in a soufflé dish or steamed in a mold, and can be unmolded if you like.

    1 medium head green cabbage, about 1¼ pounds
        (560 grams)
    1 piece of lemon zest 1 by 2 inches, including
        the white pith, or a whole walnut
    4 tablespoons (½ stick) butter
    3 onions, chopped
    8 ounces (225 grams) mushrooms, minced
    4 eggs, separated
    ½ cup (1 deciliter) bread crumbs
    ½ teaspoon allspice
    2 teaspoons salt
    6 grinds pepper
    Butter for the mold
    Flour for the mold

Quarter and core the cabbage and blanch it for 5 minutes with the lemon zest or the whole walnut in a large, uncovered pot of furiously boiling water. Drain it, chop it, and cook it, covered, for 20 minutes in ½ cup water and 2 tablespoons of the butter. Four cups of chopped raw cabbage cooks down to a scant 2 cups.

Sauté the chopped onions in the remaining 2 tablespoons butter until lightly colored. Add the minced mushrooms and cook the mixture until the liquid exudes and evaporates.

Beat the egg yolks lightly and mix with the cabbage, onions, and mushrooms, bread crumbs, allspice, and salt and pepper. Beat the egg whites until stiff and fold them in.

Butter and crumb a 6-cup soufflé mold, or a steaming mold with a tight-fitting lid. For baking, preheat the oven to 350°F (180°C). For steaming, set a rack in a large, covered kettle (or use the pressure cooker, but unweighted), add 2 inches of water, and bring it to the simmer.

This mixture will expand a little during the cooking. If you are steaming it, be sure that the mold is not more than two-thirds full; steam it in the covered kettle for 30 minutes or bake your timbale for 30 minutes in the oven. Serve it in its cooking mold or reverse it onto a warm serving plate.

## Carrots

Carrots vary enormously depending on the climate and soil in which they are grown. In southern Spain they have a very concentrated flavor due to the dryness of the soil and the intense heat. In France there is a variety grown the shape and size of a very large radish, which looks lovely when it is cooked whole and slightly glazed. Here I buy the freshest and youngest carrots I can find.

## GLAZED CARROTS

*Serves 6*

Glazed carrots are both very tasty and extremely decorative. They also often appeal to children who won't eat them any other way.

2 pounds (900 grams) carrots
2 tablespoons butter
1 tablespoon brown sugar
Juice of 1 orange

Peel the carrots and (for large ones) cut them crosswise into 2-inch lengths. Tiny carrots can be scraped and cooked whole. Boil them in salted water until they are barely tender, and drain them. In a heavy pan, melt the butter and add the sugar and orange juice. Add the carrots and cook them, uncovered, over low heat for about 10 minutes. The sugar and the sweet juice will become lightly caramelized, but if the glaze colors too quickly lift the pan off the heat. You do have to watch out for this. Keep turning the carrots so that they become evenly glazed.

## CARROT PURÉE

*Serves 6*

The reason for cutting up the carrots, in this and many other recipes of mine, is to cook them evenly. The processor makes quick work of slicing them for this recipe. (Don't julienne them in this case; the gain in time is not worth the loss of flavor.) If you have old carrots, the yellow cores are quite tough and not so sweet-flavored as the orange part, so you may want to add sugar to the cooking water. Sugar is a softener as well as a sweetener.

    2 pounds (900 grams) carrots, sliced
    2 tablespoons butter
    4 tablespoons heavy cream
    2 teaspoons sugar
    Salt to taste
    2 tablespoons finely cut dill or parsley

Boil the carrots in salted (and, if you like, sugared) water, tasting them often, until they are tender. Drain them. Mash them, adding butter, cream, and sugar, and more salt if necessary. (The purée is quickly made in the processor: Put the carrots, butter, and sugar in the container with the steel blade, and dribble in the cream with the machine running.) Serve the purée sprinkled with the dill or parsley.

## *Cauliflower*

Cauliflower is easy to cook well. The only secret is to keep it from becoming waterlogged. The best way is to steam it, but if you want to boil it, drain it very thoroughly. Here are three recipes I like, one very simple, one hearty enough to make a simple entrée; and there is a recipe for Cauliflower Fritters on page 88.

## CAULIFLOWER AU GRATIN

*Serves 6*

1½–2 pounds (675–900 grams) cauliflower
4 tablespoons flour
4 tablespoons butter
1½ cups (3½ deciliters) milk
4 ounces (115 grams) Gruyère or Appenzell cheese
About ¼ teaspoon freshly grated nutmeg
Salt and pepper to taste
3 ounces (85 grams) freshly grated Parmesan cheese

Break the trimmed cauliflower into large florets and boil or steam them until just tender. Drain them well.

Make a medium-thick Béchamel Sauce (p. 48): cook the flour in the butter, stirring constantly, until it is thickened and smooth. Add the milk and cook until the sauce has thickened (it will be quite thick) and the flour no longer tastes raw. Over low-medium heat, since it must not boil, add the Gruyère or Appenzell cheese, cut in dice or shredded, and cook slowly until it has melted into the sauce and slightly thinned it. Add the nutmeg. Taste the sauce and season it to taste with salt and pepper.

Preheat the oven to 350°F (180°C). Put the cauliflower in a buttered gratin dish and pour the sauce over it, making sure every floret is coated. Sprinkle on the grated cheese and bake for 15 minutes or until it starts bubbling, then put under the broiler for a minute or so to brown the top.

## CAULIFLOWER À LA POLONAISE

*Serves 6*

When you have a particularly nice, fresh cauliflower, this very plain recipe is excellent. I use it most often in Spain, where we get smallish, not too white cauliflowers with green cores and a full, nutty flavor.

    1 large or 2 small cauliflowers, about 2 pounds
        (900 grams) in all
    3 slices lemon
    6 tablespoons bread crumbs
    4 tablespoons butter

Trim the cauliflower(s) and steam them on a rack over boiling water with 3 slices of lemon. Steaming time varies, according to size, and whether you have 1 or 2 heads: about 12 to 15 minutes. They should have just a little crunch; test them with a small skewer. When they still feel firm, but no longer stiff, drain them. Fry the bread crumbs in the butter until golden-brown and scatter them over the cauliflower heads before serving.

## CAULIFLOWER PURÉE

*Serves 6*

I sometimes like to thicken purées, and often soups, with potato, rather than a butter-and-flour roux. But the balance of flavors is important: potato is not, after all, a neutral flavor, just mild. It is an ideal companion for cauliflower.

I cook the two vegetables separately to have better control of how soon each is done and because the last-minute combining gives a fresher, though less intense, flavor.

1 large cauliflower
2 slices lemon
2 medium baking potatoes
3 tablespoons heavy cream
Salt and pepper to taste

Break the cauliflower into equal-size pieces for even cooking. Blanch them in a large quantity of boiling water for 2 minutes, then drain them. In fresh water, add the lemon slices and simmer the cauliflower until it is soft but not soggy. At the same time, peel and dice the potatoes and simmer them in another pot until soft.

Drain both vegetables as soon as done, and dry them in their pots over heat, shaking the pots so they won't stick. In one pot, mash the cauliflower and potato together and dribble in the cream. Salt and pepper the purée to taste.

As this purée should have a little grain, I like to make it with an old-fashioned potato masher, by hand. It goes so fast, and one should never use the processor anyway for puréeing potatoes.

## BOILED SWEET CORN

*Serves 6*

I have always loved fresh corn on the cob, with a little dab of sweet butter, and a few grains of salt on each bite. Corn in this form was relatively unknown in Europe until an American GI who had fallen in love with France stayed on after the war and began growing corn for *people* (as opposed to pigs!), and soon it was all the rage. Now fresh corn appears, in various forms, at the most elegant dinners and buffets. The Baronne Alain de Rothschild served it, at a glamorous party, off the cob as a bed for poached eggs—I had *four* helpings!

12 ears of good fresh corn
2 tablespoons coarse salt (add 1 teaspoon if you use
    kosher salt, still another teaspoon if you use
    ordinary table salt)
At least 4 tablespoons suger, or to taste
8 quarts (8 liters) water at the full boil
Chilled butter and coarse or kosher salt for the table

Husk and desilk the corn as soon as you bring it home, wrap it airtight in plastic, and chill it until you cook it.

Salt and sugar the boiling water, and taste it. You should barely taste the salt at all; the sugar you should taste distinctly but faintly. Add more water if you think it's overseasoned, and bring it to the boil again.

Plunge 6 ears of corn into the water, and boil them 3–8 minutes, depending on their youth and freshness; longer for old corn, less for young. Drain the ears as quickly as possible and serve them at once, wrapped in a fresh dish towel. Repeat for second helpings.

## GREEN BEANS

*Serves 4*

If you have access to fresh garden beans, of course there is nothing better. When I can get only the regular market variety, I cook them in this perhaps slightly unorthodox way, which is very tasty with any simple meat dish.

1 pound (450 grams) green beans
Salt to taste

THE SAUCE

2 tablespoons butter
2 tablespoons flour
1 cup (¼ liter) half-and-half
Grating of fresh nutmeg
3 or more dashes of Maggi extract
GARNISH: 1 tablespoon finely cut fresh parsley

Wash, then snap the ends off, the beans. Cut them crosswise into ½-inch pieces. Cook in lightly salted water to cover for 15–20 minutes, or until they are just tender. (In a pressure cooker, cook for 3 minutes after pressure is reached.) Drain them very thoroughly.

Make a medium Béchamel Sauce (p. 48), using the proportions above, and half-and-half instead of milk. Season to taste with fresh nutmeg and Maggi extract. Add the well-drained beans, heat together thoroughly, and correct the seasoning. Serve sprinkled with the cut parsley.

## Mushrooms

Although a few years ago it was difficult to find fresh mushrooms other than the white cultivated variety, recently more and more kinds are appearing on the markets. Specialized markets offer an increasing variety of dried and even fresh mushrooms. Dried mushrooms, as they are usually imported from France, Italy, or Poland, tend to be expensive. I use them in small quantities, to give a deeper and livelier taste to many dishes, for instance, *Bigos* (p. 223), Cabbage Rolls (p. 214), and Swiss steak. They should, of course, be soaked first; every drop of the delicious soaking liquid is saved for sauces and soups.

In the Paris market, in addition to fresh cèpes, one can find chanterelles and morels and boletus, to say nothing of black truffles; in Italy, there are *porcini* (cèpes) and the famous white truffles, now occasionally available fresh in the U.S. (but at prices really immoral).

But the true heaven of mushroom lovers is Eastern Europe. I remember the tremendous expeditions led by my parents through the oak woods at Ilgovo—all very formal, each of us children with a special mushroom basket —and each mushroom we picked scrutinized by Mama or the governess. During our exile in Russia, we went in the summer to a rented dacha outside Moscow, and mushroom hunted in the surrounding forest. I still know in my bones what sort of night weather will produce mushrooms next morning, and where they like to hide.

About black truffles: they are available here, imported whole, vacuum-packed, costing an arm and a leg; they also come in cans, still expensive. But I do not recommend that you risk incarceration (or worse, confiscation!) as I once did. We were then living in New York when fresh truffles were not yet available here, and I returned from a European tour ahead of my husband, to be with the younger children and to begin preparations for Christmas. Determined to surprise Arthur with some fresh truffles, I bought beautiful ones in Paris, put them in a plastic bag, then in a box, wrapped that in layers of foil, then paper, and finally clothing, and packed the whole thing deep in a tote bag. I boarded the plane and gradually realized that the entire plane was becoming redolent with the unmistakable odor of truffles! The flight became a nightmare—and included dreadful weather that seemed like punishment from Above, but at least kept the stewardesses distracted. By some miracle we landed safely, and the customs inspector had either a bad cold or a generous nature, and my truffles and I passed undetected.

I asked Henri Soulé, owner of the original Pavillon Restaurant, to poach them in champagne, and yes, they were delicious—but my terror had been such that it even affected the taste. Never again.

Mushroom recipes are scattered throughout this book: *Lazanki* with Mushrooms and Onions on page 101; Mushroom Soup, two kinds, on pages 34 and 35; Mushroom Sauce on page 57; and several dishes flavored with mushrooms, especially those that also contain cabbage. And I love them raw, in salads, or dabbed with sour cream and red caviar. Indeed, few mushroomless days occur in my life, and all the traditional dishes of grilled, steamed, stewed, baked, and other mushrooms are my joy. But you know all these. In this brief chapter, I give you three of the delights of a Polish childhood: a nice way of doing mushrooms with sour cream, fried stuffed mushrooms rich with butter, and a delicate pickle.

## CREAMED MUSHROOMS, POLISH STYLE

*Serves 6*

This is nice served on croûtes (sliced fried bread) or with Kasha (p. 120). In fact, since mushrooms are rich in protein, mushrooms and kasha make a good entrée if you have vegetarian guests, or even if you don't.

4 tablespoons butter
2 medium onions, sliced
1½ pounds (675 grams) fresh mushrooms, sliced
2 teaspoons salt
2 tablespoons flour
½ cup (1 deciliter) sour cream
8 grinds pepper

In the butter, cook the onions until they are soft and lightly colored. Stir in the sliced mushrooms and 1 teaspoon of the salt and cook the mixture until the liquid has exuded but is only half evaporated. Sprinkle on the flour and stir it in carefully, cooking it until the mixture has thickened a good deal and no longer tastes of raw flour. Stir in the sour cream and the pepper and cook slowly for 5 minutes.

Taste, and add salt if necessary.

## STUFFED SAUTÉED MUSHROOMS

*Serves 4*

Small servings of this rich dish are particularly good with grills: fish steaks or beefsteaks, or unsauced but lively entrées like Deviled Chicken Legs (p. 234). They are also delicious served on toast as a separate course.

1½ pounds (675 grams) mushrooms
7 tablespoons butter
1 medium onion, grated, with its juice
Salt and pepper to taste
3 cloves garlic, peeled
2 tablespoons finely cut dill or parsley

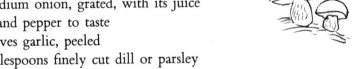

Set aside about one-third of the largest mushrooms and remove the caps. Finely mince the stems and the remaining mushrooms and sauté them in 4 tablespoons of the butter. When the juices have exuded but not evaporated, stir in the grated onion and its juice and continue to cook until the mixture is quite dry. Add salt and pepper to taste and reserve the mixture. To the sauté pan add the garlic cloves, the remaining 3 tablespoons of butter, and the reserved whole mushroom caps. Sauté the caps on both sides until golden-brown, but don't let them get dark and dry. Remove the garlic. Pack the mushroom caps with the minced mushroom mixture. In the sauté pan, heat them through, covered, over very low heat. Sprinkle the mushrooms with dill or parsley.

## PICKLED MUSHROOMS

*Makes about 2 pints*

This is a delicate and perishable pickle. I don't think you should keep it (in the refrigerator) more than two weeks. For longer storage, I substitute 3 tablespoons white vinegar for the 4 tablespoons brown cider vinegar. Nowadays, with mushrooms always available, there's no point anyway in putting up large batches. This recipe takes only a few minutes to accomplish, and I pickle mushrooms as needed: for instance, to accompany a salad of salt herring.

    1 pound (450 grams) fine white mushrooms
    2 medium onions, sliced thin
    1 teaspoon whole black peppercorns
    2 small bay leaves
    1 teaspoon salt
    4 tablespoons cider vinegar

Clean the mushrooms very well. Cut the stems even with the caps. Steam them, covered, in ½ cup water with the sliced onions, peppercorns, bay leaves, and salt. After about 5 minutes, the mushrooms should have exuded their liquid. At this point, add the vinegar, and simmer, covered, for 10 minutes longer. Taste the pickle. You may want more salt or more vinegar, or both, but be cautious.

Pour the mushrooms, spices, and liquid into clean jars. Cover the jars tightly and refrigerate them.

*Onions*

## ONIONS WITH RAISINS AND PORT

*Serves 6*

Eva made this years ago for a big family Christmas dinner to accompany a ham—extraordinarily sweet and seemingly salt-free—sent by a friend from Virginia. Onions cooked this way lend their natural sweetness to the raisins and port, and together make a caramellike glaze that is attractive as well as delicious. Try them this way as a substitute for the traditional but rather bland creamed onions often served with a Thanksgiving turkey.

24 white onions (about 1¼ inches in diameter)
1 piece of lemon zest 1 by 2 inches, including the white pith
   (to reduce cooking smell)
3 tablespoons olive or vegetable oil
⅓ cup (¾ deciliter) port
⅓ cup (¾ deciliter) cider or red wine vinegar
½ cup (1 deciliter) raisins
2 teaspoons sugar
Salt to taste
Pepper to taste

Put the *unpeeled,* untrimmed onions and the lemon zest into water to cover, bring to a boil, and simmer for 10 minutes. Drain, then put them briefly into cold water. (Discard the zest.) The onion skins will then slip off easily, but be careful to remove only the outer skin and membrane and not to cut into the first layer of onion.

In a skillet, preferably nonstick, large enough to hold all the onions closely in 1 layer, sauté them over medium heat in the oil, occasionally shaking the pan so the onions brown lightly on all sides.

Add the port, vinegar, raisins, sugar, and a light sprinkling of salt and pepper, stir well, and cover the skillet. (If it has no lid, use heavy foil.) Simmer gently, stirring occasionally, for about 15 minutes, or until the onions are tender, and the liquid has turned into a rich syrup. Serve hot, with the raisins and pan juices poured over.

## SMOTHERED ONIONS

*Makes 6 small servings*

These are so rich and full-flavored that I think of them more as a garnish than as a vegetable dish: wonderful with steak (see p. 181)! They differ from sautéed onions, because they are cooked with the lid on—literally smothered —which keeps them very soft. They should not be too dark in color.

6 medium onions, sliced fine and separated into rings
3 tablespoons butter
Salt (optional)

Sauté the onions slowly, uncovered, in the butter until they are lightly colored. Then cover and continue cooking them, over low heat, until the onions are limp: about 15 minutes. Add salt, if you like.

## *Potatoes*

My favorite vegetable need not be merely a complement for meat. The first two potato dishes here are often served with a *barszcz* (pp. 18 and 19), or with Clabbered Milk (p. 64) as the main course. And frequently I've made a whole meal of Potato Pancakes with sour cream.

This section has been confined to the recipes I think extra-choice or else a bit unusual. At one point it threatened to run away with the book.

## BOILED POTATOES WITH BACON AND ONION

*Serves 6*

6 small potatoes, peeled, or "new" potatoes, unpeeled
Slab bacon, cut in ½-inch dice
2 small onions, chopped medium-fine
1 tablespoon butter or 1 tablespoon reserved rendered
    bacon fat

In a large pot of salted water, boil the potatoes until done, for 35–40 minutes, drain them, and keep them hot. (If using "new" potatoes, peel them now.) Cook the bacon dice until they are brown and crisp. Cook the chopped onion, either in butter or in the bacon fat. Sprinkle the potatoes with the onion and bacon bits, and, if you like, drizzle a few drops of bacon fat over each.

## LITHUANIAN POTATOES

*Serves 6*

This is a simple and delicious dish of my childhood. The potatoes are partly in pieces, partly mashed and creamy, with the tiny occasional bit of raw onion and the pungent pepper adding contrast, making the whole a very unusual and tasty combination. It is especially good with broiled chops or steaks.

6 medium Idaho potatoes
3 tablespoons very finely minced raw onion
7–8 tablespoons sour cream
1 tablespoon or more coarsely ground or crushed
    black pepper
Salt to taste

Peel the potatoes and boil them whole in salted water for better "chunking." When they are just done (40–50 minutes pan-boiled, depending on their size and age; 10 minutes or so in a pressure cooker), drain them well and dry them, shaking the pot, over heat. Mix in the onion and sour cream with a wooden spoon. Some of the potato will get mashed; some will stay in chunks. Sprinkle with pepper, taste for salt, and serve.

*Note:* Boiled "new" potatoes are also very good with Mustard Sauce (p. 51).

## POMMES RISSOLÉES

*Serves 4*

These rich and flavorful morsels are most elegant with all roast meats and chops. They are just raw potato balls sautéed in butter or oil until the outsides are golden (not brown) and slightly waxy; the mealy insides are just a little firmer than a perfect French fry.

Use a nonstick pan if possible, and if you plan to serve more than 4 people, use 2 pans. This is so that the pan will be evenly heated and so that the potato balls won't be too crowded to move and turn as you shake them, which you do continuously. (Doing it with a spoon or spatula is too slow; some of the balls get brown "cheeks" while waiting their turn. But have a spoon in your free hand in case any stick or act stubborn.)

About 8 large all-purpose potatoes (to make 32 potato balls)
8 tablespoons clarified butter or very fresh oil
2 tablespoons finely cut fresh parsley

Peel the potatoes and carefully cut 32 balls with the large scoop of a melon-ball cutter. (Use the hollowed remains for soup.) Drop the balls in a bowl of water.

Full details on clarifying butter are on page 63: Briefly, you melt butter over medium heat, let the water content evaporate (it bubbles, then stops bubbling), and quickly, before it colors, skim and discard the foam, then pour off and reserve the golden liquid. Discard the white sediment.

Over medium heat, bring the clarified butter or oil to just short of the smoking point. Dry the potatoes in a kitchen towel as you drop them into the fat. To color them evenly, keep them moving all the time by jiggling the pan. If the pan has a lid, put it on while shaking. If the butter darkens or is getting too hot, lift the pan off the heat for a moment. If the butter or oil begins to smoke, drain it off, wash the pan, and resume with the same potatoes in fresh fat.

When the potatoes are an even, rich, but not dark, gold color all over, lower the heat to finish them. (The whole job takes about 20 minutes.) Taste one, to see if the centers are done. Sprinkle them with the parsley and serve at once.

*Note:* You can cheat a little by simmering the raw potato balls in water for 10 minutes, until just cooked through. Then sauté them to color them all over. They will be good but not as good.

## POMMES ALLUMETTES

*Serves 6*

These "matchstick" (sometimes called "shoestring") potatoes are good with game; I must say, however, I look on them as an extravagance to be indulged in only rarely. Anything deep-fried is expensive, since it uses so much fat; it is fattening, for the same reason; it requires your presence in the kitchen at the last minute, since deep-fried dishes should be eaten promptly after cooking; and finally, *Pommes Allumettes* must be evenly and precisely cut, by hand. I find this great fun, as I do any fine handwork, but it does take time: I am told that Escoffier prescribed little potato sticks just ⅕ inch square and have since found that what looks right to me does measure exactly that.

Nevertheless, there are times when no other potato dish will do. Delicate, golden, with a perfect proportion of crisp outside to mellow interior, *Pommes Allumettes* are really worth all the trouble. They look elegant and are delicious, especially with partridge, guinea hen, and roast pheasant.

The amount of lard or oil varies with the shape and size of your frying pot. One fries the potatoes in small enough batches so that the hot lard returns almost instantly to full heat. I suggest you do a test batch the first time and add more lard or reduce the batch size at your convenience.

6 fine, shapely, medium-size Idaho potatoes
3–4 cups (1¼–1⅔ pounds or 560–740 grams)
   fine fresh lard or vegetable oil
2 teaspoons salt

Peel the potatoes and cut them into precise sticks, with very square corners and straight sides—2 inches long, ⅕ inch square in cross section. Drop them into a bowl of lukewarm water as you cut them. This keeps the sticks white and soaks out unwanted starch.

Bring the lard or oil to medium temperature, about 320°F (160°C), in the frying pot. Dry about one-third of the potato sticks in an absorbent towel and put them in a frying basket. Submerge them in the hot lard. They will bubble and hiss; the moment this subsides, remove the potatoes and leave them to drain on paper towels while you fry the next batch. They will look floppy and they should. The next stage will make them crisp. (Up to this point they can be made an hour or so ahead.)

Moments before serving, bring the lard up to high temperature, about 380°F (195°C). Fry the potatoes again, in batches, just until they are crisp and beautifully colored. Drain them well and keep them hot while you do the next batch. Three batches will take only about 5 minutes all told. Toss the well-drained potatoes with the 2 teaspoons of salt (or more if you like) and serve them right away.

## POTATOES À LA BARBARKA

*Serves 6*

Though she could scarcely read or write, our cook Barbarka had great imagination and style; our guests were always falling in love with her. Her culinary inventions, I think, expressed her vivid personality; this dish is one of her best, and I have never seen it elsewhere.

Potatoes are peeled, hollowed, blanched, and filled with a heavily buttered mixture of minced mushrooms and onions, then baked. The butter infuses the flesh of the potato, which is delicately browned on the outside; and it is amusing to take off the potato's little "hat" and find the dark, good-smelling stuffing. As one can prepare this dish in advance, to serve with Beef Tenderloin, Roasted (p. 183) or another roast, it is practical for parties.

> 6 fine medium potatoes, as spherical as possible
>     (either baking potatoes or the big red "new"
>     potatoes will do)
> 3 medium onions, diced fine
> 3 tablespoons oil
> 1 pound (450 grams) mushrooms, minced fine
> 7 tablespoons butter
> 12 grinds pepper
> 1 tablespoon flour
> 1 teaspoon Maggi extract
> Salt to taste

Peel the potatoes, then cut off one end of each potato, so that it will stand securely in the baking dish. Cut off the other end to make a "hat," making this cut parallel with the first, so that the hat will sit level and not slide off. With a melon-ball cutter, hollow each potato to form a shell ⅜ inch thick. (This goes very easily; one can sculpt a perfectly smooth hollow. I use the discarded bits to thicken soups.)

Plunge the potatoes and their "hats" into a large pot of boiling water, and simmer for 5 minutes. One does this so that the outsides will absorb the basting butter and take on a little color. It also guards against discoloration if the potatoes are to be prepared in advance of baking. Drain the potatoes.

To make the stuffing, sauté the finely diced onions in the oil until they are softened and pale golden. Add the finely minced mushrooms, 4 tablespoons of the butter, and pepper. Cook slowly, stirring, until the mushroom juice has exuded. Sprinkle with flour and cook for 3–4 minutes more. Add the Maggi extract and salt to taste.

Preheat the oven to 350°F (180°C). Melt the remaining 3 tablespoons of butter in a low baking dish. Roll the potatoes and their "hats" in the butter to coat all outside surfaces. Fill the potato hollows with the stuffing, and set the potatoes upright in the dish. Put the "hats" on. To make absolutely sure they won't slip, I affix each one with a toothpick. Bake the potatoes for about 1 hour or until done (test with a toothpick), basting them frequently with the butter in the dish.

# RÖSTLI

*Serves 6*

*Röstli* is the Swiss name for a big thick potato pancake that is served in wedges. It is excellent with almost any kind of meat, but especially with steaks or ground meat cutlets. As it takes about 15 minutes to sauté, and as it should really be eaten hot from the skillet, allow time.

Preblanching the potatoes in their skins prevents discoloration of the flesh, which sometimes occurs in old, winter-crop potatoes after peeling.

4 large baking potatoes
3–5 tablespoons oil or lard
1½ teaspoons salt
6 grinds pepper

In a large pot of boiling water, boil the scrubbed but unpeeled potatoes for 5 minutes after the water returns to the boil. Drain and peel them and shred the flesh. (The grating disk of the processor does a good job, or use the large side of a plain grater.) Put the shreds in a large skillet with the oil or lard over medium heat. Salt and pepper them, and press the shreds into a thick mat with a pancake spatula or a wooden spoon. Their natural starch will bind them together.

After about 6 minutes, look to see whether the underside has browned nicely. When it is golden-brown, turn the pancake. The easiest way is to slide it onto a large plate or pot lid, then reverse the pan over it and quickly invert it, browned side up. Add oil if the pan seems dry and continue cooking until the second side of the pancake is golden-brown.

## POTATO PANCAKES
### *(Bliny Kartoflane)*

*Serves 6*

Served with sour cream, these pancakes are a main luncheon course all by themselves, according to my children, who love them. They are also very good with steak or game, in place of the classic *Pommes Allumettes* (p. 281), which are three times the work and require deep fat in the bargain. The pancakes are so quick to do that I regularly make them between courses; if you have things set up on the stove, a batch takes only about 5 minutes in all.

I hope you will like my way of making these without adding a binder of flour, using the natural starch instead. It gives you a purer, all-potato pancake.

4 large potatoes
½ cup (1 deciliter) water (for blender
   or processor method)
1 tablespoon onion, minced (optional)
2 eggs
Lard or vegetable shortening for frying
2 teaspoons salt (optional)
Sour cream, served separately

Peel the potatoes and grate them in the processor or blender. In the processor: Use the steel blade, not the grating disk, which shreds potatoes. Cut the potatoes into eighths and do them in 1 batch with half the water and the optional minced onion. Do it in bursts, cautiously, so as not to liquefy the potatoes. In the blender: Pour in the water first, then the optional minced onion, then half the potatoes, cut up. When the potatoes are grated sufficiently, strain them, and do the second batch in the same liquid, then combine with the first batch, liquid included. The liquid does 2 things: it keeps the grated potatoes white and it saves all their starch (which is used to hold the pancakes together).

Beat the eggs and start the fat heating in the sauté pan.

At the last minute, strain the potatoes over a bowl to catch their liquid. In seconds, the starch will settle at the bottom of the bowl. Pour off the liquid, leaving the starch in tact. Add the beaten eggs and the strained grated potatoes to the starch in the bowl, mixing them together. Add salt if you like.

If you have a large, cast-iron skillet, use that; otherwise, use the heaviest pan you have. Sprinkle it with salt (coarse, if possible) and heat until the salt starts *crackling*. Discard the salt. Put enough lard in the skillet to have it ¼ inch deep for the first batch.

Over medium-high heat, carefully drop tablespoonfuls of the potato mixture into the pan. It should "splash" a bit, to make a lacy edge. Flatten slightly to make 3½-inch rounds. Fry them, turning them once, until they are golden-brown. If you have to do 2 batches, the first batch can wait in a warm oven while you do the second, but no longer. You want these pancakes beautifully crisp. Serve with sour cream.

## RUTABAGA WITH DICED BACON SKWARKI

*Serves 6*

Rutabagas are very large yellow turnips and when peeled are light cantaloupe color. (They are occasionally sold waxed, so peel them thoroughly.) Cooked, they are yellow, and a bit sweet.

For many years, never having seen the word "rutabaga" spelled in English, I pronounced it rather like "Rutberger," which was the name of a potter who lived in the village near my home in Lithuania, on a hill that seemed to be made entirely of the red clay with which he made his pots. As a child, entranced, I would often sit watching him at his wheel as his hands molded and gave shape to the clay. It was really both a magical and a sensual experience and could well be one of the reasons I have always loved doing things with my hands—sculpting, embroidering, drawing, and, most of all, taking real pleasure in the handwork of the kitchen. Although I realize that all the fantastic machines we are coming to take for granted are wonderful time and energy savers, I can't help feeling a little nostalgic for the days when speed was somewhat less essential than the more personal touch of human hands.

What has all this to do with rutabagas? For one thing, no machine I know of will cut vegetables into ½-inch dice as neatly and quickly as a good, sharp, thin-bladed French knife, or cut slab bacon into nice ¼-inch cubes for *skwarki,* "little squares."

Rutabagas may be served just buttered, or mashed and blended half and half with mashed potatoes. They are especially good and attractive cooked in dice and served with bacon *skwarki.* For more about *skwarki,* see page 65.

1 rutabaga (about 2 pounds or 900 grams)
½ teaspoon salt, or to taste
2 tablespoons butter (optional)
Sugar to taste

THE BACON SKWARKI

¼ pound (115 grams) slab bacon,
   or 6 *thick* slices regular bacon

Carefully peel the rutabaga and cut into ½-inch dice. Put them into a pot with cold salted water to cover. Bring the water to the boil, turn down the heat, cover the pot, and cook for 20 minutes, or until tender. Test for doneness with a fork. (In a pressure cooker, cook only 5 minutes after pressure is reached.) Drain the rutabaga very thoroughly and return to the pot. Toss with optional butter.

Meanwhile, cut the slab bacon into dice just over ¼ inch, cubed. Sauté them, in butter, if you like, preferably in a nonstick pan, until they have browned, but not burned. Remove the *skwarki* with a slotted spoon and drain on paper towels.

Add a little salt and sugar to taste to the rutabaga. When ready to serve, sprinkle it with the bacon and, if you like, dribble a little of the rendered bacon fat over all.

*Variation:* Toss with 1 teaspoon finely minced fresh ginger.

## *Spinach*

The important thing about this vegetable is to cook it as little as possible.
Here are the two ways I do it most often.

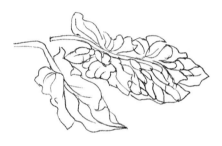

## ÉPINARDS EN BRANCHES
### (Leaf Spinach)

*Serves 6*

2 pounds (900 grams) fresh spinach
1 tablespoon butter and 1 tablespoon lemon juice, or
  1 tablespoon olive oil and 1 whole clove garlic

Wash the spinach and remove the larger stems. Plunge it into a soup kettle
full of lightly salted, furiously boiling water. Cook for about 15–20 seconds,
or until the spinach is just barely limp. Drain it well, then sauté it briefly,
not more than 5 minutes, in the butter and lemon juice, or in the oil with
garlic (which you then discard).

This is good cold with a Vinaigrette (p. 294) and quartered hard-boiled
eggs.

## CREAMED SPINACH

*Serves 6*

This is a purée and should be garnished with "croutons," which in this case mean triangles of crustless white bread, sautéed in a little oil and butter.

2 pounds (900 grams) fresh spinach
1 tablespoon flour
1 tablespoon butter
½ cup (1 deciliter) light cream or half-and-half
1 teaspoon sugar
Salt and pepper to taste
Dash of Maggi extract
¼ cup (½ deciliter) heavy cream

Wash the spinach, stem it carefully, and boil it as for *Épinards en Branches* (preceding recipe), but for 2 or 3 minutes. Drain it very well. Chop it fine or pass it through a vegetable mill. (Use the processor only if you want the purée particularly fine.) Cook the flour in the butter, stirring, until it is thickened and smooth; then add the light cream or half-and-half, and cook, stirring, until the sauce has thickened and the flour no longer tastes raw. Add the spinach and cook about 5 minutes longer. Season to taste, using sugar, salt, pepper, and Maggi. At the last minute, add the heavy cream, mix well, and just heat through.

## *Zucchini*

I like zucchini best when they are quite young—they need very little cooking and their shiny green skins are particularly appetizing. This is an extremely adaptable vegetable, equally delicious hot or cold, cooked or raw, or as part of combinations, such as ratatouille.

Larger zucchini are perhaps best sliced and deep-fried.

## STUFFED ZUCCHINI, HOT AND COLD

*Serves 6*

Stuffed with similar mixtures of seasoned, chopped hard-boiled eggs, these look most attractive, hot on a platter of roast meat or cold on a buffet table.

HOT ZUCCHINI

   3 hard-boiled eggs
   2 tablespoons butter, softened
   2 tablespoons finely cut chives or green scallion tops
   Salt and pepper to taste
   6 small zucchini (5–6 inches long)
   2 tablespoons bread crumbs
   1 tablespoon freshly grated Parmesan cheese

Chop the eggs fairly fine. Mash them with the butter, the chives or scallions, and salt and pepper.

Poach the washed, unpeeled, and untrimmed zucchini in lightly salted water for about 4–5 minutes. Trim off the ends, and cut the zucchini in half the long way. Preheat the oven to 350°F (180°C). Scoop out the seed portions and a little of the flesh with a spoon and fill the zucchini "boats" with the egg mixture. Mix the bread crumbs with the Parmesan and sprinkle lightly over the eggs. In a buttered ovenproof dish, heat them in the oven for 10–15 minutes, then put them under the broiler for a few minutes just until the tops brown. Serve immediately.

COLD ZUCCHINI

3 hard-boiled eggs
2 tablespoons mayonnaise
2 tablespoons finely cut chives or green scallion tops
Salt and pepper to taste
6 small zucchini (5–6 inches long)
Pimiento for decorations

Follow exactly the directions for hot zucchini, but add the mayonnaise to the chopped hard-boiled eggs and let the zucchini "boats" and eggs cool before stuffing. Refrigerate, not more than an hour or so (so the egg mixture doesn't dry), and decorate with strips of pimiento before serving.

## DEEP-FRIED ZUCCHINI

*Serves 6*

6 medium zucchini
1 teaspoon salt
About 3 tablespoons flour
Oil for frying—about 2 cups (½ liter),
    depending on your pot
½ teaspoon minced garlic
5 grinds pepper
1 lemon, cut in 6 wedges

Slice in ¼-inch rounds the unpeeled zucchini, sprinkle with the salt, and let sit until some juice exudes. Dry the slices on paper towels and flour them lightly, patting off the excess. Deep-fry them in very hot oil, about 375° F (190°C): hot enough to brown a bread cube in 1 second. Drain the slices on paper towels, sprinkle them with minced garlic, pepper, and salt, if you think, after tasting, that they need it. Serve with lemon wedges.

*Variation:* Zucchini make good fritters, following the general rule for Eggplant Fritters (p. 89).

# VEGETABLE JULIENNE

*Serves 6*

This simple-sounding recipe makes an excellent dish for a winter meal, accompanying ground meat dishes such as Beef Cutlets, Spanish Style (p. 184), ground Lamb Cutlets (p. 200), or Meat Loaf (p. 219).

   1 medium leek, white part only
   1 small celery root (celeriac)
   2 medium carrots
   2 small parsnips
   2 tablespoons butter
   1 tablespoon tomato paste, or more to taste
   1 teaspoon sugar
   1 teaspoon salt, or to taste
   4 grinds pepper

Cut the leek in fine crosswise slices and separate them into rings. Wash and drain them well.

Slice the celery root for easier peeling. Peel the carrots and parsnips. Cut these root vegetables into inch-long sticks thinner than paper matches, using a rotary cutter or the processor fitted with the julienne blade. Or if, like me, you enjoy cutting by hand, just use a big, sharp knife. Sauté them in the butter until they are medium-soft.

Add the leek to the sauté pan, mix well, and sauté the vegetables a minute more. Sprinkle on about 2 tablespoons water, cover the pan, and simmer over very low heat for about 10 minutes. Mix in, off heat, the tomato paste, the sugar, salt, and pepper. Taste the dish very carefully and add more seasoning if you need it.

# Salads

My family likes a salad at every meal, usually as an accompaniment to the main course, rather than a course by itself. (But when we are serving sauerkraut with the meat, I omit salad and often serve applesauce or baked apples instead.) This group of salad ideas includes a few, like celery root and black radish, that are usually served as hors d'oeuvres but can just as well be treated as relishes.

As for dressings, mine are quite simple and ordinary. I always include a tiny bit of sugar and use American cider vinegar when it is obtainable (in France it often isn't); otherwise red wine vinegar.

As for herbs, they are important in all my cooking, so I discussed them at the beginning, in the Sauces and Notions chapter, page 72. Briefly, I think this: for a dressing, crush herbs; for a garnish, finely cut (don't chop) them.

*Salad Dressings*

## VINAIGRETTE

I prefer vinegar to lemon and use oil in a proportion of 3 to 1, with equal amounts of salt, sugar, and pepper.

*Variations:* Add equal amounts of crushed chives, tarragon, and parsley; add finely cut shallots; add dry English mustard beaten with the yolk of a hard-boiled egg (sometimes I use my own mustard-honey combination, p. 51).

## SOUR CREAM DRESSING

½ cup (1 deciliter) sour cream
1 tablespoon vinegar
1 tablespoon finely cut chives or scallions
½ teaspoon sugar
½ teaspoon salt

Thoroughly blend together all ingredients.

# MAYONNAISE

2 egg yolks
½ teaspoon confectioners sugar
1 cup (¼ liter) olive oil
1 tablespoon vinegar or lemon juice
½ teaspoon salt
¼ teaspoon white pepper

Whisk or blend the egg yolks until they are pale and very thick. Add the sugar and beat until it is dissolved. Add the oil by drops, beating or whisking all the time, until the mixture is thick enough to mound a little on your fingertip. Then you can add the oil by tablespoonfuls, still beating or blending constantly. When the mixture is thick, add the vinegar or lemon juice, salt and pepper, taste, and correct the seasoning.

### Variations

*Sauce rémoulade:* To each cup of mayonnaise add 1 tablespoon each of finely chopped capers, finely cut mixed fresh herbs, and finely diced *cornichons* (the little French sour pickles, not "sweet tiny gherkins").

*Sauce verte:* Instead of putting the salt into the mayonnaise, add it to the following herbs in a mortar: to each cup of mayonnaise add 1 tablespoon each of crushed chives, chervil, and tarragon. For a more intense green color, crush 1 tablespoon minced watercress leaves with the herbs, or add 2 drops of green vegetable coloring. The watercress also adds a little bite. Refrigerate the sauce for a day before you use it.

*Pink mayonnaise:* Add ketchup, tasting carefully, as brands vary. I don't use it just for the color; I love the taste. See page 151 for similar recipes for Green Mayonnaise and Pink Mayonnaise.

*Note:* If you are using bottled mayonnaise, taste carefully for salt before adding any more.

## Two Relishes

These can be part of a variety of hors d'oeuvres, or garnishes for cold meats, or they can be served with an entrée on small individual side plates.

You might also think of Pickled Mushrooms (p. 276) when you are planning this sort of food.

### BLACK RADISH RELISH

*Makes 1 cup*

Unpeeled, this radish looks like a coal black turnip, but inside it is snow white. Milder and sweeter than the red, tastier than the white, black radishes make a very fresh-tasting little condiment. Those who like beer will love it with black radish relish dabbed on a bit of black bread, accompanied by a slice of some good cold sausage.

3 black radishes, medium-size (like a medium beet), peeled
1½ teaspoons salt
2 tablespoons very finely cut scallions or fresh chives
⅓ cup (¾ deciliter) or more sour cream

In the processor (with the grating disk) or by hand, grate the peeled radishes. Mix the pulp with the salt. Tie it up in rinsed cheesecloth or a dish towel, weight the parcel (an 8-ounce can will do), and let it sit for 30 minutes or so in a colander. Quite a lot of moisture will exude. Squeeze out more. The radish now is very crisp and delightful to chew. Add the finely cut scallions or chives and the sour cream, taste, and correct the seasoning.

*Note:* The radish has a very pungent odor and must be covered tightly when refrigerated. You might also want a little extra ventilation when grating!

## CELERY ROOT (CELERIAC) RELISH

*Makes 1 cup*

1 small celeriac
2 teaspoons salt
Dijon-type mustard, to taste
About 4 tablespoons Mayonnaise (p. 295)

Celery root is best peeled by cutting it into slices, so that you can get cross sections of its annoying surface crannies. Cut or process it in fine julienne, sprinkle it with the salt, mixing well, and let it sit for an hour. Discard any exuded liquid: there may be none, but the celery root will have become softer. Pat the julienned root dry. Mix it with mustard-flavored mayonnaise (use less salt if using commercial mayonnaise).

## *Green Salads*

Five principles sum up a good green salad; clichés or not, I really cannot omit them.

1. Choose an interesting mixture of greens, some tender, some crisp; some mild, some assertive.
2. Wash them well and dry them carefully, keeping them chilled until used.
3. Tear the leaves; they look more three-dimensional somehow! Cut leaves seem to flatten and get soggy.
4. Do not dress and toss the salad until the last moment— preferably do it at the table.
5. For tossing salads, be sure to use a bowl larger than you think you need!

## Combination Salads

One summer while shopping in the shady whitewashed market hall in Marbella, I was fascinated by great piles of melons emitting most delicious aromas. There were cantaloupes, white-skinned melons with green flesh, and yellow ones with orange meat inside. I don't even know their names, but I bought one of each, carved them into balls, added a fresh crisp cucumber from my own garden, and mixed it with a light pink mayonnaise dressing. The result was most pleasant, refreshing, and won the approval of my family.

Here are a few other ideas, probably familiar to you, but they might inspire variations: add a few walnut meats to an apple and heart of celery salad; cut endives in crosswise slices, soak them briefly in ice water so they won't be bitter, drain, then mix with diced apples and mayonnaise; slice raw mushrooms over young crisp green beans; try string beans with artichoke hearts; grapefruit or orange sections with avocado; endive and sliced beets and sieved hard-boiled egg; watercress with crumbled bacon and hard-boiled egg; avocado with melon, papayas, and oranges. And for winter days and meals, a popular Lithuanian salad, which is plain sauerkraut fresh or from the can, served with its juice, and sprinkled with a little sugar—nothing else added!

## *Vegetable Salads*

One can get bored, though not for long, with green salads and with hot vegetables. So, for a change, I serve vegetables dressed like salads: not very cold, and never in large quantities. It's nice sometimes just to have a little bowl of some lively cool vegetable, quite sharply seasoned, beside one's entrée plate or as a bridge between courses.

### BEAN SPROUTS SALAD

To soften the sprouts just a little, pour boiling water over them and drain them immediately. They combine well with paper-thin slivers of white Spanish or Bermuda onions, which have been soaked briefly in ice water. Or add fine shreds of ham and/or cheese. I don't use a regular dressing, just a sprinkle of soy sauce.

### CARROT AND APPLE SALAD

Scrape young crisp carrots and shred fine. Peel an equal amount of apples and shred. (The little Mouli rotary grater does this perfectly, or the fine shredding disk of the processor.) Mix the shreds with mayonnaise, using as little as possible. Taste and add a little sugar, salt, pepper, and vinegar or lemon juice to taste. Mix in well, with a handful of seedless raisins.

### RED CABBAGE SALAD

Cut it in very fine, almost hair-fine shreds, sprinkle it with salt, and let it rest for an hour. Then press out the excess liquid and season the cabbage with vinegar, sugar, and (cautiously) additional salt.

## CUCUMBER SALAD

Fat, ordinary cucumbers I peel and split in half lengthwise, to get out the seeds; then I slice the flesh into half-moons. Those long, firm, thin-skinned hothouse cucumbers, I just peel and slice about ⅛ inch thick. For either kind, the slices are sprinkled with salt, allowed to sit for 15 minutes or more in a colander, weighted with a heavy pot or a can on a plate, then drained carefully. Season them with Sour Cream Dressing (p. 294), or just vinegar, sugar, and finely cut dill.

## GREEN BEAN SALAD

This recipe does not produce the bright green, almost raw stack of matchstick-thin, immature green beans you may be thinking of. It is intended for the too-big everyday green bean, and it tastes decidedly "cooked"—rich and nutty, in fact—and is olive green in color. Cut your big beans crosswise into ½-inch cylinders, a shape that holds dressing well. Put them in the pressure cooker with ½ cup water, a pinch of salt, and a sliver of garlic. Cover the pot and cook for 1 minute after pressure has been reached. Quickly stop the cooking, drench the beans in cold water, and drain and dry them well. They are nice in a Vinaigrette with finely cut herbs (p. 294).

## RED PEPPER SALAD

To peel red peppers, broil them, turning them once or twice, until they are charred all over. This will also add a pleasant smoky flavor. Then let them cool until they can be touched. Remove the skins, stems, cores, and every single seed. Cut the peppers in ⅓-inch strips and marinate them briefly with thin onion rings in just enough oil to coat them. Sprinkle on vinegar to taste, a pinch or two of salt, and mix well.

## HOT POTATO SALAD

My recipe is just the classic one, but here are 2 hints. First, if you haven't got the proper waxy or boiling potatoes, you can get much the same texture by cooking ordinary peeled potatoes in a steamer. I prefer to cook the potatoes just before serving and peel and dress them while they are still hot. But if the potatoes have to be cooked in advance and are cool (but not refrigerated), one can just heat up the oil, vinegar, pepper, salt, and minced onions (or scallions or shallots), then gently add the cubed cooled potatoes to the warm pot, and combine it all. Taste and adjust seasonings.

## ZUCCHINI, WATERCRESS, AND
## RED ONION SALAD

Eva makes a salad that is both attractive to the eye and interesting to the palate. Wash but don't trim fresh, firm zucchini, and poach them in unsalted water for 2 minutes per inch of thickness (try to find even-size ones). A pinch of baking soda in the water preserves their color. Plunge them into cold water, trim, then slice them crosswise into ⅛-inch slices. Wash the watercress and dry thoroughly, removing the thicker stems. Peel and slice red onion *paper thin,* separating the rings, then at the last minute toss everything together with a Vinaigrette dressing (p. 294).

Kisiel

Bananes Flambées

Fruit and Cream, Broiled

Fruit with Lemon Cream

Raspberry Cream

Coconut and Raspberry Jelly

Barbarka's Caramel Mousse

Pears with Sabayon or Vanilla Sauce

Poires Belle Hélène

Lemon Bavarian Cream

Chocolate Mousse

Banana Custard

Crème Brûlée

Caramel Custard (Flan)

Crème Mocha

Coffee Custard

Steamed Coffee Pudding (or Soufflé)

Steamed Chocolate Pudding (or Soufflé)

Steamed Lemon Pudding (or Soufflé)

Rice Pudding

Pâte Sablée

Lemon Custard Tart

Strawberry Tart

Apple and Caramel Tart

Apple and Almond Tart

Three Mazurkas with Pâte Sablée—
   Orange, Vanilla-Cream, and
   Chocolate Icings

Almond Mazurka

Glazed Apple Tart

Chrust

Racuszki

Pastry Cookies and Jam Turnovers ("Jammies")

Schmoor (with Pâte à Choux)

Apple and Banana Dessert Fritters

Crêpes with Jam or Sugar or Filling

Cheese and Walnut Filling

Lemon Filling

Crêpes Suzette

Omelette Viennoise

Clafoutis with Sour Cherries

Sucharki Ilgowskie (Ilgovo Rusks)

Babka (Sweet Raisin Bread)

Cheese Cake

Nanny's Luscious Lemon Cake

Honey and Spice Cake

Chocolate Cake

Sand Torte with Orange Butter-
   Cream Filling

Torte Orzechowy (Walnut Cake)
   with Chocolate-Butter Filling

Almond and Coffee Torte

Coffee Glaze (for Almond Torte)

# Desserts

When a meal has been copious, I like to end it with fruit, especially in summer. Otherwise, I think it is more satisfying to have a dessert. Then you don't get too hungry between meals, so in the end you eat less and feel better.

For guests it often amuses me to serve two or three desserts, partly to show off and partly to give friends the fun of choosing between, say, a *crème brûlée,* a raspberry and coconut jelly, and a lemon tart. Greedy people—I love greedy people—will enjoy all three.

Most of my desserts are uncomplicated, and they are usually a major element in the meal; you will find several such everyday dishes at the beginning of this chapter: simple fruit desserts, jellies, and egg-based custards and puddings. It was hard to limit the group of pastries that follows these: baked ones and poached ones, tarts, pies, turnovers, cookies, dumplings, and *pierogi,* and Mazurkas, the traditional Polish confections one eats almost like candy. And then the pancakes and fritters! The doughs and batters I use, both for desserts and for savory dishes (as in the Little Entrées chapter), are few in number and very simple; but once you have made them, you will realize how adaptable they are, and hundreds of improvisations will occur to you. You need never repeat yourself, unless compelled to by popular demand— the Lemon Custard Tart (p. 331), for instance, is one people seem to remember for years.

Between these desserts and the cakes, I have tucked in one unclassifiable recipe for *Sucharki,* or rusks (p. 356). They were a daily staple at Ilgovo, the house of my mother's family, and for all I know, the recipe is centuries old. Very ancient, too, are most of the cake recipes that follow. But I seem never to be able to restrain myself from inventing, improvising (sometimes even improving) recipes. Even as we were testing and double-checking the Steamed Coffee Pudding (p. 324) for this book, I saw some nice fresh lemons in the refrigerator and was suddenly inspired to try a variation (p. 326) with lemon, one of my favorite flavors (along with coffee, chocolate, vanilla, apricot, raspberry, black currant). I made the lemon steamed pudding on the spot and served it at dinner. My two daughters and I devoured every bit of what we decided later, somewhat embarrassed, would serve six.

# KIŚIEL
## (pronounced keesh'l)

*Serves 6*

Because it is so simple and so pure, nothing more than a tart red fruit juice slightly thickened, *kiśiel* used to be considered a nursery dessert in its native Russia. In fact it is an excellent way to end the many rich courses of a copious dinner. I like to serve it warm, in soup plates, with heavy cream passed separately. You swirl in a little cream with just one stir (never mix it), and there is something pleasing about the contrast of red and white, warm and cold, tart and bland, velvety and satiny, as they mingle in your mouth.

Two 10-ounce (285-gram) packages "quick thaw"
   frozen raspberries
Water, if necessary
2–3½ teaspoons potato starch
   (also known as potato flour) or cornstarch
Sugar to taste
Heavy cream, as an accompaniment

All other quantities must be adjusted to the kind of juice you use. The flavor should be intense, and the sweetness must not be cloying. For the juice of packaged frozen raspberries (my favorite version), thaw the raspberries, then cook them over medium heat, in their juice, until the berries are cooked through inside and have darkened slightly in color. This takes about 10 minutes' simmering. A pink scum may foam up on the surface, but it will disappear later. Strain the berries, pressing them only very lightly. The 2 packages will yield a scant 2 cups of clear, not pulpy, juice. Add to this enough water to make 2½ cups (6 deciliters). Refrigerate ½ cup (1 deciliter) of the liquid and, when cold, mix it carefully with the potato starch or cornstarch. Strain the starch mixture into the reserved juice, taste it, and add sugar if you wish. Bring it to a boil, stirring (not whisking—that can lighten the color), and stir it for 5 minutes until thickened to the consistency of a medium-thick sauce.

I serve *kiśiel* warm; if you plan to serve it cold, use only 2½ teaspoons potato starch, for the liquid thickens as it cools. Serve with heavy cream.

*Variations:* The juice from several cans of sour cherries (which you might have on hand after making *Clafoutis,* p. 355, for instance) makes a nice and very traditional *kiśiel.* Or you can use fresh cranberries. Cook 1 quart cranberries in a heavy pot in about 3 cups water to cover until they are mushy, then strain the berries and their juice, not pressing down too hard. Add water to make 2½ cups, and sugar to taste. Use the same proportions of juice and starch as above. If you plan to serve it cold, use only 2 teaspoons starch. Cranberries are full of pectin, and the liquid will jell lightly as it cools.

## BANANES FLAMBÉES

*Serves 6*

This is the sauce I use also for Crêpes Suzette (p. 351); it is very fresh and orange-y, and I prefer it with only a discreet amount of alcohol, so that the clear orange taste is not smothered. I find that a little brandy brings out more of the flavor of orange liqueur than you would get by using a double amount of liqueur and omitting the brandy.

    1½ cups (3½ deciliters) freshly squeezed orange juice
    3 tablespoons lemon juice
    3–4 tablespoons grated orange zest
    6 tablespoons unsalted butter
    ¾ cup (1¾ deciliters) sugar
    6 bananas, ripe but not overly so
    4 tablespoons orange liqueur (Grand Marnier, Cointreau,
       or another)
    4 tablespoons brandy

In a large skillet place the orange and lemon juice, the grated orange zest, the butter, and the sugar. Cook for a few minutes to the consistency of a light syrup. Peel the bananas. If any fibrous threads adhere to the flesh, remove them. Split the bananas lengthwise and cut them crosswise into manageable segments, say about 3 inches long.

Add the bananas to the skillet, and, turning occasionally, cook over low-medium heat for about 10 minutes, until they are soft but not mushy.

Just before serving, warm the skillet until the bananas are heated through and the sauce is bubbling. Warm the liqueur and the brandy together, ignite them, and add them to the sauce. Turn the banana pieces in the sauce until the flames are extinguished, and serve at once.

## *Two Fruit and Cream Desserts*

The first of these has a thick topping of unsweetened whipped cream, over which you sprinkle brown sugar, which is then lightly glazed. The effect is rather like an English "fool," with the added charm of little morsels of caramel.

## FRUIT AND CREAM, BROILED

*Serves 6*

5 cups (1¼ liters) sliced fresh or canned fruit (well drained)
2 cups (½ liter) heavy cream, whipped
½ cup (1 deciliter) or more brown sugar

Arrange the fruit in an ovenproof dish. Cover with stiffly whipped, unsweetened cream. Refrigerate the dish for several hours, or until very cold.

Before serving, remove the dish from the refrigerator to take the chill off. Preheat the broiler. Distribute the brown sugar in a thin layer over the cream; I usually press it through a strainer as I shake it above the dish. With the broiler door left open, broil the dish just until the sugar melts. Most of the cream stays on top; a little mingles deliciously with the fruit.

## FRUIT WITH LEMON CREAM

*Serves 6*

The delicately flavored cream is nice with a rather sweet, soft fruit: fresh ripe strawberries that you can dip in the cream, or canned apricots, or a well-chilled applesauce made by processing cored baked apples, skins and all. I like to serve the cream in individual goblets or punch cups, and pass the fruit in a serving dish.

Whipping an egg white with the cream seems to stabilize it, so that it will safely hold quite a bit of liquid (in this case, lemon juice and sherry) in suspension.

2 cups (½ liter) heavy cream
1 egg white
½ cup (1 deciliter) sugar
Grated zest, and juice, of 1½ lemons
3 tablespoons Amontillado sherry
5 cups (1¼ liters) fruit

Put the cream, egg white, sugar, lemon zest, lemon juice, and sherry in a large bowl and whip until stiff. Refrigerate it for several hours, if possible in individual goblets or cups, and serve it with the fruit.

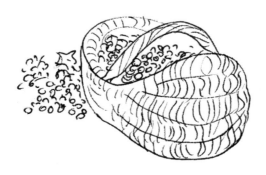

## RASPBERRY CREAM

*Serves 6*

This is a simple, easy, mousselike dessert, beautifully pink and very appealing
to children.

>   Two 10-ounce (285-gram) packages frozen raspberries
>       in juice
>   1½ tablespoons (1½ standard envelopes)
>       unflavored gelatin
>   ½ cup (1 deciliter) water
>   1 cup (¼ liter) heavy cream

Thaw the berries and sieve out the seeds. Measure the pulp and juice; you
will have about 2 cups. If you have more, add an extra pinch of gelatin.

Soften the gelatin in ½ cup water. Heat the raspberry juice and dissolve
the gelation in it. Let the mixture cool to room temperature.

Whip the cream until it is stiff. Fold in the raspberry mixture and
refrigerate the mousse until it is set, about 4 hours. This can be unmolded
for serving, but usually I just serve it in the bowl.

## COCONUT AND RASPBERRY JELLY

*Serves 8*

The idea for this pleasant dessert first came to me on a hot, dusty noonday
in New York, when I was trying to imagine a refreshing surprise to give
my daughter after her hard day's work in the hospital. In the hotel kitchenette I had two pouches of frozen raspberries, and the thought of that intense,
tart-sweet flavor became as nagging as an unfinished melody. What would

complement it? Then I remembered Barbarka's two-layer fruit jelly, whose white base was made with almonds and milk, and thought of coconut. (In California for many years I made it with fresh loganberry juice and coconut milk from the Farmer's Market.)

A full-dress version, using fresh coconut, is described in a note following the recipe. But I will begin by showing you the easiest possible way: Use canned coconut juice (or coconut cream) and make and serve the dessert in a glass bowl that will hold 2 quarts (2 liters). It can also be made in a mold or ring mold for easier serving, but then be sure to make the raspberry layer first so it will be on top when unmolded. Actual working time is only 10 minutes or so, but since one layer must jell before you add the second layer, begin about 6 hours before serving.

THE COCONUT (OR BOTTOM) LAYER

*Makes 4 cups (1 quart or 1 liter)*

2 tablespoons unflavored gelatin
　　(2 standard envelopes)
4 cups (1 liter) coconut liquid*
Sugar, if necessary
3 drops, precisely, of almond extract

Soften the gelatin in 1 cup of the coconut liquid. Heat the remaining liquid to the simmer, add the gelatin mixture, stir until thoroughly dissolved, and taste it. Add sugar to taste. When the mixture has cooled a little, add 3 drops of almond extract, no more, and stir it in. (For precision, I measure it with an eyedropper.) Pour this mixture into your serving bowl and chill it until it is set, about 3 hours. For much faster jelling, you can put the bowl in a larger bowl of ice cubes and ice water, and refrigerate them.

*For convenience I generally use canned sugarless coconut juice and sweeten it to taste. My favorite brand is Mapro's, imported from Singapore. You may also use canned coconut cream (Coco-Lopez is good), which is condensed and sweetened. Combine a 15½-ounce can coconut cream with 2 cups half-and-half, omitting sugar and almond extract from recipe.

THE RASPBERRY (OR TOP) LAYER

*Makes 4 cups (1 quart or 1 liter)*

Four 10-ounce (285-gram) packages frozen raspberries
   in juice
2 tablespoons unflavored gelatin (2 standard envelopes)
⅓ cup (65 grams) sugar

You need not thaw the raspberries in advance. Place them in their juice, with 1 cup water, in a saucepan over medium heat. Bring to the boil and simmer for 10 minutes, long enough to cook the raspberries through. Meanwhile, soften the gelatin in 1 cup cold water. Strain the cooked raspberries and their liquid into a large measuring vessel: add sugar, and press down only lightly on the pulp, so that the liquid remains perfectly clear. Add enough water to it to make 4 cups (1 liter). Return the liquid to the saucepan, heat it, and add the gelatin mixture, stirring it off heat until the gelatin is thoroughly dissolved.

Chill the raspberry mixture only until it is syrupy. If it begins to set, reheat it briefly, and chill again. When the coconut mixture is firmly set, gently and slowly spoon on the raspberry mixture, and chill the dessert until it is jelled, about 3 hours.

*For an unmolded jelly:* It is always more attractive to have the light, translucent layer on top, so make the raspberry mixture before you make the coconut one. To avoid raspberry dribbles down the sides, plan for easy unmolding by filming the 8-cup (2-liter) mold with a tasteless oil like vegetable shortening. Unmold by reversing the mold onto your serving plate. If the jelly doesn't slide right out, give the mold and plate one firm shake. In an emergency, you can cautiously warm the mold by briefly swathing it in a dish towel wrung out in hot water.

*Note on serving:* I don't make this dessert more than 2 days before serving, as after that time the red layer leaks a little color into the white.

*Fresh coconut:* This makes the dessert better still, but the process is a bit more laborious. It is not difficult, though. Buy 2 coconuts, shaking them to be sure they are full of juice. With a hammer and a small screwdriver or tenpenny nail, pierce the 3 sunken "eyes" at the pointed end, and enlarge the holes for quick draining. Drain the coconuts through a strainer into a measuring vessel. Bake the emptied coconuts for 15 minutes (no more) at 350°F (180°C). A few good whacks with a hammer will easily crack the hairy outer shell, which then comes off easily. Peel or cut off the brown inner skin. With the grating disk in the processor, flake the coconut meat. Add enough milk to the strained coconut juice to make 4 cups (1 liter). Scald the liquid and pour it over the grated coconut meat. Let the mixture cool, extract all the liquid by wringing in a dish towel, and proceed to make your jelly. The fresh coconut mixture will separate after a few hours, so jell it fairly promptly.

## BARBARKA'S CARAMEL MOUSSE

*Serves 8*

This is an eggless, creamy yet airy dish, stabilized with gelatin and—not in Barbarka's version but in mine—flavored subtly with coffee. You scarcely taste the coffee; you taste the somehow expanded flavor of caramel. A few droplets of caramel will usually condense at the bottom of the mold so that, when the pudding is turned out, its surface is flecked with dark gold. The texture is both light and velvety.

You can make this dish a day in advance, but do not freeze it.

2 tablespoons (2 standard envelopes) unflavored gelatin
½ cup cold water
1 cup (1 deciliter) boiling water
1 cup plus 1 teaspoon sugar
2 teaspoons instant coffee
2 cups (½ liter) heavy cream

Put the gelatin in a large bowl and pour the cold water over it to soften it.

In a heavy frying pan—nonstick is a great help here—over medium heat, melt 1 cup of the sugar and caramelize it to a dark amber color, slowly, stirring constantly. (For full details about making caramel, see page 66.)

Carefully, off the heat, pour ½ cup boiling water into the caramel, stirring constantly; it will fizz but don't worry. Dissolve the instant coffee and the 1 teaspoon of sugar in the remaining ½ cup boiling water and pour over the softened gelatin, stirring until it is completely dissolved. Now pour the caramel into the coffee-gelatin mixture, and stir well; then refrigerate until cooled to room temperature. Then set the bowl in a larger pan full of ice cubes and water and put it where you can monitor the jelling, which goes fast near the end. (To keep it jelling evenly, give it an occasional stir. None of it must set before you use it.)

Whip the cream stiff enough so that you can stand a spoon upright in it. When the gelatin mixture has become a cold, uniform syrup that clings to your fingertip or coats a spoon, fold in the whipped cream. Keep the bowl slightly tilted toward you, to be sure you are incorporating all the liquid, which has a tendency to filter down through the cream and settle at the bottom.

Thoroughly rinse an 8-cup (2-liter) mold with cold water, shake off extra drops, and pour in the gelatin-cream mixture. Refrigerate the mousse until it is softly firm (about 6 hours), and unmold it to serve.

## PEARS WITH SABAYON OR VANILLA SAUCE

*Serves 6*

If you have perfectly ripe fresh pears, chill them, peel them, sprinkle with lemon juice, and use them for this excellent dessert. But the canned ones are awfully good. Most of the best restaurants in Paris use canned pears. Chill them, drain them well, and pour over them one of the two sauces. The sauce may be hot (for an exciting contrast) or cold (for advance preparation).

SABAYON SAUCE

*Makes about 1½ cups*

This sauce, served hot in a goblet as soon as made, is a dessert in itself, better known by its Italian name, *zabaglione.* Sometimes, however, I make it with dark rum for a slightly lighter taste.

    4 egg yolks
    ⅓ cup (75 grams) sugar
    ½ cup (1 deciliter) very rich Marsala wine
        or dark rum

Beat the egg yolks and sugar until they are as thick as possible. Slowly, beating constantly, add the Marsala or dark rum. Now place the sauce over but not in hot water, and continue beating, as it warms, until it is as thick as mayonnaise. If you plan to use it cold, remember that it will thicken as it chills. Be sure to keep scraping the bottom and walls of the pot as you cook.

VANILLA SAUCE

*Makes about 2 cups*

This basic custard sauce is useful for all kinds of fruit desserts and sweet soufflés.

    3 egg yolks
    ½ cup (100 grams) sugar
    1½ cups (3½ deciliters) cream, half heavy and half light
    ½ teaspoon vanilla extract, or ½ vanilla bean

Beat the egg yolks with the sugar until thick and pale. Add the cream and cook the custard, stirring constantly, over hot water until the mixture coats a spoon. Let it cool a little and add the vanilla. If you use vanilla bean, halve it crosswise, split a half pod and scrape it so that the seeds will float into the sauce; remove the half bean pod just before serving.

### *A Pear and Sauce Variation: Poires Belle Hélène*

*Serves 6*

This is a classic dessert, easy to make at home, with a fine balance of flavors. It is best served in individual dishes. On a portion of very good vanilla ice cream (use 1½ pints for 6), set a small poached pear or (well-drained) canned pear half. Drizzle with a thin, hot, bittersweet chocolate sauce.

THE CHOCOLATE SAUCE

> 6 ounces (180 grams) fine bittersweet chocolate,
>    for instance, Tobler "Tradition"
> ½ cup (1 deciliter) water
> 1 tablespoon dark rum
> 1 teaspoon brandy

Over hot, not boiling, water, melt the chocolate with the water. Off heat, stir in the rum and brandy. Serve hot.

## LEMON BAVARIAN CREAM

*Serves 8–10*

After they had tasted it at my house, Prince Rainier and my beloved friend the late Princess Grace of Monaco adopted this dessert as a family staple. As well as delicious, it is adaptable: you can serve it in a big bowl, or unmolded, or in individual goblets, or as a filling for meringue shells. It freezes well too. I made it up after tasting an American lemon meringue pie for the first time. Not yet having encountered a lemon chiffon pie, I thought the topping had not enough taste, and the middle, too much.

6 or 7 lemons

1 tablespoon (1 standard envelope)
   unflavored gelatin

8 eggs, separated

1 cup (200 grams) plus 3 tablespoons
   or more sugar

2 cups (½ liter) heavy cream

Grate the lemons delicately, avoiding the white pith, to make 4 table-spoons grated zest. Squeeze 1⅓ cups (3¼ deciliters) lemon juice. Soften the gelatin in ⅓ cup of the lemon juice. Put 8 egg yolks with 1 cup of the sugar into the top of a double boiler. Add the remaining cup of lemon juice and the grated zest. Place the mixture over, not in, hot water. Cook, stirring constantly, over low heat until the mixture is thick and coats the spoon. Dissolve the gelatin-lemon mixture in 3 tablespoons boiling water, and stir it into the egg-lemon mixture. Cool it slightly and taste it for sweetness; I like it quite tart. When the mixture has cooled to room temperature, refrigerate it; but take it out of the refrigerator as soon as it is cold, before it begins to set. Check it a few times.

Meanwhile, beat the egg whites until they are foamy. Still beating, gradually add the remaining 3 tablespoons of sugar, and continue beating until the whites are stiff but not dry. Cover the bowl airtight with plastic wrap, to wait until the cold gelatin mixture is a thick, uniform syrup that clings to your fingertip and coats a spoon. You can hasten this by putting the gelatin bowl in a larger bowl filled with ice cubes and ice water. Stir the gelatin mixture occasionally, so that it thickens evenly.

When the gelatin is almost ready, whip the cream. It will have more volume if you keep it very cold. Fold the egg whites into the gelatin mixture, then fold in the whipped cream, and refrigerate the mousse until it is softly set. (It will never become stiff; nevertheless, after thorough chilling, it is sturdy enough to unmold.)

*Variation:* You can reserve the whipped cream and pass it separately with the mousse made of egg whites only, which of course tastes much more of lemon. I often do this when there are dieters among my guests. In this case you may prefer to add a little sugar to the whipped cream and make the mousse with a little less.

# CHOCOLATE MOUSSE

*Serves 6*

This simple but sinful dessert should not be served after a rich dinner! We have always liked our chocolate on the bitter side of sweet and the dark side of brown; we judge restaurant mousse by its color even before trying it. When I make it, I add the little specks of orange zest to give the tongue some little surprises. See the end of the recipe for two other variations on the theme.

8 ounces (225 grams) good bittersweet chocolate
   (Tobler "Tradition" for instance)
½ cup (1 deciliter) water
2 tablespoons sugar
½ cup (1 deciliter) heavy cream
1½ teaspoons grated orange zest
4 eggs, separated
½ cup (1 deciliter) heavy cream, whipped
   (optional)

In the top of a double boiler over but not in simmering water, or in a heavy saucepan over *very* low heat, melt the chocolate with the water and the sugar, stirring constantly. Still stirring, add the heavy cream and the grated orange zest. Off heat, add the egg yolks and incorporate them thoroughly. Stirring constantly, put the pan back over the hot water or low fire, and cook the mixture for a few moments; it will thicken somewhat.

Cool the chocolate mixture, but do *not* refrigerate, while you beat the egg whites. When they are stiff but not dry, stir one-third of them into the chocolate mixture, then carefully but thoroughly fold in the rest.

Pour the mousse gently into individual bowls or cups. Refrigerate 2 hours or more. Before serving, if you like, decorate with the additional whipped cream.

*Variations:* Eva folds 2 teaspoons grated unsweetened chocolate at the same time as the egg whites, and/or substitutes 1–2 tablespoons rum, crème de cacao, or Kahlua for an equal amount of water when melting the chocolate. Be sure to use a little less sugar if using sweet liqueurs.

## BANANA CUSTARD

*Serves 6–8*

Because we once had a surplus of bananas, rapidly becoming overripe, I invented this dessert. Now it is the other way around: because the dessert is so good, I deliberately buy and reserve bananas for it. You cannot make it successfully with nice spotless bananas, the kind best for eating in the hand. Nor can you simulate overripe bananas by precooking them; they get soft, but don't develop much aroma. One is obliged to wait until they become covered with light brown freckles and have a rich perfume.

3 good-size bananas, very ripe but not blackened
4 eggs
7–8 tablespoons sugar
1 teaspoon vanilla extract
1 cup (¼ liter) heavy cream
1 cup (¼ liter) light cream
3 slices crustless white bread, diced and lightly toasted
A few preserved cherries for decoration (optional)

Preheat the oven to 325°F (165°C). Peel and slice the bananas and lay the slices in an ungreased 9-inch Pyrex or porcelain pie dish. Beat the eggs with the sugar and vanilla. Scald the heavy and light cream and add it, beating, to the eggs. Pour this custard over the bananas. Scatter the toast dice on top, pressing down gently until each is in, not on, the custard. Bake for about 30 minutes, or until a knife inserted in the middle comes out clean. Serve lukewarm, decorated, if you like, with preserved cherries drained of any liquid.

# CRÈME BRÛLÉE

*Serves 8–10*

*Crème Brûlée* is <u>*crème brûlée,*</u> I insist, elegant and luxurious from top to bottom, and made with heavy cream, golden Jersey cream if you are lucky, under its crackling, gleaming brown-sugar glaze. It is quite easy to make, and this recipe has several tips gained from long experience. Long, because this dessert is an unfailing success. Even dieters ask for second helpings. So I make *crème brûlée* as often as my conscience permits. (I have even made it in ice-cube trays in a New York hotel, cooling it on the outside window sill, hoping the pigeons wouldn't walk on it.)

Bake the custard well before you serve it, so that it will be thoroughly chilled when you glaze it; but glaze it just before serving.

I often serve fruit with it, and sometimes cookies—or both.

4 cups (1 liter) heavy cream
10 egg yolks
2 tablespoons white sugar
2 tablespoons vanilla extract
1 cup (200 grams) light brown sugar

Preheat the oven to 300°F (150°C). Scald the cream and set it aside. Beat the egg yolks. Beat in the white sugar and the vanilla. Pour the cream into the yolk mixture, beating constantly; then pour the custard into a Pyrex or other gratin dish.

Set the gratin dish in a bain-marie (a large roasting pan of boiling hot water) and bake the custard for about an hour; but check it for doneness after 45 minutes. The surface should be pale gold; don't let it get brown. When it is done to this point, remove it from the bain-marie and let it sit until it has cooled to room temperature. Refrigerate it several hours or overnight. It will become firmer as it chills.

For the glaze, a lot of people use dark brown sugar, but I think the light kind is less overpowering. It is worth taking great pains to spread the sugar very evenly over the custard, to a depth of just ⅓ inch, right to the edges, with no bare spots. The best way is to press the sugar through a strainer, to avoid lumps, then smooth it. Return the dish to the refrigerator.

Light the broiler (but do not preheat). Set the custard dish in a larger dish filled with ice cubes and ice water. The colder the custard as a whole can remain, the colder will be the top surface. If the top surface gets too warm, it may admit some of the broiled sugar, which then oozes down through the custard.

Run the custard, in its cold bath, under the broiler. Leave the broiler door open and keep constant watch. It takes at most 2 minutes for the sugar to melt and caramelize. If any sugar begins to blacken, it is glazing too fast. Remove the dish, lower the broiler rack, return the dish, and continue. When the whole sugar surface is dark amber and bubbling, it is done. Remove the dish. In 5 minutes the custard will have cooled the sugar, which hardens into a dark brown crust, and the *crème brûlée* is ready to eat.

*Three Simple Custards*

## CARAMEL CUSTARD (FLAN)

*Serves 6*

For detailed remarks on making caramel, see page 66.

1½ cups (300 grams) sugar
¼ cup (½ deciliter) boiling water
4 eggs
2 cups (½ liter) milk or half-and-half
1 teaspoon vanilla extract

Caramelize 1 cup of the sugar: Melt it in a heavy pan and remove it from the heat when it bubbles and then begins to turn amber. Let it sit a moment, then dilute it with the boiling water. Pour some of this caramel syrup into a custard mold or custard cups, and tilt and turn it (or them) to coat the inner surfaces.

Dilute the remaining caramel a little, stirring in another ¼ cup boiling water to use for a sauce. Preheat the oven to 350°F (180°C). Beat the eggs to blend them thoroughly. Heat the milk with the remaining ½ cup sugar to the simmer, and pour it over the eggs, beating them as you do so. Add the vanilla, mix well, and pour the mixture into the mold or cups.

Set the mold or cups in a roasting pan containing about an inch of hot water and bake for 35 minutes, or until set. (You may find it easier to add the water after the pan containing the mold or cups is on the oven rack.) Let the custard cool to lukewarm before serving, and serve it with the reserved syrup. Or cool it to room temperature and unmold it with its syrup, to which you add the syrup you have reserved.

## CRÈME MOCHA

*Serves 6*

This is made and served just like Caramel Custard (preceding recipe), except that the syrup is different. To make it, you dissolve 4 ounces (115 grams) bittersweet chocolate and 1 tablespoon instant coffee in 1½ cups (3½ deciliters) hot water. Pour some of this into the mold or cups and reserve the rest for your sauce.

## COFFEE CUSTARD

*Serves 6*

This is the simplest of the three, and perhaps the best. Since the custard, which is similar to the others and not very sweet, has no sauce, I like to serve it with something a little sugary but tangy, like gooseberry jam or an English sour-cherry preserve.

In this case I prefer half-and-half to plain milk. As in the Caramel Custard recipe (opposite), heat 2 cups of it and stir in 4 tablespoons instant coffee with ½ cup sugar until dissolved. Pour this over 4 beaten eggs. Omit the vanilla extract. Bake as for Caramel Custard and serve in its mold, quite warm.

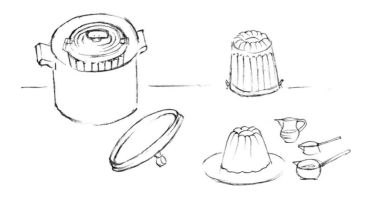

## STEAMED COFFEE PUDDING (OR SOUFFLÉ)

*Serves 6–8*

This warm, moist, delicate molded dessert is quite unlike any other I know. It has long been a favorite with my family, all generations, and many friends, and I still find myself inventing variations with different flavors and sauces. You will find here recipes for a chocolate and a lemon version. The same recipe works perfectly as a soufflé, but the texture is different, slightly dryer, with the top a bit crusty. Try it both ways.

The pudding must be made in a special steam-pudding mold, which is metal, and has a close-fitting top that either clamps or screws down. (Do not try to improvise one.) These molds are not hard to find and can be used, with or without the lid, for other things, jellies, etc.

Serve the pudding with whipped cream (either ruched around the pudding base or simply in a bowl), a bowl of raspberry or currant syrup, and a smaller bowl of warm melted butter—just a small spoonful per person.

As steamed puddings must be unmolded as soon as they are done, and served immediately, it is important to gauge with some accuracy the eating time of the rest of the meal. Let the guests wait a few minutes, not the pudding. *Note:* When testing for doneness, it helps to have a slightly musical ear, as you will see when you make the recipe.

1 tablespoon instant coffee
1½ teaspoons instant cocoa powder
1 cup (¼ liter) hot water
3 tablespoons flour
3 tablespoons butter
4 eggs, separated
Butter for the mold, if you are baking the pudding
¼ cup (½ deciliter) bread crumbs
Flour for the soufflé mold
Pinch of salt
¼ cup (60 grams) sugar

Dissolve the instant coffee and cocoa powder in the hot water. In a small saucepan cook the flour in the butter, stirring constantly, until thickened and smooth. Add the coffee-cocoa mixture and cook, stirring constantly, until you have a smooth, medium-thick sauce. With the saucepan over a low fire, add the egg yolks, 1 by 1, stirring constantly. When they are all incorporated, remove from the fire and set aside to cool to room temperature.

Butter a 6-cup mold and line it with bread crumbs. Have ready a large kettle with a tightly fitting cover and set in it a steam rack or trivet. Have on hand a kettle of boiling water. *Or,* for baking the pudding as a soufflé: Butter and flour a 6-cup soufflé dish and preheat the oven to 375° (190°C).

Beat the egg whites until foamy. Add the pinch of salt. Continue beating, gradually adding the sugar, until the whites form stiff, shiny peaks. Stir one-third of the whites into the cooled sauce and fold in the remaining whites.

Spoon the mixture into the buttered and crumbed 6-cup pudding mold, which will be two-thirds full; it must not be fuller. Cover the mold tightly and set it on the steaming rack in the kettle. Pour into the kettle enough boiling water to reach halfway up the sides of the mold. Tap the mold and note the sound it makes for comparison later. It should sound a bit hollow. Set the kettle on high heat until it begins to steam, then lower it; just keep the water simmering, for 45 minutes all told. Tap the mold again—it should now sound "full"! Remove the lid of the mold.

To unmold, carefully *center* your serving plate on the open mold and invert it deliberately but gently. Lift the mold off. Serve immediately.

*Or,* for a soufflé, spoon the mixture into the 6-cup soufflé dish and bake for 30 minutes, or until done. The center should have risen about 1½ inches above the rim and browned slightly.

## STEAMED CHOCOLATE PUDDING (OR SOUFFLÉ)

*Serves 6–8*

Use the same recipe as for Steamed Coffee Pudding (preceding recipe), but omit the cocoa powder and substitute 4 ounces (115 grams) semisweet chocolate for the instant coffee. Melt the chocolate in the hot water as you did for the coffee pudding. Serve this dish with Vanilla Sauce (p. 315).

## STEAMED LEMON PUDDING (OR SOUFFLÉ)

*Serves 6*

This is a slightly different version of steamed pudding, using milk. It is still extremely delicate. Heavy cream and/or a fruit sauce or syrup is, again, delightful.

3–4 lemons
3 tablespoons unsalted butter
3 tablespoons flour
1 cup (¼ liter) milk
About ⅓ cup (75 grams) plus 2 teaspoons sugar
½ teaspoon salt
4 eggs, separated
Butter for the mold
Bread crumbs or flour for the mold

Carefully grate the lemons to make 3 tablespoons of zest. (Do it on a fine grater and be careful not to grate any of the bitter white pith.) Then squeeze the lemons to make 5 tablespoons of strained lemon juice.

In a small saucepan make a roux with the butter and flour, and cook it for a few moments until the flour no longer tastes raw. Add the milk, stirring constantly, and cook over a low fire until you get a very thick mixture. Stirring, add the lemon zest and juice, ⅓ cup of the sugar, and the salt.

Taste the mixture for sweetness and sourness, adding a bit more sugar or lemon juice, if you like, to taste. Cool the mixture for about 5 minutes, to allow the flour to expand a little.

Add the egg yolks, 1 by 1, each time mixing to incorporate them thoroughly. Beat the egg whites until they are stiff but not dry, gradually adding the remaining 2 teaspoons sugar toward the end. Stir one-third of the egg whites into the lemon mixture, then fold in the rest.

Pour the mixture into a prepared buttered-and-crumbed mold and follow all remaining directions for Steamed Coffee Pudding (p. 324) for cooking, then unmolding.

If you wish to make the recipe as a soufflé, follow the Steamed Coffee Pudding directions on page 325. Note that the cooking time for the soufflé is shorter than for the pudding.

# RICE PUDDING

*Serves 6*

I still love the bland warmth and the simplicity of all the porridges and puddings of my childhood (mine and my children's), served with plenty of sweet cream: tapioca, semolina, bread pudding—the whole lot. I even brought home to Paris once a parcel of their own special semolina given me by the Savoy Hotel in London, where this sort of old-fashioned dish is appreciated and properly made.

Among such dishes is rice pudding. This recipe, though not too unlike the Savoy's very good one, is a plain, pleasant formula I remember from home. It uses cooked rice; if I have a little left over and am alone, I bake myself a mini-pudding in a custard cup.

Serve it warm with cream and/or fruit syrup such as currant or raspberry.

3 cups cooked white Rice (p. 122)
1½ cups (3½ deciliters) or more milk or light cream
3 egg yolks
½ cup (100 grams) sugar
1½ tablespoons grated orange rind, or to taste
½ cup (1 deciliter) or more raisins
1 teaspoon vanilla extract

In a double boiler over barely simmering water, or just in a very warm place, soak the rice in the warm milk or medium cream until the liquid is absorbed. If you think the rice can absorb a little more, add it. (And if it doesn't get absorbed, no harm is done.) This can take an hour or longer.

Preheat the oven to 325°F (165°C). Beat together the egg yolks and sugar until they are thick and pale. Add the orange rind, the raisins, and the vanilla, and combine the mixture with the soaked rice.

Pour the pudding into a buttered baking dish (a 6-cup soufflé dish is fine), and bake for about 30 minutes or until done. The pudding should have a golden-brown top and will be quite firm.

# $\mathcal{P}astries$

### Four Tarts with Pâte Sablée

This egg-yolk dough produces a golden, crisp, cookielike pastry, which does not get soggy when filled with fruit. It can be made and shaped with the fingertips, need not be chilled before baking, and holds its form in the oven. In other words, this kind of pastry is as easy as it is refined, and you can teach a child of six in one session to produce an impeccable tart that is more fun to make than mud pies. And much more fun to eat.

## PÂTE SABLÉE

*Makes a 10-inch shell*

1 stick (4 ounces or 115 grams) unsalted butter
  at room temperature
3 tablespoons sugar
2 egg yolks
1 cup (140 grams) plus 3 tablespoons flour
½ teaspoon salt

*To make the dough by hand:* Cream the butter, using a wooden spoon or your fingers. It doesn't have to be as fluffy as butter creamed for a cake, just evenly soft and easy to work. Cream in the sugar, then the egg yolks, then the flour and salt, with the spoon or your fingers. As soon as it is evenly blended, mass it into a lump. To pick up dough crumbs, roll the lump around the bowl, collecting all adhesive bits. If very dry bits remain, brush them together with your fingertips, sprinkle with a few drops of water, and press them into the dough mass.

*To make the dough in a processor:* Start with very well-chilled butter and beat the egg yolks with 1 tablespoon ice water. Cut the butter into ½-inch dice, and keep chilled. Put the flour, salt, and sugar in the processor bowl, fitted with the steel blade. Process to blend them. Distribute the cold butter dice over the flour. Process in about 4 short bursts of 1 second each. (A second can be measured by saying "Mississippi" slowly.) Now turn on the machine and instantly pour the egg yolk and water down the feed tube. Turn off the machine as soon as the dough is evenly colored and has begun to mass. Take out the dough and pat it into a lump.

*To form a tart shell:* Though you can of course roll the dough, I like to form it with my fingers. Put the lump of dough in an ungreased slip-bottom tart mold or a flan ring sitting on a baking sheet. Flatten the dough with the heel of your hand. As the dough spreads out, dimple it with your fingertips in quick staccato jabs. The "dimples" should be almost transparently thin and the ridges between them about ⅜ inch thick. The walls of the tart should also be ⅜ inch thick, unless you have a fluted mold. (This makes a more secure structure than a plain flan ring, so you can make the walls thinner.) At the base of the walls, press the dough well in. If the dough crumbles or tears anywhere, simply pat on a bit more and dimple it again. So long as it stays cool enough not to feel greasy, this dough cannot be overworked. If the butter does begin to melt under the heat of your fingers, sprinkle it with a teaspoonful or so of additional flour. Preheat the oven to 400°F (205°C).

*To bake the tart shell:* You don't have to chill it first, but I do if there is time. Bake it for about 12 minutes, or until golden all over.

*To bake a filled shell:* Set the oven to 350°F (180°C). Baking times vary with the filling: usually about 30 minutes.

## LEMON CUSTARD TART

*Serves 6–8*

Once you have grated and squeezed the lemons, this golden custard filling can be made in one second in the blender. It tastes best when lukewarm; bake it while you're having dinner.

3–4 lemons
3 tablespoons unsalted butter, softened
⅓ cup (¾ deciliter) bread crumbs
3 eggs
1 cup (200 grams) sugar
1 cup (¼ liter) heavy cream
One 10-inch tart shell of *Pâte Sablée* (preceding recipe)
    glazed with 1 egg beaten with 1 tablespoon water,
    then partially baked at 400°F (205°C) for 8 minutes,
    or until it is a very pale gold

Grate the lemons carefully, using the "fine" side of your grater and applying very little pressure to be sure of avoiding the bitter white pith. You should have 3–4 tablespoons. Squeeze the lemons to make ¾ cup (1¾ deciliters) juice.

Preheat the oven to 350°F (180°C). Pour the lemon juice, grated zest, butter, bread crumbs, eggs, sugar, and cream into the blender, and blend just long enough to mix them thoroughly.

Pour the custard into the half-baked tart shell, not quite filling it since the lemon custard expands during baking. Bake it for about 20 to 30 minutes. It is done when the filling has risen somewhat, all over. It will be uniformly set and golden-brown. Let the tart cool for 10 minutes before you serve it.

## STRAWBERRY TART

*Serves 6–8*

This begins with a fully baked shell. I line it with a thin layer of *crème pâtissière,* on which I set perfect hulled strawberries that have been dipped in melted currant jelly. A mouthful of succulent strawberry, rich custard, and crisp pastry is simply delicious.

THE CRÊME PÀTISSIÊRE

> 4 egg yolks
> ¾ cup (150 grams) sugar
> 1¼ cups (3 deciliters) heavy cream
> 1 tablespoon vanilla extract, or ½ split, scraped vanilla bean
> One 10-inch fully baked tart shell of *Pâte Sablée* (p. 329)
> 2 pints (½ liter) large, ripe, unblemished strawberries
> 1 cup (¼ liter) red currant jelly, melted

In the top of a double boiler, off heat, beat the egg yolks with the sugar until they are thick, light, and very pale. In a saucepan bring the cream (with the vanilla bean if you are using it) to a boil. Off heat, beating steadily, pour the cream over the egg mixture. Set the double boiler top over, not in, simmering water over medium heat. Cook and stir the custard until it coats the spoon. If you are using vanilla extract, add it now. Let the custard cool to room temperature. It will thicken as it cools; don't refrigerate it, or it will get too thick to spread. Remove the vanilla bean, if you used it.

Pour the cooled *crème pâtissière* into the tart shell and refrigerate for 10 minutes, or until the cream firms slightly. Carefully wash, dry, and hull the berries. Dip them 1 by 1, in the melted currant jelly, and arrange them, pointed ends up, on the cream. Serve at room temperature.

*Variations:* You may omit the *Crème Pâtissière,* fill the tart shell with fruit, and serve whipped cream, if you like, separately. You may substitute raspberries for the strawberries.

## APPLE AND CARAMEL TART

*Serves 6–8*

This is best served hot, almost bubbling: a prebaked shell of *pâte sablée* filled with sugared bits of apple sautéed in butter and topped with caramel.

> 6 tart apples (Northern Spies are ideal, or perhaps
> Jonathans—if you use a bland apple like
> Golden Delicious, first sprinkle the pieces with
> lemon juice)
> 2 tablespoons (30 grams) butter
> 1 tablespoon grated orange or lemon zest
> ¾ cup (150 grams) sugar, or to taste
> One 10-inch fully baked tart shell of *Pâte Sablée*
> (p. 329)

Peel and core the apples, divide them in eighths, and cut them in uniform pieces the size of a fingernail and ⅛ inch thick. Sauté the apple pieces slowly in butter, mixing in the grated zest and about ¼ cup of the sugar, to taste, until they are colored but still rather crisp. Fill the tart shell with the hot apples. Melt the remaining ½ cup sugar in a heavy skillet, stirring constantly, until it colors, and immediately drizzle the hot caramel over the hot apples. (For details about caramel, see page 66.) Serve at once.

## APPLE AND ALMOND TART

*Serves 6–8*

This is unusual in using an unbaked shell of *pâte sablée.* The filling of apples, topped with almonds and sugar, becomes slightly crystallized on top, giving you a nice contrast of textures.

   7 tablespoons unsalted butter
   ¾ cup (150 grams) sugar
   3½ ounces (100 grams) or ⅔ cup blanched almonds,
      ground fine
   4–5 tart apples
   One 10-inch tart shell of *Pâte Sablée* (p. 329)
   2½ ounces (75 grams) or ½ cup sliced almonds

Cut the butter into small pieces; add the sugar and the finely ground almonds, and mix them with your fingertips, with a rubbing gesture, until they are the consistency of rough meal.

Preheat the oven to 350°F (180°C). Peel, core, and cut the apples as for Apple and Caramel Tart (preceding recipe). Put them in the pastry shell. Cover them with the ground-almond mixture. Sprinkle this with the sliced almonds.

Bake the tart for 35–40 minutes. Serve it lukewarm.

## *Mazurkas*

A mazurka is not only a Polish dance, it is one of a group of Polish confections, and probably of just as ancient origin. At least three or four mazurkas are always part of the cold buffet one serves at Easter. Usually they are large sheets of rich pastry topped with a very sweet, almost candylike icing. The three icing recipes I give you here are my favorites among the dozen or so in the little leather-covered notebook my mother filled for me with her culinary heirlooms. Another mazurka, an almond one, is made with a special dough of pulverized almonds.

## THREE MAZURKAS WITH PÂTE SABLÉE

*Makes a large mazurka, 9 by 14 inches*

One recipe of the "short," cookielike *Pâte Sablée* (p. 329) will line your largest jelly-roll pan or five little 4- by 6-inch pans. You can bake mazurkas on cookie sheets, but the edges won't be as neat. Roll the dough if you like, but I prefer to "dimple" it with my fingertips (see *Pâte Sablée*). Bake this pastry base in a preheated 400°F (205°C) oven for about 12 minutes, or until crisp and golden-brown. Then spread it with one of the following icings.

ORANGE ICING

    2 juice oranges
    1 lemon
    ½ pound (225 grams) sugar

One uses juice oranges because they have less white pith than navel oranges, and this icing shouldn't be too bitter-tasting. Cut the oranges and lemon into chunks, skins on, and discard the seeds. Process them to a pulp in the processor with the steel blade. In a heavy pot, mix the fruit pulp with the sugar and cook over low heat, stirring often, for 30 minutes or so, until the mixture is glossy and thick. Spread it on the hot *pâte sablée* right after baking, let the mazurka cool, and serve it cut in small squares.

VANILLA-CREAM ICING

This mixture, without vanilla, also supplies a candy called *kalouga* by Alice B. Toklas. She says to pour the hot mixture on an oiled surface and to let it cool before cutting into pieces. I agree with her; it makes a nice sort of fudge. I don't know where she got her recipe—not from me, at any rate.

    1 whole vanilla bean
    2 cups (½ liter) heavy cream
    2 cups (400 grams) sugar

Split the vanilla bean lengthwise and scrape it, so that the seeds will be released into the mixture. (You can substitute about 2 teaspoons vanilla extract.)

In a heavy skillet, cook the cream and sugar slowly, stirring constantly, until the sugar is dissolved. Add the vanilla and continue cooking until the mass gets thick and blond-colored. (A candy thermometer will read 238°F (114°C); a drop of the mixture will make a firm, elastic ball on a cold plate.) Be careful, as you keep stirring, not to let it burn. Fish out the vanilla bean and spread the vanilla cream on a hot prebaked sheet of *pâte sablée.* The icing will become firm and fudgelike as it cools. Cut it when cooled into small squares.

CHOCOLATE ICING

This makes a shining glaze ¼-inch thick.

> 6 ounces (180 grams) best bittersweet chocolate (for
>    instance, Tobler "Tradition")
> ¼ cup (½ deciliter) water
> ⅓ cup (¾ deciliter) heavy cream
> 2 teaspoons unsalted butter

Melt the chocolate with the water over low heat. Add the cream and butter and raise the heat to medium. Let a little moisture evaporate, but remember that this mixture will thicken as it cools. Take it off the heat when it has the consistency of thick honey. Pour it immediately over the whole surface of a sheet of prebaked *pâte sablée.* When the icing is cool, use a sharp knife to cut the mazurka into small squares.


## ALMOND MAZURKA

Arthur's Parisian friends, especially the Rothschild family, were very kind and welcoming to me after our marriage, and invited us often to sumptuous meals. We returned their hospitality, but of course in our own style. We lived then high on Montmartre, in a tiny pavilion that had been Arthur's bachelor quarters. As he had nearly always eaten out (or had given elegant parties for which he ordered in the specialties of the best restaurants in Paris), the only "kitchen" was a tiny cubbyhole, primitively equipped with a two-ring gas burner for coffee making, adjoining his valet's rented room on the ground floor of the building across the small garden. (Another such room, previously his dining room, and reached through the window by little steps, became a nursery in 1933, and from 1935 to 1938 housed our two eldest children *and* their nanny!) After a few months of cooking on those two burners, I allowed myself the luxury of a real, if tiny, stove with a small oven. This experience proved to be wonderful training for cooking in the many hotel kitchenettes I was to encounter in my subsequent life.

Meantime, in my Montmartre cubbyhole, I cooked the simple, good Polish dishes I knew, of which this mazurka was one of the most popular; Baron Edouard de Rothschild loved it and asked his wife, Germaine, to arrange for me to teach it to their chef.

An appointment was made. Germaine had never set foot in the kitchens of her great house, so her butler guided us through the halls and salons, down to an establishment that seemed to me the size of a ballroom, past a regiment of white-clad *sous-chefs* and *marmitons,* into the Presence of the Chef Himself. I felt utterly ridiculous, setting out my little parcels of sugar, eggs, and almonds. The chef stood in stony silence as I began to explain my simple recipe. In my terror, I seemed to see his starched *bonnet* growing a foot taller with every instruction I gave.

His composure remained unbroken until I began to pat the dough into the pan with my fingertips. "Never," said he, choking with indignation, "does a professional chef permit himself to touch the food with his bare hands." I don't know if the great chef ever tried it my way, or even at all, but I went right on cooking it, and everything else, using hands or tools without prejudice, according to which was more efficient for the particular job. Nowadays I am grateful for the processor at the grinding and mixing stage of this recipe, which is based on a pastry of pulverized almonds. For the topping of caramelized almonds, I prefer to sliver the nuts with my knife for a more irregular and lively texture and appearance.

1 pound (450 grams) blanched almonds
3 drops (no more) almond extract (you can use an eyedropper)
1 pound (2 cups plus 5 tablespoons, or 450 grams) sugar
½ cup (1 deciliter) egg whites (6 or 7, depending on eggs)

Butter and flour a jelly-roll pan 11 by 8 inches. Or you can use a 9-inch pie plate.

Grind to a powder two-thirds of the almonds, that is, ⅔ pound. Reserve the rest. Mix the ground almonds with the almond extract and half the sugar (reserving the rest), and all the egg whites (which are not beaten before mixing). Beat the mixture with a wooden spoon until you have a stiff, smooth paste.

Preheat the oven to 300°F (150°C). In the processor grind and mix ⅔ pound almonds with ½ pound (1 cup plus 1 tablespoon) sugar until they are very finely ground. Sliver the remaining ⅓ pound almonds and set aside, and place the remaining ½ pound sugar in a heavy skillet.

Add only ⅓ cup egg whites; otherwise, the paste will be too liquid. Add 3 drops of almond extract, and process the mixture to a paste.

Spread the paste in the buttered and floured jelly-roll pan or pie plate. I do it with my fingertips, in "dimples," which smooth out during baking.

Bake the almond dough in the preheated oven for 35–40 minutes, or until it is firm and pale golden-brown.

*The topping:* Prepare it while the dough is still hot. This topping gets hard and crackly as it cools.

When you have removed the almond pastry from the oven, set it aside and start melting the remaining sugar over medium heat. Stir constantly, and cook it to a pale golden-brown. (For details on making caramel, see page 66.) At once, off heat, stir in the slivered almonds. Quickly spread the mixture over the (warm or lukewarm, but not cold) dough.

When the topping has cooled enough to touch, cut the mazurka into squares or wedges with a very sharp knife.

## GLAZED APPLE TART

The crust for this tart is made with the rich, semiflaky cream cheese dough used for *Coulibiac,* for which you will find a detailed recipe on page 113.

This is not a sweetened dough. For desserts, sweet turnovers, and so on, I use it just as you would use an American pie pastry, but with care to chill it after it is formed. It is so very rich that it shrinks during baking, so I take the simple precaution of rolling it to an ample size. Otherwise there is nothing difficult about this flavorful pastry.

THE CREAM CHEESE DOUGH (a summary recipe)

*For a 9-inch shell*

1 stick minus 1 tablespoon (100 grams) unsalted butter
1 cup (140 grams) flour (with more available)
1½ teaspoons sugar
½ teaspoon salt
3½ ounces (100 grams) cream cheese
1 egg for glazing crust

Chop the butter into the flour, sugar, and salt, until it has the consistency of rice. Coarsely work in the cream cheese. (If you are using old cream cheese, you may need a few drops of water.)* The dough should look heavily streaked with white. If not using immediately, mass it together, wrap it airtight, and refrigerate it. Bring to room temperature before rolling out.

Flour the board and the pin, form the chilled dough into a flat cake, and roll it quickly, working from the center outward, sprinkling on more flour if you need to. It must remain streaky and "marbleized," and the circle should be an inch wider than your pie dish or ring. Fit it in, allowing for

---

*In a processor with the plastic or steel blade this takes seconds. Be sure to stop immediately when the cream cheese forms a ball.

should be an inch wider than your pie dish or ring. Fit it in, allowing for shrinkage at the edges. If you prefer, to minimize shrinkage, put the dough lump into the pie dish or ring and "dimple" it as directed on page 330 of the *Pâte Sablée* recipe.

Chill the dough in the dish or ring for 15–30 minutes. Preheat the oven to 350°F (180°C).

Mix the egg with 1 tablespoon water, and brush over the crust (you may not need all the egg mixture). Prebake the crust for 8–10 minutes, then, without cooling it, put in the apples.

THE APPLE "FILLING"

2 large apples, cored, peeled, and sliced thin lengthwise
1 tablespoon sugar
1 teaspoon grated lemon zest
½ cup (1 deciliter) quince, crabapple, apple,
 or red currant jelly

Arrange the slices in a circular pattern on the crust, starting with the outside edge and working toward the center (see illustration). When finished it will look like a large flower, or a large, double pinwheel. Sprinkle the sugar and the grated lemon zest over the apple slices evenly, and return the tart to the oven. Bake for another 20–25 minutes, or until the crust is fairly brown and the apples are cooked.

While the tart is warm, melt and heat the jelly and pour it over the apples to cover them completely. Cool slightly. If possible, eat the tart without refrigerating at any point: the cold changes the textures too much. A screen-type cover is good for keeping unwelcome creatures away without humidifying the tart.

## CHRUST
("Kindling" favors, pronounced h'*roost*)

*Makes 8 dozen pieces*

As far back as I can remember, the traditional *Chrust* appeared on holiday tables. I seem to associate them most with the Tuesday ("Mardi Gras") before the beginning of Lent—the last "fat" day before the lean forty days no child ever looked forward to! The great mounds of delicate little twisted strips, sprinkled with confectioners sugar, really look like little twigs of kindling with a frosting of snow! Fragile to the touch and crumbly to the bite, these light and delicious favors literally melt in your mouth. You will find the eight dozen does not last very long, and you will be glad to have enough to send some home with your holiday guests.

1 egg
2 egg yolks
1 tablespoon vinegar
2 tablespoons rum
2 tablespoons sugar
¼ teaspoon salt
⅓ cup (¾ deciliter) sour cream
2 tablespoons unsalted butter, softened
2 cups (280 grams) flour, with more available
2 pounds (900 grams) lard for frying,
    or 1 pound lard and 1 pound vegetable shortening
Confectioners sugar for sprinkling

Do not use a processor for mixing. The motor's warmth melts the butter.
In a large mixer bowl, briefly beat the egg and egg yolks, then add the vinegar, rum, sugar, salt, and sour cream. Blend well, then add the softened butter and blend again. Add the flour, 1 cup at a time, blending each thoroughly. Keep mixing (with an electric beater, if possible) until the mixture becomes too stiff. If you have a dough hook, change to that from your beating attachment; if you don't, remove the mixture to a floured

board and knead it by hand, adding a little more flour if the dough will absorb it. By hook or by hand, beat or knead it until it forms a ball, and leaves your hands quite clean after kneading. (If you want more detailed instructions for kneading, look under Noodles, p. 98.)

Rest the dough under an inverted bowl for about 10 minutes, then cut it into about 5 pieces. One piece at a time, on the floured board, roll the dough out in the thinnest possible long strip, adding a bit more flour if it seems too sticky. If your strip gets too long to handle, cut it in half, and keep rolling until it won't get any thinner. Cut the strip into "ribbons" an inch wide, or a bit less. Then cut each ribbon into 3½-inch lengths. Cut a slit down the center about 1 inch long, then pass one end through the slit and back in the same direction.

Heat the lard in a heavy kettle or Dutch oven to 350°F (180°C), or until a cube of day-old bread browns in 45–50 seconds. Fry the little favors in the hot fat, turning them so both sides puff and turn light golden-brown —this happens very fast, in 10–15 seconds, so do only as many as you can watch, turn, and remove without burning any. As they are done, remove them onto a large surface covered with paper towels, and drain them very thoroughly. When your first batch is done and drained, sprinkle it all over (both sides of the favors) with confectioners sugar, and set aside.

Start rolling out the second piece of dough, and repeat the entire process until the dough is used up. If you don't wish to fry all of it at once, you can wrap the pieces of dough individually, and refrigerate or freeze them until you are ready to fry them.

## RACUSZKI
### (pronounced Rah'tsoosh-ki)

*Makes about 36 pieces, 2 inches in diameter*

The dough for these light and delicious little golden-brown puffs is very similar to the *pâte à choux* or *choux* paste, given for French Dumplings (p. 90), but with somewhat different proportions. *Racuszki* are best while still slightly warm, sprinkled with confectioners or granulated sugar and served with gooseberry, raspberry, or sour cherry preserves on the side—or a fruit syrup.

¾ cup (¼ liter) water
½ stick (2 ounces or 60 grams) unsalted butter
1½ teaspoons granulated sugar
½ cup (70 grams) flour
3 eggs
1½ teaspoons grated orange or lemon zest
Pinch of salt
2 pounds (900 grams) lard or vegetable shortening
   (or half of each)
Sugar for sprinkling (confectioners or granulated)

In a saucepan, boil together the water, butter, and sugar. Then, off heat, add all the flour at once and stir vigorously until the mixture is thoroughly blended and lump-free. Return to heat over a medium fire, and cook, stirring constantly, until the mixture forms a ball and comes off the sides of the pan. Cool the mixture slightly—5 or 10 minutes—then add the eggs and incorporate them very thoroughly with the flour-water mixture. Stir in the grated orange or lemon zest and the salt.

In a deep-frying kettle or Dutch oven, melt the lard or shortening, and heat slowly to 350–365°F (180–185°C), or until a day-old 1-inch bread cube turns golden-brown in 60 seconds.

Dip a metal "basting" spoon into the hot fat. Then with the tip of the spoon take up an oval-shaped piece of dough just under a tablespoon in volume. (For forming and dropping *racuszki* dough into fat, see instructions for French Dumplings, p. 90.) Do not crowd them in the fat, as they will about triple in size. Fry them for about 1 minute, then turn them over and fry another minute, or until both sides are equally golden-brown. Be sure the fat remains at the correct frying temperature.

As each puff is done, remove it with a slotted spoon and drain very thoroughly on paper toweling, changing it several times. Transfer to a serving platter and sprinkle with sugar. Pass preserves or syrup separately.

*Note:* You may fry the *racuszki* an hour ahead, keep them warm in a very slow oven, and sprinkle the sugar over them at the last minute.

## Pastry Cookies and Jam Turnovers ("Jammies")

If I have leftover *pâte sablée* when making a tart shell or a mazurka, I form the trimmings into nice "short" cookies. You will remember that this dough is infinitely reformable and can be reworked as much as you like, provided it doesn't get so warm that the butter melts. (In that case, refrigerate it for 15 minutes.) It is much easier to roll when chilled, but you can always shape it with your fingers. Cut out your cookies, place them on a baking sheet, brush them with beaten egg for a glaze, and sprinkle on each one a large pinch of chopped almonds mixed with sugar. Bake them at 400°F (205°C) for about 10 minutes.

Full details about *pâte sablée* are on page 329.

*Almond dough* (see the recipe for Almond Mazurka, p. 337) makes a good short cookie to serve with fruit. Chill the dough, then roll it as thin as you can, cut it in squares, and bake it at 400°F (205°C) until done (about 8 minutes). You can make these cookies into minimazurkas by spreading them with the bittersweet Chocolate Icing on page 337.

*Cream cheese dough* (see the recipe for Glazed Apple Tart, p. 340) is not sweet, and so I like to combine it with jam for little turnovers. Remember that this dough is semiflaky. Therefore, if you are reassembling trimmings and scraps, roll them into a ball and cool for 15 minutes in the refrigerator. Then roll out again.

From this sheet, cut long strips 4 inches wide. Down the middle of each strip make a continuous band, 1 inch wide, of bitter marmalade or apricot preserve. Then flip one long edge of the dough strip over the jam to meet the other edge, and seal the joined edges and the ends of the dough strip with your fingertips or the tines of a fork.

At this point, the long thin turnovers (which are sliced after baking) can be refrigerated until you are ready to bake them. They are best eaten right out of the oven.

Just before baking, preheat the oven to 375°F (190°C) and glaze the turnovers with an egg beaten with 1 tablespoon water. Bake them for about

15 minutes or until they are golden-brown. With a sharp knife, cut them crosswise into slices, and serve.

Full details about cream cheese dough are on page 340.

*Pâte à choux* leftovers make *schmoor.* I don't know whether the silly name is traditional or a family joke. Our cook Barbarka used to smear leftover dough on a baking sheet, strew it with raisins, slivered almonds, and sugar, and bake it at 400°F (205°C) for about 8 minutes. What you get is an irregularly puffy, shiny sheet that you cut into squares and serve as cookies. Not elegant, perhaps, but children love it.

Full details about *pâte à choux* are on pages 92–93.

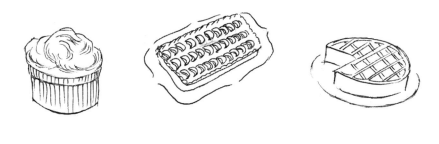

# $\mathcal{D}$umplings and $\mathcal{D}$essert $\mathcal{P}$ierogi

Entrée dumplings made with farmer cheese (*Serniki* I, the firm kind on page 93, and *Serniki* II, the delicate, egg-enriched kind on page 95) make a very pleasant dessert, sprinkled with sugar and cinnamon and served with sweet or sour cream. I like them warm.

*Pierogi,* just to remind you, are made very like wontons or ravioli of a dough similar to noodle dough, which is quickly poached in boiling water. With a sweet filling, like the one made of farmer cheese and walnuts on page 350 (where it fills dessert crêpes), the *pierogi* can be served for dessert with a sprinkling of sugar and sour cream.

Full details about *pierogi* dough are on page 105.

# APPLE AND BANANA DESSERT FRITTERS

*Serves 6*

One crisp and tart, one mellow and fragrant, these are delightful served together from the same dish. I sprinkle them with a little sugar, since the batter has none.

If you have to make a quick dessert or sweet snack, these are even more practical than crêpes, since the batter, because it is leavened with baking soda, doesn't need to sit before you use it. It is exactly the same batter I use for entrée fritters (described in full detail on page 86). I offer a summary recipe below.

### THE FRUIT

Two apples and 3 bananas should be plenty for 6 servings. Peel and core the apples and slice them into disks not more than ⅓ inch thick. The bananas should be fully ripe, with a few brown specks. Peel them, remove any fibrous strings, split them lengthwise, and cut them crosswise into quarters (or sixths, for very long bananas). Lay the fruit pieces on towels to dry while you mix the batter.

### THE BATTER

½ cup (70 grams) flour
½ cup (1 deciliter) heavy cream
¼ cup (½ deciliter) milk
2 eggs, separated
¼ teaspoon salt
¼ teaspoon baking soda
Vegetable shortening for frying
½ cup (100 grams) or more sugar for sprinkling

Beat well together the flour, cream, milk, egg yolks, and salt. Beat the egg whites until they hold together in soft peaks. Stir the baking soda into the flour mixture and fold in the egg whites.

Unless you use 2 frying pans and a lot of shortening, you will have to do the fritters in 2 batches, as the pan must not be crowded. So have a hot ovenproof dish to keep them warm.

In a sauté pan, melt enough shortening to cover the bottom by ¼ inch, and bring it to quite high heat. With a long fork, dip each piece of fruit into the batter to coat well. Without shaking off excess batter, slide the fruit into the hot fat. Turn them once. Remove the fritters with a skimmer, drain them on paper towels, put them in a hot ovenproof dish, and serve them at once, sprinkled with sugar.

# Dessert Crêpes

For full details on making crêpes, see pages 78–80. The summary recipes here are just to remind you about quantities.

# CRÊPES WITH JAM OR SUGAR OR FILLING

*Serves 6*

Serve the crêpes in a stack, with the garnish on the side, so that the crêpes don't get soggy. (But sometimes, if they can be eaten soon, I do sprinkle warm crêpes with sugar and layer them in a dish; then the sugar melts deliciously in their warmth.)

1 cup (140 grams) flour
Scant cup (¼ liter) milk
¾ cup (1¾ deciliters) heavy cream
¼ teaspoon salt
2 eggs
About 3 tablespoons vegetable shortening,
    vegetable oil, or Clarified Butter (p. 63)

Beating vigorously, combine thoroughly the flour, milk, cream, and salt. Beat in the eggs. Let the batter rest for 30 minutes.

Cook the crêpes over high heat in a lightly greased 7-inch crêpe pan. Pour a scant ¼ cup of batter into the hot pan, tilting it to cover the bottom evenly. Cook until the upper surface looks dry and the lower surface golden-brown. Turn or flip over the crêpe to cook the second side. Each crêpe is cooked in less than 2 minutes. If you aren't going to use them right away, warm the whole stack, wrapped in foil, for 10 minutes in a moderate oven, just before serving.

With these I like a not too sweet jam, like gooseberry, or else apple butter, or a nice sour-sweet conserve we used to call *powidla*. It is made of prune plums (the small blue ones with bright orange flesh). Cut the plums small, removing the stones but leaving on the skin. Weigh them, and mix them with half their weight of sugar. If you don't have a scale, here is a rule of thumb for conserving any stone fruit: for 4 cups of fruit, minus stones, allow 2¼ cups of sugar. Let the sugared fruit sit overnight at room temperature, then simmer it until the fruit looks "jammy." Refrigerated in a tightly covered jar, this will keep for months.

## *Filled Crêpes*

The following filling recipes, serving 6 people, are Polish and were contributed by my friend Fela Krance, who illustrated this book.

## CHEESE AND WALNUT FILLING

*Makes about 2¼ cups*

1½ cups (3½ deciliters) farmer cheese
1 cup (¼ liter) ground walnuts
  (or you can use pecans)
6 tablespoons sugar
1 tablespoon grated lemon zest
1½ teaspoons vanilla extract

Combine the above ingredients and put about a soupspoonful on each crêpe. Roll up the crêpes, sprinkle them with sugar, and keep them warm in an ovenproof dish until ready to serve.

## LEMON FILLING

*Makes 1½ cups*

This is a tart lemon curd, a thick sauce you spread on the middle of each crêpe. Roll them and arrange them on a hot fireproof dish, then sprinkle them with confectioners sugar and flame them by pouring on warmed brandy and setting it afire.

Grated zest and juice of 3 lemons
5 egg yolks
½ cup (100 grams) granulated sugar
2 tablespoons confectioners sugar
3 tablespoons brandy

Keep the pancakes hot.

In a double boiler, stirring constantly, cook together the lemon zest and juice, the egg yolks, and the granulated sugar, until the sauce thickens and coats a spoon. Taste for balance of sweet and sour. Spread a little on each hot pancake, roll them, sprinkle on the confectioners sugar, warm the brandy, pour it over the crêpes, and ignite it.


## CRÊPES SUZETTE

*Serves 6*

For this dish I use thin, delicate pancakes, yellow with egg yolk, with the egg whites beaten stiff and folded in. See pages 78–80 for details on crêpe-making in general.

But the special point about my version of this classic dish is the balance of flavors in the sauce. Don't, please, add to the amount of liquor—at least, not until you have once tried the recipe. I do feel that the dish loses all its fresh flavor and its charm if the sauce is overdosed with spirits. Moreover, I don't like the pancakes to be soaked with sauce, so I prefold them before saucing them, merely coating the outer surfaces.


THE CRÊPES

6 tablespoons flour
4 egg yolks
2 cups (½ liter) milk
1 teaspoon sugar
⅛ teaspoon salt
2 egg whites
2 tablespoon clarified butter for the pan

Full details on clarifying butter are on page 63. Briefly, melt butter over medium heat; it will bubble as the water content evaporates. When the bubbling stops, immediately pour out the clear liquid and reserve it. Discard all whitish sediment.

Beat together thoroughly the flour, egg yolks, milk, sugar, and salt. Reserve the egg whites, keeping them closely covered at room temperature. Let the egg-and-flour mixture stand for at least 30 minutes. Then beat the whites until they form stiff peaks and fold them into the batter.

Heat a 7-inch (or smaller) crêpe pan over rather high heat. Film it with clarified butter (adding more as needed) and ladle in about 3 tablespoons batter, just enough to cover the pan surface thinly, as you tilt the pan this way and that. Cook the crêpe about 90 seconds on the first side, or until the surface begins to look dry, then turn it and cook about 30 seconds on the second side. Repeat until you use up all the batter.

Do not stack the pancakes until they are cool, or they will stick together. You can of course make the crêpes in advance and refrigerate them, stacked flat and closely wrapped.

THE ORANGE SAUCE

1 cup (¼ liter) freshly squeezed orange juice
Juice of 1 lemon
Zest of 2 oranges, grated very fine
6 tablespoons butter
½ cup (100 grams) granulated sugar

*For the flaming:*

2 tablespoons confectioners sugar
2 tablespoons orange liqueur (Grand Marnier, for instance)
1 tablespoon brandy

In a frying pan, combine the orange and lemon juice, the orange zest, the butter, and the granulated sugar. Cook them over medium-high heat until the liquid is reduced to a light syrup.

Most cooks seem to put the pancakes into the hot sauce, and then fold them into quarter-circles (2 folds) right in the pan. I'd rather not: they drink up too much of the sauce and get soggy. Nor do I make the sauce at the table. But people do enjoy seeing it flamed, so now and then I get out a chafing dish and combine the sauce and the pancakes in the dining room. If you do this, you begin by lighting the fuel, so that the "blazer," the chafing-dish pan, has a chance to get warm. Then bring in a prearranged tray with a dish of pancakes already folded, a stack of warm dessert plates, a bowl of orange sauce, a bowl or shaker of confectioners sugar, the orange liqueur, the brandy, a ladle to heat the liquors in, and a taper or box of matches. You will also need 2 spoons to turn and serve the pancakes.

When you are ready to serve the crêpes, pour the sauce into the blazer over medium heat. Add the crêpes, already folded into quarter-circles, and turn them quickly to coat them with the sauce. Sprinkle them with the confectioners sugar. Pour the orange liqueur and the brandy into the ladle and rest the bowl of the ladle in the hot pan, among the crêpes, to warm. Light a match or taper, ignite the liquor (if it doesn't flame at once, warm it a moment longer), tip it into the sauce, and spread the flames around with your serving spoons.

One serving (on a warm plate!) consists of 2 or 3 pancakes and a serving spoonful (2–3 tablespoons) of sauce.

## OMELETTE VIENNOISE

*Serves 6–8*

This is not an omelette, or a cake, or a soufflé, but it has elements of all three. It looks like a jelly roll, but is more fragile: it should be served the day it is made, though even next day, in its somewhat deflated state, it tastes very good. I serve it either for dessert or at tea time.

4 eggs, separated
½ cup (100 grams) sugar
2–3 drops of almond extract
1 teaspoon vanilla extract
Pinch of salt
2 tablespoons flour
1 tablespoon appropriate liqueur: Cointreau, Grand Marnier,
    Cassis, or rum (optional)
About ½ cup (1 deciliter) of a lively tasting, not too sweet,
    jam or preserve (gooseberry, sour cherry, etc.)
Confectioners sugar

This recipe precisely fills a jelly-roll pan 7 by 11 by 1¼ inches, but you can use a slightly larger one. Thick or thin, the "omelette" is very easy to roll. Prepare the pan by buttering it and lining the bottom with buttered waxed paper.

Preheat the oven to 350°F (180°C). Beat the egg yolks and sugar until they are thick, pale, and very light. Add almond extract, vanilla extract, and salt, mixing well. Sprinkle the flour over them and fold it in. Beat the egg whites until they form stiff peaks and fold them in. Spread the mixture in the pan, smooth the top, and bake it for about 15 minutes, until it has about doubled in volume, the top is pale gold, and the edges have shrunk a little from the pan.

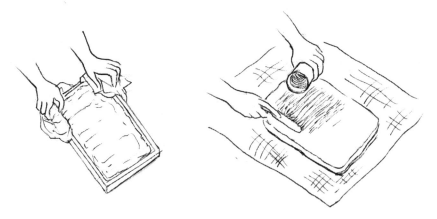

Stir the optional liqueur or rum into the jam or preserves. Spread a dish towel flat, sprinkle it with confectioners sugar and invert the pan onto it.

Peel the waxed paper off the cake. Spread the bottom of the cake (now the top side) with the jam or preserve. Quickly roll up the cake, while it's still warm; rather, compel it to roll itself by lifting the towel at one end, which

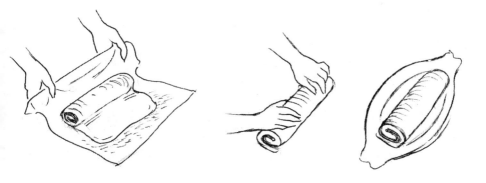

nudges it over, and continuing the motion, gently, down the length of the cake, gathering the towel up behind it. Set the rolled cake on a serving plate, and, while it is still warm, sprinkle it with confectioners sugar. Serve as soon as you can.

## CLAFOUTIS WITH SOUR CHERRIES

*Serves 6*

This simple dessert, somewhere between a pudding and a cake, is quick and inexpensive for large parties. The recipe can safely be doubled for a larger dish; just bake it 10 minutes longer. Since it is best served lukewarm, I usually mix it in the morning and start it baking just as the guests arrive.

*Clafoutis* is delicious made with almost any fruit. My favorite is sour cherries, but any not-too-syrupy canned fruit will do—as long as you drain it well. You can also use fresh fruit, or even frozen—thawed and drained —if necessary. Try it with blueberries, Italian plums, sliced peaches, or apricot pieces.

4 eggs, lightly beaten
½ cup (100 grams) sugar
¼ teaspoon salt
4 tablespoons flour
½ stick (2 ounces or 60 grams) unsalted butter, melted
1 cup (¼ liter) half-and-half
1 teaspoon vanilla extract
One 1-pound (450-gram) can drained, pitted sour cherries,
   or other fruit (see above)

Preheat the oven to 350°F (180°C). Butter a small gratin dish. Combine the beaten eggs, sugar, salt, flour, melted butter, half-and-half, and vanilla extract. Drain the cherries or other fruit, and lay them in the dish. Pour the pudding mixture over them. Bake for 30–35 minutes. The *clafoutis* will puff, but will sink down a little.

## SUCHARKI ILGOWSKIE
### (Ilgovo Rusks)

*Makes about 150 pieces*

One of my earliest memories is the sound of the rusk drawer—a metal-lined, round-bottomed bin built into the woodwork of the kitchen corridor—being opened just before tea time at Ilgovo. It contained quantities—hundreds—of small, rather sweet buns that were split and dried after baking and stored in layers interspersed with granulated sugar. They kept for weeks at a time and were always served at tea and often at breakfast, but we never tired of them. And lately, just on a whim, I searched for the recipe in my mother's little notebook and baked an enormous batch to bring to a house party at a château. I set them in a big basket on the hall table and noticed with pleasure that no passerby could resist scooping up a few little rusks as he or she went through the hall.

After almost three centuries and many invasions and occupations, the manor house at Ilgovo still stands on its bluff above the Niemen. This recipe may be as old as the house and remains for me a sweet memory of years gone by.

1 cup (¼ liter) milk
1½ cups (300 grams) plus 1 tablespoon sugar
1 teaspoon salt
2 packages active dry yeast
4 cups (570 grams) flour
1 stick (4 ounces or 115 grams) unsalted butter, softened
4 eggs

Warm the milk with 1 tablespoon of the sugar and the salt until it is the temperature of a rather hot bath (105–115°F, if you have one of those useful "instant" thermometers). In the bowl of an electric mixer put the 2 packages of yeast and pour on the milk mixture. When the yeast is well dissolved and creamy, add 1½ cups of the flour. Stir it in well, then cover the bowl airtight with plastic wrap and let it stand in a warm place until it looks swollen and puffy. This takes only 15 minutes or so in a slightly warm oven, about 100°F (38°C).

To the batter add the well-softened butter, 2 of the eggs, 1 cup of the sugar, and the remaining 2½ cups of flour. Beat the dough at medium speed for about 15 or 20 minutes, until it comes off the sides of the bowl. Let it stand, covered, at the temperature of a warm room until it has doubled in volume: about 1½ hours.

Between your floured palms roll the dough into balls the size of a large walnut, and space these on baking sheets, leaving them enough room to double in size without touching. At room temperature this will take an hour or less. Preheat the oven to 350°F (180°C) about 10 minutes before the rusks are ready to bake. The best indication that yeast dough is ready is the feeling (to your fingertip) that it has developed a skin, thin and smooth as a flower petal, that scarcely resists the lightest touch.

Beat the remaining 2 eggs with 1 tablespoon water. Using a feather or a pastry brush, paint the risen dough balls with this glaze. Bake them for 25–30 minutes, until they have swollen and colored a rich brown. Let the little buns cool. Then slice them in half horizontally and dry them for several hours or overnight in a warming drawer or a very slow oven.

Store them, sprinkling each layer with the remaining ½ cup of sugar, in airtight metal boxes or tins. They will keep for weeks.

## BABKA
### (Sweet Raisin Bread)

*Makes 2 large loaves or 2 kugel-shaped babkas*

In our family, throughout the years, this *babka* has been the most popular companion to coffee, chocolate, tea, milk—or almost anything else! When baked as a loaf, we called it bread, but made in a kugel shape, a sort of tall mold with a hole in the middle, sprinkled with rum and covered with frosting, it became one of the traditional Easter sweets—together with the Mazurkas (p. 335) and tortes and other goodies such as *Chrust* (p. 342) or *Racuszki* (p. 343).

*Babka* has one very special quality: it disappears mysteriously, and very quickly, no matter where you try to hide it, so one should always bake two at a time. I remember when we lived in California and the children were still small, I sometimes baked as many as eight loaves in a day. This was before we had these wonderful, powerful dough-mixing machines, so the whole family had to work at kneading—at least those who did were entitled to more.

A *babka* (or several) in the oven fills the house with a most romantic, cozy, old-fashioned smell and puts everyone into a good mood and a holiday spirit; even if there is no special occasion at hand a *babka* seems like the friendliest thing to have around for unexpected guests, or midnight snacks.

Among its many virtues are the fact that it keeps very well, can be refrigerated or frozen, and even when it is beginning to dry a bit, unlikely as that usually is, it becomes absolutely delicious toast, the raisins warm and plump, making it lovely for breakfast or tea.

An honored tradition in our family is the fine art of "slivering," applicable also to mazurkas and several other sliceable sweets. Having insisted audibly that one "can't any more" and obviously engrossed in a profound conversation, one toys idly with the knife—which quite naturally tries to "straighten" a crooked slice, or scrape up "messy" crumbs, etc. Entire *babkas* have been "slivered" away while no one was having any.

THE "STARTER"

> 2½ packages active dry yeast
> ½ cup (1 deciliter) warm water (115–120°F/46–49°C)
> 1 tablespoon sugar

THE DOUGH

> 4 cups (570 grams) flour
> 1½ cups (3½ deciliters) milk, warmed to about 100°F (38°C)
> 1 teaspoon salt
> 1 cup (200 grams) sugar
> 10 egg yolks
> 1 stick (4 ounces or 115 grams) unsalted butter, softened
> 1 tablespoon grated orange zest
> 1 tablespoon grated lemon zest
> 4 drops of almond extract
> 1 ample cup (¼ liter) raisins, both dark and golden
>   (soak in water or rum, if overdry)

THE UNBAKED DOUGH GLAZE

> 1 egg
> 1 tablespoon water

THE BABKA FINISHING GLAZE

> 1 tablespoon rum
> 1 tablespoon water
> 1 cup (200 grams) confectioners sugar
> 1 teaspoon lemon juice, or to taste

In a small bowl dissolve the yeast in the warm water with the tablespoon of sugar. Let it stand while you continue: it will "start," or foam, slightly.

To make the dough, put 2 cups of the flour, the warm milk, and salt in a large mixing bowl and mix until smooth. Add the yeast mixture and stir in well. Then add the sugar, egg yolks, the softened butter, the orange and lemon zest, the almond extract, and the remaining 2 cups of flour and mix thoroughly. With dough attachment or hook on the mixer, beat the dough for about 15 minutes, or until it begins to detach itself from the dough hook and the sides of the bowl.

With a scraper, push the dough down into the bowl, cover lightly with a dish towel, and let stand at normal room temperature where it will not be disturbed. *Avoid* warm places such as the top or back of the oven, or near a radiator. In about 3–4 hours, it should have doubled in bulk.

Punch the dough down and add the cup of raisins, mix them in as thoroughly and evenly as possible.

Butter and flour 2 large (or 3 small) loaf pans or 2 kugel forms. Fill them about one-third with the dough. (If you have a little extra dough, butter and flour any appropriate little pan, glass or metal, and use for overflow.)

Let the dough rise again in the pans or forms until it nearly fills them —1–1½ hours. Ten minutes before they are ready to bake, preheat the oven to 350°F (180°C) and glaze the tops with the egg-and-water dough glaze. Bake for 35–40 minutes, until the tops are golden-brown and a straw or tester comes out clean from the centers. Bake a few minutes longer, if necessary.

When done, remove the pans or forms from the oven, cool the *babkas* in the pans for 10 minutes, then invert them onto cooling racks. Let them cool thoroughly. If made in loaf pans, they are fine as they are. Turn right side up if they were made in kugel forms and glaze them: Heat the rum and water in a small pan and pour into the confectioners sugar in a bowl. Add the lemon juice and stir the mixture until it is spreadable, adding a little more hot water, if necessary. Spread over the tops of the kugel-shaped *babkas*.

# Cakes

## CHEESE CAKE

*Serves 8–10*

This is a velvety, creamy cheese cake with a cookie crust and a firm, glossy topping of sour cream. I tasted it for the first time when my daughter Alina was born in Los Angeles; George Cukor asked his Hungarian cook to bake this, her specialty, and he sent it to me at the hospital. After that, with the help of our housekeeper Kate, I set to work to duplicate it. It was a great novelty to me, and I promptly "exported" it to Europe, where it was received with great enthusiasm.

Make this a day ahead. It needs to mellow and will be easier to slice.

About 35 Nabisco "Nilla" wafers, to make 1¼ cups
   (3 deciliters) when crumbed
6 tablespoons butter
12 ounces (340 grams) Philadelphia cream cheese
2 eggs
⅔ cup (130 grams) sugar
1 teaspoon vanilla extract
1 teaspoon lemon juice

THE TOPPING

1 cup (¼ liter) sour cream
4 tablespoons sugar
1 teaspoon lemon juice
1 teaspoon vanilla extract

Crumb the "Nilla" wafers by rolling them with a rolling pin (or better yet in the processor). Melt the butter. In the 9-inch pie plate, preferably Pyrex, blend the crumbs and the melted butter and pat them evenly over the bottom. To shape the sides of the shell, one can fit a second pie plate into the first and rotate it, pressing down, until the crumbs have climbed up the sides. Chill this crust for 30 minutes or so, until the butter has hardened.

Preheat the oven to 350°F (180°C). Beat, blend, or process until smooth: the cream cheese, eggs, ⅔ cup sugar, 1 teaspoon vanilla, and 1 teaspoon lemon juice. Pour the mixture into the chilled shell. Bake for 30 minutes; it will be done when the mixture does not wobble when you jiggle the oven rack. The surface will be pale golden, and the custard will have swollen to fill the shell completely.

Leave the cake at room temperature until it has cooled—about 20 minutes. The filling will sink a little, making room for the topping.

To make the topping, mix together the sour cream, 4 tablespoons sugar, 1 teaspoon lemon juice, and 1 teaspoon vanilla extract. Pour this onto the filling and smooth it level. Bake it for 5 minutes, or until the sugar has dissolved. Cool the cake at room temperature, then chill it until the topping is firm and shiny.

# NANNY'S LUSCIOUS LEMON CAKE

*Serves 6–8*

After baking this cake, which is flavored with lemon peel, one makes holes in the top and squirts them full of lemon syrup. Consequently, each slice has attractive vertical streaks of slightly candied cake, and every bite has two textures. "Will *not* make cake soggy," wrote June Clancy, a delightful Irish woman who was kind enough to contribute her unusual recipe to my book after I had tasted it one day at tea. I too like it best at tea time.

7 tablespoons unsalted butter, softened
1 cup minus 2 tablespoons (175 grams) sugar
1¼ cups (175 grams) flour
1¼ teaspoons double-acting baking powder
4 tablespoons milk
2 tablespoons grated lemon zest
2 eggs
Pinch of salt

THE SYRUP

6 tablespoons sugar
4 tablespoons lemon juice
2 tablespoons granulated or confectioners sugar
   for sprinkling

Before mixing the batter, preheat the oven to 350°F (180°C). Butter and flour a cake tin or loaf pan of 6-cup capacity and line the bottom of the pan with buttered and floured waxed paper.

In a large bowl, combine the soft butter, sugar, flour, baking powder, milk, lemon zest, eggs, and salt. Rapidly beat the mixture until it is smooth. Scrape it into the prepared pan and smooth the surface with a spatula.

Bake the cake for about 45 minutes, or until a toothpick comes out clean. Cool it for 15 minutes, in its pan, on a rack, while you make the lemon syrup: Over low heat simmer together 6 tablespoons sugar and the lemon juice, until they form a light syrup. Prick the top of the cake, going down about two-thirds of its depth, with a large (clean) screwdriver, or skewer (or best of all, a chopstick), then gently spoon the syrup over it, making sure that all the little "mine shafts" fill up. Leave the cake to cool to room temperature, then sprinkle it with the 2 tablespoons granulated or confectioners sugar.

## HONEY AND SPICE CAKE
### (*Piernik,* pronounced pye*h*r-neek)

*Makes a thick 9- by 13-inch slab*

This is a very old recipe, actually my grandmother's, which my mother wrote down in a little notebook for me many years ago—along with as many other family "heirloom" recipes as she managed to bring out of Lithuania after the war.

A *piernik* is a flat cake that comes out extremely hard when just baked and feels as though one could never even bite into it—but—it is supposed, according to all the old recipes, to be put away for 2 weeks or more, during which it actually absorbs moisture from the atmosphere and becomes perfectly soft. And if one is impatient and wants to eat it right away, although it is a bit difficult to cut, it will actually melt in your mouth!

One of its chief virtues is the fact that it will keep indefinitely; if you make several at once, you can give them as winter holiday presents and know that they will be even more delicious weeks after the candles are out and the tinsel put away.

Serve pieces of buttered *piernik* with tea or at breakfast or a festive buffet brunch.

The mixture is very stiff. If possible use a heavy-duty mixer on a stand. I use the processor only to grind the walnuts, which I do with a ¼ cup of the sugar, so that they will not become oily. The blender, if you prefer it, also grinds nuts well.

1 cup (¼ liter) honey
½ teaspoon each: powdered ginger, powdered cloves,
    powdered cinnamon, powdered nutmeg
1 large pinch of ground black pepper
3¾ cups (500 grams) flour
2 jumbo (or 3 large) eggs
1 teaspoon baking soda
3 tablespoons vodka
1 cup (¼ liter) walnuts, ground fine with ¼ cup sugar

Preheat the oven to 350°F (180°C). Butter and flour a baking tin 9 by 13 by 2¼ inches.

In a saucepan, melt the honey with the ginger, cloves, cinnamon, nutmeg, and ground pepper, and bring it to a full boil. At once, while it is very hot, pour the mixture over the flour in the mixer bowl, beating as you do so with the flat beater blade. When the mixture is perfectly blended, add the eggs 1 at a time, blending each in turn completely. Let the mixer go on beating at medium speed while you dissolve the baking soda in the vodka. Add the soda–vodka mixture, then the nuts, beating only until they are well combined. Pour the batter into the baking tin and smooth the surface.

Bake for 1 hour, then lower the oven heat to 300°F (150°C) and continue baking for about 30 minutes, or until the cake has shrunk faintly from the sides of the pan and the edges are a little browned. Reverse the cake onto a dish towel spread over a rack, but do not remove the pan until the cake is cool. Let the cake sit overnight. Wrap the towel around it, using a second towel, if necessary, to cover the cake, and store it at room temperature for a week. It will soften a little. For longer storage, up to 3 months at least (overall), wrap the cake airtight when it has softened and store it at room temperature.

## CHOCOLATE CAKE

*Serves 8–10*

This recipe, from Helen Szell, is for a small, firm, dense, not too moist or sweet cake, almost black in color, and having a wonderfully deep flavor. No wonder: I asked a friend who collects cookbooks to look for comparisons, and she could find no other cake with such a high proportion of chocolate and butter to flour. It's very easy, and the cake keeps well, slices well, and freezes well.

I like to serve it in thin slices with a fruit dessert, or on a plate with mixed cookies for tea.

1½ sticks (6 ounces or 180 grams) unsalted butter
¾ cup (150 grams) sugar
5½ ounces (160 grams) Baker's semisweet chocolate
3 eggs, separated
¾ cup (105 grams) flour
*Babka* Finishing Glaze (p. 360) (optional)

Cream the butter until soft, add the sugar, and cream them together until they are light and fluffy. Over very low heat, melt the chocolate. Let it cool to just above room temperature (so it doesn't harden), and add it to the butter and sugar. One at a time, beat in the egg yolks. Gradually add the flour, stirring it in thoroughly, to make a smooth batter.

Preheat the oven to 350°F (180°C) and butter and flour a 6-cup loaf pan. Beat the egg whites until they form stiff, shiny peaks. Stir one-quarter of the beaten egg whites into the batter, and fold in the remaining three-quarters. Spoon the batter into the prepared loaf pan.

Bake at the lower-middle level of the oven for about 40 minutes. When the cake is done, a toothpick will come out clean, the edges of the cake will have just barely shrunk from the sides of the pan, and the top may be lightly cracked.

Leave the cake pan on a rack for 10 minutes, then unmold it.

The cake needs no frosting, but if you like, when the cake has cooled, you may glaze it with the *babka* glaze.

## SAND TORTE

*Serves 12–16*

A very old-fashioned cake, pale creamy yellow, whose firm, dense texture is midway between a butter cake and a pound cake and whose delicate flavor should not be masked by too much icing. It is often served just sprinkled with confectioners sugar. I think a thin glaze of bittersweet chocolate and a filling of orange butter cream are nice complements to the mellow taste of butter and almond.

In the old days, this kind of cake was baked in a very large springform pan and separated into layers. Since the icing hides one's cuts, I separate the cake by cutting it in half vertically and then slice the halves horizontally into layers. If I'm using layer pans, I peek when the cake is two-thirds done, and move them around if one is baking faster.

2 sticks (8 ounces or 225 grams) unsalted butter
1 cup (200 grams) sugar
8 eggs, separated
4 ounces (115 grams) flour (1 cup plus 6 tablespoons
    cake flour, or 1 cup plus 3 tablespoons all-purpose
    flour)
4 ounces (1 cup plus 2 tablespoons) potato starch
    or cornstarch
½ cup (1 deciliter) ground blanched almonds
1 tablespoon grated lemon zest
3 drops of almond extract
2 tablespoons kirschwasser or white rum

Preheat the oven to 325°F (165°C). Cream the butter, adding the sugar gradually, then the egg yolks 1 by 1 after the sugar is well incorporated. This mixture should be nice and fluffy. Sift together the flour and starch and add the mixture gradually, beating to incorporate it very well. Add the ground almonds, lemon zest, almond extract, and liqueur. Beat the egg whites into stiff peaks, and fold them into the batter.

Butter and flour an 11-inch springform mold. Pour the batter in and bake for about 1 hour. When the cake is done, a toothpick will come out clean, and the edges will have shrunk slightly from the pan. Or bake the cake in three 8-inch layer pans, or two or three 9-inch layer pans, for 20–25 minutes.

PROCESSOR METHOD

With the steel blade, grind the almonds with ⅔ cup sugar and the lemon zest. Add the mixture to the mixed flour and starch. Without cleaning the processor bowl, process the egg yolks with ⅔ cup sugar until thick and pale yellow. (They don't get quite so fluffy as by hand beating, but don't worry.) Cut the butter in small pieces and process it with the yolks and sugar. Add the almond extract and liqueur. By hand, or with a mixer using the flat blade, combine the flour and nut mixture with the butter and yolk mixture. Beat the egg whites until stiff, with a beater, *not* the processor. (I add a pinch of salt for maximum volume, compensating this way for the slightly less fluffy processed yolks.) Fold them into the batter, and bake the cake as above.

When the cakes are done, invert them immediately onto cake racks to cool. When the layers are completely cool, turn them right side up, and either sprinkle the individual layers with sugar and use them as two or three separate tea cakes, or make them into *one* layer cake by filling with orange butter cream or apricot preserves and glazing with chocolate (see Chocolate Mazurka Icing, p. 337).

ORANGE BUTTER-CREAM FILLING

*Makes enough for three 9-inch layers*

"Enough" means enough to cover two 9-inch circles, not to frost the top and sides of the cake.

    1 egg
    2 egg yolks
    ½ stick (2 ounces or 60 grams) unsalted butter
    1¼ cups (250 grams) sugar
    1 tablespoon grated orange zest
    3 tablespoons fresh orange juice (or 1 tablespoon
        frozen concentrated orange juice)

Beat the egg and yolks together lightly. Combine all the ingredients in a saucepan, or in the top of a double boiler, over, not in, simmering water. Cook this mixture, beating constantly, over low heat until it is quite thick. Off the heat, beat it until it is cool (it thickens a bit more as it cools).

## TORTE ORZECHOWY
### (Walnut Cake)

*Serves 16–20*

This rich, dark, nut layer cake is perfect for large parties, since one serves it in small pieces. As a rule I cut a circular core, about 1½ inches from the edge, then cut the circular rim in truncated wedges and the core in pointed wedges.

For this cake, I use the processor to grind the nuts and the big mixer (fitted with the whip) for the eggs.

This is one of my mother's best recipes, one we have always made for special events such as birthdays and Christmas.

1 pound (450 grams) walnut meats, ground to powder
   (makes 6 cups/ 1½ liters, not pressed down)
1½ cups (300 grams) sugar
11 eggs, separated
½ cup (1 deciliter) heavy cream
Grated zest of 1 large orange
½ cup (1 deciliter) unseasoned bread crumbs
⅓ teaspoon salt
4 tablespoons dark rum
Shelled walnuts for decoration (optional)

Butter and flour three 9-inch layer pans or one 10-inch springform. If you grind the walnuts in the processor (or blender), grind them with ½ cup of the sugar to prevent oiliness.

Preheat the oven to 350°F (180°C). Beat the egg yolks and sugar together until they become very pale and form the ribbon. Add the cream. Mix together the grated nuts, orange zest, bread crumbs, and salt. Beat the egg whites until stiff and fold them into the yolk mixture. Then, little by little, sprinkle the nut mixture over the batter, gently folding it in until evenly combined. Distribute the batter equally among the 3 layer pans or spoon it into the springform.

Bake the layers for 25–30 minutes. Halfway through baking, exchange the layers from the upper to the lower racks, from the front to the back, of your oven, so that all will bake evenly. The springform version takes 50 minutes to bake.

Let the cake cool for 5 minutes in the layer pans, then unmold the layers onto racks. In the springform pan, cool the cake for 20 minutes, then unlatch and remove the wall of the pan.

To cut a large cake into layers, cut it vertically in half, then cut each half into 3 equal layers. When you reassemble the circles, the frosting will hide the cuts.

Before filling and frosting the cake, sprinkle the layers with the rum. They should then sit for 30 minutes (to absorb the rum) before you assemble the cake. Spread the lower layer of cake with half the Chocolate-Butter Filling (following recipe), put another layer of cake on that, and spread with the rest of the filling. Top with the third layer, then frost the assembled cake with the Chocolate Mazurka Icing on page 337. Decorate, if you like, with halved walnuts.

CHOCOLATE-BUTTER FILLING

    4 ounces (115 grams) semisweet chocolate
    1 stick (4 ounces or 115 grams) unsalted butter
    2 tablespoons dark rum
    Pinch of salt

Melt the chocolate over very low heat. Cream the butter and combine it with the chocolate (which should be cool enough to touch comfortably) and the rum and salt.

*Note:* This cake freezes perfectly, but must be given plenty of time to thaw, since the chocolate-butter filling will be hard otherwise. Keep the cake in the refrigerator, with cut places covered with plastic wrap, to prevent the butter from melting or softening too much.

*Variation:* Use raspberry jam as filling between two of the layers. Make less Chocolate-Butter Filling accordingly.

## ALMOND AND COFFEE TORTE

*Makes two 9-inch layers*

This delicious cake is another "family heirloom" from my mother's little handwritten notebook, a recipe of *her* mother's, next to which is written my mother's comment: *"Delicious!"* It is a kind of cousin to the preceding walnut torte recipe, but with slightly different flavors and textures. Both tortes are excellent candidates for "slivering" (see *Babka* on p. 358) or nibbling. These cakes are very rich and festive and go a long way, as one can eat only a little at a time. I occasionally make both and give each guest a thin sliver of each, watching, delighted, as they try to decide which is better, how they differ, and ask for more to help decide!

5 ounces (140 grams) almonds, shelled, unblanched
   (i.e., brown skins left on)
5 ounces (140 grams) blanched almonds (without skins)*
2 cups (400 grams) sugar
10 eggs, separated
1 tablespoon vanilla extract
1 teaspoon almond extract
¼ cup (½ deciliter) finest ground regular coffee
   (if you have a grinder, use rich beans, and the
   finest grind setting)

In a processor bowl with the steel blade, put all the almonds, skinned and unskinned, and ½ cup of the sugar. Grind them until they are very fine and fluffy. (They can also be done in a blender, in 2 batches, also with the sugar,

---

*If you prefer, buy all the almonds with skins. Measure out 5 ounces (140 grams), put them in boiling water, and simmer for about a minute. Run under cold water. The skins will slip right off. The skinned almonds must be *very thoroughly dried* before you grind them.

or in a nut grinder, without.) Remember that you want a powdery texture, as the nuts take the place of flour in this cake. Adding sugar to the processor or blender keeps the nuts from becoming oily and heavy. Be very careful not to grind too long, or you will have nut-butter instead of nut-flour!

In a large mixer bowl, beat the egg yolks with the remaining 1½ cups of sugar until they are thick and pale. Add the vanilla and almond extracts and the finely ground coffee (or ground coffee beans). Beat this mixture for 5 minutes; it will be very stiff.

Preheat the oven to 375°F (190°C). Beat the egg whites until stiff but not dry. Stir one-third of them into the nut mixture, to loosen it somewhat. Fold the remaining egg whites in thoroughly. Butter and flour two 9-inch layer pans or two 9-inch springform pans. Divide the cake batter evenly between them. Bake them on the center rack for 35–40 minutes. You may want to change their positions during baking, turning them and exchanging them front to back of the oven so they bake evenly. When the cake is done, a straw or tester inserted in the centers should come out clean. (For testing, I found long, toothpick-thin wooden skewers used for Japanese dishes to be perfect—no burnt fingertips!)

Cool the layers in their pans on racks for 5 minutes, then turn them out on the racks and cool thoroughly.

THE FILLING

    2 tablespoons instant coffee
    2 tablespoons boiling water
    1 stick (4 ounces or 115 grams) unsalted butter
    ½ cup (100 grams) confectioners sugar
    1 tablespoon rum

Dissolve the instant coffee in the water and cool thoroughly. Have the butter cool, but not frozen. Cut it into small pieces and cream it in a small bowl with the sugar and the rum. Add the coffee mixture and blend well. Keep the filling cool and just spreadable—don't let the butter start melting. Spread the filling on one layer, and put the second layer on top of it.

## COFFEE GLAZE
### (for Almond Torte)

¾ cup extra-strong coffee
   (4 level teaspoons dry regular instant)
⅔ cup (130 grams) granulated sugar
1 cup (200 grams) sifted confectioners sugar
5 tablespoons rum

In a saucepan, combine the coffee and granulated sugar. Bring this mixture to a boil; then, over a low flame, stir until it thickens to a syrupy consistency.

Put the confectioners sugar into a nonmetal bowl. Gradually, stirring continuously with a wooden spoon, pour the coffee mixture over it. Continue stirring until the icing is very smooth. Add the rum and stir well again. Spread over the torte as soon as possible. Refrigerate the iced torte until ready to serve.

# *Menus*

FOR A SMALL DINNER PARTY BEFORE THE THEATER OR CONCERT

(This is quickly served, eaten, and cleaned up.)

Beef Stroganoff
Boiled Rice
Glazed Carrots

Cucumber and Melon Salad

Poires Belle Hélène

SUPPER AFTER A CONCERT

(This can be prepared in the afternoon. You return from the concert, heat the *barszcz* for 5 minutes, and while people are eating their soup, the chicken cutlets and the noodles and mushrooms are warming up in a slow oven. Moreover, it is a menu that can be easily prepared for large numbers.)

Clear Barszcz (served in cups)

Chicken Cutlets with lingonberries
Lazanki with Mushrooms and Onions
Carrot salad and endive, apple, mayonnaise salad
Assorted cheeses

Omelette Viennoise

Chocolate Mazurkas

Fruit

A "HUIT À MINUIT" BUFFET FOR 40 PEOPLE

(Most of this can be done in easy stages, in advance, up to a week ahead.)

Large Coulibiacs
Bigos with Smothered Potatoes
Fish Cutlets with Tomato Sauce

Pâté Barbarka

Choice of vegetable salads

Tort Orzechowy
Lemon Bavarian Cream
Cut-up fresh fruit with kirsch

A LARGE BUFFET PARTY

Carp in Jelly, Sauce Verte, horseradish
Goulash with Caraway Seeds
Pierogi with Cheese and Potato Filling
Kasha with Mushrooms

Celery Root Relish      Cucumber Salad
Zucchini, Watercress, and Red Onion Salad

Assorted cheeses, breads

Cheese Cake      Mrs. Szell's Chocolate Cake
Coconut and Raspberry Jelly

BUFFET LUNCH,
POSSIBLY FOR LOTS OF PEOPLE

(Everything can be eaten with a fork.)

Chicken Medallions with Dill and Cream
Lazanki with Mushrooms
Chicken Liver Pâté in Aspic

Fish Salad with Potato and Egg
Several vegetable salads, including watercress
(which keeps better than mixed green salad)

Chocolate Mousse     Fresh Strawberries

A SUMMER BUFFET

Cold Poached Striped Bass, Sauce Verte
Lemon Chicken en Chaud-froid

Cucumber Salad     Zuccini, Watercress, and Red Onion Salad
Carrot and Apple Salad     Green Bean and Raw Mushroom Salad

Raspberry Cream, with fresh raspberries

A SMALL SIT-DOWN DINNER

Jellied Chicken Soup with Black Caviar
Beef Tenderloin, Roasted
Assorted steamed vegetables
Pommes Rissolées

Bibb and Boston lettuce salad,
lemon and oil dressing

*Crème Brûlée*

A LUNCH FOR "SPECIAL" GUESTS

Oeufs Farcis à la Polonaise
Tripes à la Varsovienne      Vodka
Marrow and Matzo Dumplings, or boiled potatoes

Mixed green salad

Coffee Custard with Gooseberry Jam

SIT-DOWN LUNCH

Avocado with Melon, Papaya and Oranges

Veal Piccata
Épinards en Branches
Fresh Noodles

Strawberry Tart

A DINNER (OR LUNCH) PARTY

Melon or Watercress Soup
Guinea Hen with Sour Cream
Pommes Allumettes

Green Salad

Lemon Soufflé

Shrimp with Dill and Sherry

Roast Leg of Lamb
Purée of Beets (Polish beets)
Pommes Rissolées

Tossed green salad

Barbarka's Caramel Mousse

MENU FOR A HOT DAY

Chlodnik

Fried Fish, Spanish Style
Sweet Corn
String Beans with Artichoke Hearts

Coconut and Raspberry Jelly

SUGGESTIONS FOR TEA

Babka    Nanny's Luscious Lemon Cake
Chrust    Orange Mazurka    Omelette Viennoise
Almond and Coffee Torte    Sucharki Ilgovskie

Salt Herring Salad

Chicken Broth, with French Dumplings

New York Cut Steaks
Lithuanian Potatoes or Potato Pancakes
Green Beans

Green Salad, and Cucumber Salad with Vinegar and Dill

Steamed Coffee Pudding
Caramel Vanilla-Cream mazurka

Carp in Jelly
Lemon Chicken
Boiled Rice
Asparagus

Tomato Salad

Apple and Caramel Tart

Tomato Soup

Crêpes with Beef Filling, Sautéed
Green Salad
Artichokes Vinaigrette

Barbarka's Caramel Mousse

Celery Soup
Kasha with Mushrooms and Mushroom Sauce
Mixed green salad
Fruit and Cream, Broiled


Cabbage Rolls
Steamed Potatoes
Salad
Crêpes with Jam or Sugar


Boiled Beef with Horseradish Sauce
Boiled potatoes, carrots, leeks, cabbage, turnips, etc.
Cheese Dumplings (Serniki I) with Sugar and Sour Cream


Clear Barszcz, Crêpes with Calf's Brain Filling
Cabbage Timbale with Mushroom Sauce
Lemon Custard Tart


Mushroom Soup with Barley
Lamb Cutlets
Asparagus
Kiśiel


Adam's Vegetable Soup
Eggplant Fritters
Roast Leg of Lamb, cold
Green Salad
Clafoutis

# Index

A NOTE ABOUT THE AUTHOR

Nela Rubinstein, the youngest daughter of the Polish conductor and musician Emil Mlynarski and his wife Anna Hryncewicz, was born on her mother's Lithuanian family estate. She grew up in Warsaw, where she studied dance, and in 1932 she married the pianist Arthur Rubinstein. During their fifty years of marriage they had four children and made their homes chiefly in Paris, Los Angeles, and New York. The Rubinsteins traveled all over the world together, and Mrs. Rubinstein now lives in Paris and New York and spends summers in Marbella, Spain.


A NOTE ON THE TYPE

The text of this book was set via computer-driven cathode ray tube in Bembo, the well-known monotype face. The original cutting of Bembo was made by Francesco Griffo of Bologna only a few years after Columbus discovered America. It was named after Pietro Bembo, the celebrated Renaissance writer and humanist scholar who was made a cardinal and served as secretary to Pope Leo X. Sturdy, well-balanced, and finely proportioned, Bembo is a face of rare beauty. It is, at the same time, extremely legible in all of its sizes.

Composed by The Haddon Craftsmen, Inc.
Allentown, Pennsylvania

Printed and bound by The Murray Printing Company,
Westford, Massachusetts

Typography and binding design
by Dorothy Schmiderer